THE COMPLETE GUIDE TO *CLIMBING* (BY BIKE) IN THE NORTHEAST

A guide to cycling climbing and the most difficult climbs in the northeast United States

Help Keep This Guide Up to Date

Diligence was put forth by the author to provide as accurate as possible the information contained in this guide. However, things change over time (roads close, starting and/or points are re-routed, etc.).

If you encounter alternate conditions from those stated here or have additional climbs to include and/or suggestions for improvement please send those to:

extreme.press@yahoo.com

Other climbing guides by the author include:

50 Climbs (By Bike) in Utah
The Complete Guide to Climbing By Bike (2nd Edition)
The Complete Guide to Climbing By Bike in California (2nd Ed)
The Complete Guide to Climbing By Bike in Colorado
The Complete Guide to Climbing By Bike in the Southeast

Information on these guides can be found at the website: **www.usacyclingclimbing.com**

Complete Guide to Climbing by Bike Series

THE COMPLETE GUIDE TO *CLIMBING* (BY BIKE) IN THE NORTHEAST

A guide to cycling climbing and the most difficult climbs in the northeast United States

John Summerson

Extreme Press
405 Kettle Court
Winston-Salem, NC 27104
336 659-7600
Extreme.press@yahoo.com

An Extreme Press Guide

May, 2015

All photos by the author unless otherwise noted

Library of Congress Control Number: 2015930482

ISBN 13: 978-0-9792571-6-2

"The best climbers do not suffer less; they just suffer faster" Chris Boardman

Back cover - Prospect Mountain Highway in New York

Table of Contents

Connecticut

Maine

Massachusetts

New Hampshire

New York

Vermont

Preface

If one is looking for a single characteristic that might best describe the climbing among the many mountains of the northeast United States, it may be steep. The paved ascents in this region tend to be more vertical than any other in the U.S. In fact, there is more 20% grade here than in any other region of the country. Having collected climb data from all over the United States while preparing the book 'The Complete Guide to Climbing By Bike' and with interest in climbing growing, I realized that many worthwhile climbs were being left out of the nationwide guide simply because they were not among the very most difficult. This was particularly evident in the Northeast U.S. which contains a large number of challenging ascents.

While no one knows the local climbs better than those that live nearby, I think this database is comprehensive but unlikely complete. At the least this data is now available in one place for those seeking this information. Today I still get a sense of satisfaction from finding another particularly challenging hill to climb so please send any other climbs worthy of mention to the author for (hopefully) future editions.

USE LOW
GEAR
NEXT
1 1/2 MILES

Introduction

Road bike cycling is one of the most popular sports in the world and the biggest challenge within the sport, and its most intriguing aspect, is hill climbing. Major professional cycling tours such as the Tour de France and the Giro d'Italia are usually won and lost in the mountains. But why climb the hill?

Climbing is also the most difficult part of cycling, requiring great energy and effort and on tough hills or going all out, producing pain. Why, then, do cyclists routinely engage in a painful activity that can result, as they themselves describe, in great suffering for the sole purpose of reaching the top? In the case of professional riders it could be argued that they are paid to do it. For others answers may include losing weight, improving one's racing ability or fitness level, or getting back to where you started. But I think the real answer is because it's there. This simple phrase sums up the main reason people undertake physical challenges. Be it mountain climbing, distance running or peak-bagging by bike, the main reason cyclists will tolerate the pain is for the physical and mental challenge itself. Simply put, hills are there to be beaten.

For years, major cycling events such as the Tour de France have evoked the image of the lone rider struggling up sheer alpine pitches, straining their physical limits.

Cycling greats such as Eddy Merckx, Bernard Hinault and Lance Armstrong, while very complete all-around riders, became legends in the sport in large part from their climbing exploits. The mountains add an almost mythic quality to races as the riders are seen overcoming obstacles that extend beyond the actual asphalt, rock and dirt upon which they climb. Even average cyclists feel the allure of attempting difficult climbs and achieve tremendous satisfaction from a successful summit. It sounds pretty simple. Find a mountain with a paved road to the top and then pedal up it. However, hill climbing is not easy, as certain climbs involve ascents of thousands of vertical feet. Elite riders can race to the top but success for most involves just getting there.

As the northeast United States has many challenging hills to conquer, this book is meant to be a resource for road bike hill climbing and to describe the most difficult climbs in the area. Other ascents are included for reasons such as a steep grade or some other unique aspect.

Climbing

No one may know when the first significant hill was climbed on a bicycle but the first documentation of major ascents occurred in stage races which originated in Europe, the oldest being the Tour de France. It is interesting to note that the first two Tours (first held in 1903) did not include any mountain passes. Bikes were heavy, single speed (and brake) behemoths while many roads were unpaved. Some felt that the riders of the day could not complete big climbs and that adding them to the race route would ruin the Tour.

It was not until 1905 that significant climbs were added, the very first being the Ballon d'Alsace in the Vosges Mountains. In 1910 the first major, high altitude passes were added (four major climbs in the Pyrenees Mountains including the now famous Tourmalet) which resulted in a great deal of criticism directed at race organizers that the routes were too difficult. As is often the case human potential was underestimated as many riders of that era conquered the climbs in dramatic fashion. In contrast, 1910 was also the year that the broom wagon was introduced to sweep up those who could not finish the stage.

In 1911 the first major climb in the Alps was added (Col de Galibier) with spectacular results. Instead of being a detriment, the uphill duels captured the public imagination and added to the popularity of the event. The race route

every year thereafter has contained many significant climbs. Other major tours that followed also began to include hills along their routes. In 1933 the Tour de France and the Giro d'Italia (Italy's national tour) began recognizing the best climbers in the field (Spain's Vicente Trueba was the first winner in the Tour along with Alfredo Binda in the Giro). Most of the major stage races now recognize this accomplishment as the cyclists earn points based upon their finish in a climb and its difficulty. The cyclist with the most accumulated points is awarded the Polka Dot Jersey as the winner of the king of the mountains competition.

The performances of great early climbers such as Alfredo Binda, Fausto Coppi and Charley Gaul continued to increase the popularity of the major tours. These events made climbs such as the Tourmalet and L'Alpe d'Huez in France and Stelvio in Italy as well known to cycling fans as the Daytona Speedway or Yankee Stadium are to U.S. racing and baseball fans respectively. The mountains allowed bike races to become truly great as the event rose beyond the personal concerns of the cyclists to reflect life as a whole. Today hill climbing is more popular than ever and within multi-stage races those with hilltop finishes are usually the most anticipated and best attended stages of the race. Spectators know that hills offer the best opportunity to view the drama within the peloton as it struggles through the most difficult and important element in any race.

Climbing adds the mythic quality of overcoming obstacles that continues to be associated with the major cycling tours and which has produced many memorable moments. Ascending difficult hills is about struggle and perseverance and it is these aspects that have made conquering the mountains the heart and soul of cycling.

Scenic Route 52 in New York

About This Guidebook

Road bike cycling and hill climbing in particular are enjoying a surge in popularity in the U.S., perhaps due to the success of the major road bike races and Lance Armstrong and/or the ongoing fitness/physical challenge craze in this country. In spite of growing popularity however, there is little published information on the location of area road bike hill climbs and very little accurate data on the length and elevation gain of these climbs. Many roads are hilly but that is not the intent of this guide. The location, description and profiling of major individual hills in the Northeast U.S. is its aim. As such, I set out to publish a guide for those cyclists looking for this information and to collect data for climb comparison purposes. You may have many of these hills all to yourself as the majority are not well known.

In addition to listing the location of climbs, I wanted to provide accurate data on their length, grade, elevation gain and other statistics. While there are various data available it is important when compiling data to reduce the variability of measurement that can occur from multiple sources and to apply consistent definitions to hill climbs. The listed statistics for climbs often vary as different people use different starting and ending points and less than accurate measurement procedures. At times climb gradients are reported inaccurately or overestimated such as when the maximum grade is sometimes considered the average grade. In addition, climbs are sometimes profiled by using mapping software to analyze roads that have been superimposed upon a topographic map. Roads are at times not accurately laid down within map contours which can result in less than accurate measurements. The measurements in this guide were all obtained directly on each climb and compiled by one source. That said, keep in mind that truly precise data is hard to come by and errors in measurement and recording are bound to happen.

There are hundreds of climbs in and around the mountains of the Northeast (states covered are Connecticut, Maine, Massachusetts, New Hampshire, eastern New York and Vermont) so obviously they all cannot be included in these pages. What this guidebook does attempt to include are the most difficult road bike climbs in the area that are open for bikes (see appendices for rankings). Other ascents are described due to a steep grade, or other unique aspect such as outstanding scenery (along with significant climbing), cycling history or some combination of the above. Appendices in this guide rank climbs by overall difficulty, average grade, elevation gain and several other categories. The author has first hand knowledge of 170 out of the 172 (99%) described climbs in this guide. Climbs with estimated statistics are noted. It is a difficult task to attempt to record and document all of the significant climbs within the Northeast so if noteworthy ascents were left out please send the appropriate information to the author.

While some of the ascents in this guide are for the serious road cyclist only, there are many moderate climbs for the rider looking to improve their climbing skills and/or fitness level. Be sure to know your fitness and ability level before you tackle the longer and/or more difficult hills in this book. Start with the shorter, less steep climbs and progress from there. As all are located in the mountains, the scenery along the way is usually spectacular and will help ease the pain of a tough ascent.

Defining A Hill Climb

Along with the location and statistics of Northeast U.S. climbs, this guide will attempt to standardize the definition of a hill climb. That is, what constitutes a climb, what are the starting and ending points and, if multiple approaches, the shortest route to the top. The start and finish of most climbs are generally easy to define as they have definite beginnings and endings. Others are a bit vague, particularly along shallow-grade stretches of road. The starting point of these types of climbs is considered to be the transition from flat to a definite climb or a significant change in elevation for very gently climbing stretches of roads. A good example of the latter is the north side of Red Mountain Pass in Colorado along Route 550 (one of the most spectacular climbs in the U.S.).

Route 550 actually begins to climb many miles to the north of its listed start in Ouray, CO. However, the grade is so slight that the author believes this should not be considered a hill climb. Once in Ouray it is quite clear where the true hill begins as there is a significant change in grade right in the middle of town.

Another topic worthy of discussion regarding climb definitions is a clarification of their ending points. Most climbs have an easy-to-define end such as Mount Washington in New Hampshire which dead-ends very close to the top of the mountain. However, some do not. For climbs that do not dead end, the top is considered when the road descends from that point (such as mountain passes), or if it reaches a significant flat without significant climbing beyond it. A good example of the latter is Devils Kitchen in NY. At its listed top the road flattens out. Over the next few miles the road rolls up and down before peaking at an altitude that is slightly higher than the listed climb peak. However, the additional climbing is not constant and is over such shallow grade that the additional riding does not constitute climbing in the author's mind.

Another issue in defining climbs is how flat sections and/or descents along the route factor in. A climb can have small flats and/or infrequent small descents and still be considered a continuous ascent as long as the vast majority of the route is uphill (< 10% of the route is flats/descents). Many major hill climbs have small flats or

The top of Bear Mountain near New York City

Beginning the final stretch on Mount Equinox in Vermont

descents along the way but these sections always lead to significant additional climbing. Some very good rides with serious elevation gain however contain multiple flats/descents and are not included. These would include Route 130 in South Carolina; a very entertaining ride that climbs a significant distance but that has too much of its route along flat and/or descending terrain.

Some climbs may have a single major flat/descent (no more than one mile in length) if there is extended, significant climbing both before and after the flat/descent. For example, Mount Mitchell in North Carolina has a single major descent along its route but because there is significant climbing both before and after the descent it is considered a single climb. If a climb has more than one major flat/descent along its route it is considered two separate climbs. For instance, Route 168 from Fresno to Kaiser Pass in California has more than 8000 feet of elevation gain along its route but there are several major descents along the way so the route is actually several different climbs. Mount Hamilton near San Jose, California is another example; it contains three uphill sections between two fairly major descents and while the climbing sections are worthy in themselves, the route from bottom to top is not considered by most to be one hill climb.

Definitions of Terms

This guide will use several terms to describe each climb which are defined below:

Total elevation - This is the elevation gained in feet from the starting point to the top of the climb. If a climb has descents within it this additional climbing is not included in the total elevation gained. Elevations were measured using global positioning satellite (GPS) positions from which a very accurate elevation was then determined by plotting the fixed point using a topographic software program.

Length - This is the distance of the climb in miles. If you are retracing your route back to the starting point, in order to determine the total distance of the ride, simply double the climb's length. Climb lengths were measured by automobile odometer (at least two measures and averaged) and cycle computer.

Average Grade (maximum grade) - This is the average percent grade or steepness of the climb and is expressed as a percentage (8%). The grade assigned to each hill is the average grade over the entire climb. The higher the percent grade, the steeper the climb. Percent grade is determined by dividing the elevation gain by the length of the climb. The maximum grade is just that. The measured maximum gradient must extend all the way across the road (a very steep inside corner that could be bypassed for instance does not qualify) and be at least three feet in length. As cycle computers are not a particularly accurate device for measuring maximum grade, this parameter was assessed by hand by gradiometer. In the listed climb descriptions the distance and elevation data only reflect the contiguous portion of the road that is part of the climb. If the climb includes small flats or descents, they are included in the distance but do not contribute to the net elevation gain. Thus the average grade may not in some cases accurately represent the true nature of the climb. That is, there are usually sections on the climb that are steeper than the average grade along with sections that are less steep than the average grade.

Rating - There are several formulas available to rank climbs. All have shortcomings and have received criticism. In major races such as the Tour de France climbs are ranked using a numeric scale from 4 (easiest) to 1 with an extra classification describing the most difficult climbs as hors categoire or 'beyond category'. There are general guidelines for these categorizations that involve length and grade. However there are not precise definitions for each category and often the ratings are not applied consistently. In addition, climbs are often ranked according to their placement within a race stage meaning that a climb towards the end of a stage may be categorized as a 2 when the same climb may be a 3 (easier) if placed at the beginning of the stage. You may also have noticed that more recently certain climbs used in the Tour de France have been receiving a more difficult rating than for previous tours (call it hill inflation perhaps), regardless of their placement in a stage.

The elevation reached within a climb is not taken into account in this and most other ratings systems as well. As increasing elevation has deleterious effects on physical performance, this factor should be taken into consideration. The point here is that a more accurate formula is needed and the one listed below is an attempt to more precisely quantify the difficulty of a climb and has taken into account the climb's elevation gain, average grade, altitude, surface and grade variability:

Average grade x total elevation gain x altitude adjustment (see altitude adjustment description) x grade variability (see grade variability adjustment description).

Altitude adjustment: Altitude research indicates that human performance shows a noticeable performance detriment beginning at approximately 2000 feet elevation of approximately 1% with subsequent performance deficits with increasing altitude and duration of activity. There are other elements that affect performance at altitude but vary by individual and at this point in time are very difficult if not impossible to quantify. The author acknowledges that the adjustment presented here is an estimation of the effects of altitude on hill cllmbing performance.

Grade variability adjustment: If a climb has two or more segments where the grade of the segment exceeds the average climb grade by at least five percentage points the rating is adjusted by 0.025 (assumption that grade variability results in a slightly more difficult climb) for each of those sections. Very few climbs meet this criterion.

As you can see from the climb rankings there is very little difference in the numeric rating of many of the climbs. So little in fact that you will have a very difficult time discerning the differences while on the bike. All that having been said, there are too many variables involved to precisely rank a climb numerically and it is not the main intent of this guide to do so. While the author believes this rating system is an improvement over other models it is hoped that these ratings, while serving as a general guide to compare climbs, will also serve to spur debate and perhaps eventually a truly accurate rating system.

Directions - The starting point for almost all directions for climbs listed in this guidebook is the nearest town, some of which are very tiny places. A good road map will be helpful to locate and reach many of these locations. I would recommend the North American Road Atlas from AAA as it contains a town index for each state but any national/state highway road map will do.

Rules of the Road

- Wear a helmet.
- Follow the same driving rules as motorists and be sure to obey all traffic patterns and road signs.
- Wear bright colors so you are more visible to motorists.
- Ride single file on busy roads so that motorized vehicles can pass.
- Use hand signals to alert motorists to your next move.
- Ride with traffic and not against it.
- Make eye contact with drivers and assume they do not see you.
- Try to avoid riding in foggy, rainy or windy conditions.
- Be alert for sewer grates, manhole covers, cattle guards, oily pavement, gravel, wet leaves and ice.
- Give parked cars a wide berth.
- Many of these listed climbs are fairly long rides so go prepared with an extra tube along with pump, tool kit, rain gear, food and plenty of fluids at all times.
- It is usually best to ride with a partner or partners. In case of emergency one rider can go for help if needed.

Pre-Ride Check:

- Check the tires for proper inflation.
- Check the brakes for proper traction.
- Check all quick releases to make sure they are tight.
- Check the chain for tightness.
- Check all nuts and bolts.
- Spin your wheels through frame and brakes.
- Make sure you have all necessary gear for the particular climb/ride.
- Bring a positive attitude along whenever possible.

A warning in Vermont

Improving Climbing Ability

For new cyclists, hill climbing is one of the most daunting aspects of riding. More experienced cyclists, however, enjoy climbing and regard tough hills as a challenge. It is a great feeling to make a solid climb and then enjoy the descent down the other side. The simplest way to improve your climbing technique and the best training for climbing is to climb; that is, to incorporate hills into your rides. However, don't start climbing big hills until you have built up an adequate cycling fitness base. Try to accumulate a significant amount of relatively flat riding first. At that point add shorter/moderate grade hills to your rides and work your way up to the longer and/or steeper climbs. Incorporating hills in your riding will not make them any shorter but eventually they will feel that way.

Cycling Techniques for Climbing

Improving your basic cycling techniques can also improve your climbing ability. It is important to maintain a smooth, steady rhythm as you pedal up the hill. Unless very short in length, start a climb with as slow a pace as possible. This will allow you to develop a rhythm which not only includes the pedaling cadence but breathing as well. Breathe slowly and deeply as this will help establish a smooth pedaling cadence. Obviously in your pedal stroke it is much easier to apply force to the pedals when your foot is on the down stroke. However, this results in uneven power output contributing to slight accelerations and decelerations of the bike which becomes exaggerated when climbing. To remedy this try to lift your knee and drag your foot backwards across the bottom of the pedal stroke, pulling upwards slightly on the upstroke and pulling the pedal forward across the top of its rotation.

There are several other factors to consider when climbing. First, make sure you have the right gears. At least a 39-tooth small chain ring in front and a 25-tooth rear gear (a 27 or 28 (or a triple) is even better if you will be riding consistently on steep hills). Upon encountering a hill, do not shift too soon as this can result in a momentum loss from a high RPM spinning effect. Conversely, you must not end up in a gear that is too large which tends to tire the rider out. The proper climbing cadence varies among individuals. The idea with gearing is to maintain a cadence that is comfortable, shifting as you tire and the RPM's start to drop. Basically, if the gradient varies on the climb adjust your gearing so that your cadence and level of effort are maximized.

Another factor is whether to sit or stand during the ascent. Seated is more energy efficient but a standing position can produce much more power. A simple rule to start with is that if the hill is long, climb in the saddle, and if short or while attacking, stand. Reality dictates that on most challenging hills you will do both. For most of the climb you will find it is more efficient to sit in the saddle. Put your hands on the top of the brake hoods or handlebars and keep them relaxed. Try to change their positioning periodically. The upper body should not be crunched forward too far and the shoulders should be open. This will allow for easier breathing as the climb continues. Relax your upper body as well, as this will decrease oxygen demands. Your weight should be over the cranks to maximize power during the pedal stroke. Try not to bounce on the pedals as you shift from side to side. Developing a rhythm that combines pedaling and breathing will make a big difference in your climbing efficiency. At times you will need to stand such as on very steep sections or when sprinting past a fellow rider. Just before you stand, shift to a higher gear as you can generate more power in this position (shift back when you sit down again). As you come off of the saddle continue with an even pedal stroke and push your hands forward. Come out of the saddle on the down stroke to minimize loss of momentum.

Specific Training for Hill Climbing

While the physiology of human performance training is much more understood today than in the past, training is still as much art as science. That is, there is more than one way to improve performance. However, perhaps the more important considerations are time and commitment. Time to train is obviously limited for most. With that in mind it is paramount that this limited time is put to good use. Intensity is the key with adequate rest for recovery. Particularly with hill climbing which involves very intense bursts of effort, adequate recovery is essential to avoid overtraining and burnout. In addition, train consistently for best results. Develop specific climbing goals and a plan to reach those goals. Listen to your body and back off if needed. Commit to climbing success and it will likely follow.

Good climbers have certain attributes that contribute to their success. All have an endurance base and have developed solid power to weight ratios which gives the ability to generate greater amounts of force with each pedal stroke. They also have high anaerobic endurance which results in greater levels of lactic acid tolerance. Training to improve climbing ability should focus on these physiologic aspects.

Build a Base

As previously mentioned make sure you have a solid cycling base before adding significant climbing to your riding and attempting the interval routines described later in this section. You should complete many miles of distance riding on mostly flat terrain to build your endurance base before moving on to more specialized routines that target climbing ability. The amount of time needed will vary by individual, ranging from several months to several years of regular road cycling

Scenic climbing in New York

Steep grade on Mount Washington

depending on age, health and fitness level. After a period of mainly flat riding, add moderate hills to your regular endurance rides. As you progress, add longer and steeper hills.

Power to Weight Ratio

Climbing ability has a strong correlation with power to weight ratio; in fact it is perhaps the most accurate predictor of climbing success. As you may have noticed, the climbing specialists on the pro tour are almost all very lean (the late Marco Pantani comes to mind). Thus, climbing can be improved by increasing power, losing body weight or, for the greatest results, a combination of the two. Even a relatively small weight loss (3-5 lbs) can produce significant improvement. Much information is available regarding losing weight so this guide will not attempt to add to that body of knowledge. Just keep in mind that weight loss can lead to reductions in power output (to maintain power lose as much fat and as little muscle as possible). Increasing cycling power will be touched upon in the following sections and comes about through specific training.

Regarding the advantages of lower weight, do not forget your bike. As long as component stiffness is not compromised (stiffer rims and frames flex less during use and thus take less energy to push up hills) reducing your machine's weight will improve its ability to climb as well. Rotating weight is the real key so you will see the biggest gains from reductions in this area. Use the lightest rims, pedals and shoes you can afford. Tires with smoother and thinner treads and stronger sidewalls will also help.

Improving Lactate Threshold

Lactate threshold is the point at which lactic acid begins to accumulate above moderate levels, resulting in fatigue in the affected muscles. This quickly results in the inability to continue to perform at this level of work. Most riders know the heavy legged feeling after a hard bout of work when you must slow down in order to keep going. The goal of training is to raise the point at which lactic acid accumulates enough to affect performance. All things being equal, the higher your lactate threshold, the faster the pace you can hold on climbs. While lactate threshold can be measured directly it correlates well with heart rate and is normally between 75-90% of maximum heart rate. The goal of climbing-specific training should be to increase that percentage towards the top of the range. A simple way to estimate your lactate threshold is to perform two bouts of work. When rested and motivated and after a good warm-up, perform a twenty minute time trial at maximum effort and record your average heart rate. Repeat this test under similar conditions. The average heart rate for both efforts is a close approximation of your heart rate at your lactate threshold. Providing you have a sufficient aerobic endurance base (see 'Build a Base' above) lactate threshold training should improve your climbing ability. This is very demanding training however and will require proper recovery between bouts so don't forget to include easy days on the bike when needed.

Interval Routines

A very effective way to increase your power and to raise your lactate threshold in order to improve climbing ability is through the use of intervals. Intervals are relatively short bursts of more intense effort followed by a recovery period. Several of the below routines should be interspersed (start at the top of the below list and progress down) within your regular riding training (1-3 times per week) depending upon the season. Use them more frequently for pre-season training; tapering off before races. Add/delete routines as needed. Recovery between intervals should be easy, high cadence spinning on mostly level ground.

Big gear climbs - On various hill grades shift up one cog from normal (harder gear) for 1-2 minutes. Keep cadence at least 50 RPM and stay seated.

Cruise intervals - 3 to 5 intervals for 6-12 minutes each on a moderate grade (3-5%) at or just below your lactate threshold. Recover for 2-4 minutes. Gradually add minutes to each interval.

Anaerobic endurance intervals - 3-5 intervals for 2-4

minutes each on a 6-8% grade, gradually building the intensity, with cadence of at least 60 RPM. Intensity should be above your lactate threshold for the second half of the interval. Recovery should be double the interval length.

Extended Climbing at Lactate Threshold - On a steady and moderate grade, climb for 15-30 minutes at or just slightly above your lactate threshold. Gradually add minutes up to 30 (or the longest hill you may need to climb).

Sit/Stand intervals - On a moderate hill and at a comfortable cadence, alternate seated and standing climbing of equal intervals. After thirty seconds in the saddle, stand on the pedals for 30 seconds. After another minute of climbing in the saddle, stand for one minute, etc. Gradually build the intervals up to 4-5 minutes each.

Hill Sprints - Perform 5-10 sprints for 10-15 seconds at maximum effort. Gradually move from moderate to steeper hills. Recover for five minutes between each sprint.

Hill Jumps - While climbing a moderate hill do 4-5 sets of 3-5 jumps for ten crank turns (both feet) at maximum effort. Recover for one minute between each jump and five minutes between each set.

Advanced Hill Jumps - On a moderate grade perform 3-5 two minute sets, attacking every thirty seconds for ten pedal strokes. Stand for the attacks which should be at maximum effort; stay seated otherwise. Recover for five minutes between sets.

Weight Training

One factor linked to climbing success is leg strength. Particularly if you cannot put in year round riding on hills, weight training sessions should be added to your weekly routine. Ideally hit the weight room 2-3 times per week in the off season and once per week in season, tapering off before races or big rides. Increasing upper body strength has the potential to reduce upper body fatigue and increasing lower body strength will give you the ability to push a bigger gear over the same hill. The below exercises will give you the most benefit for your time spent in the gym. Do not include both squats and leg presses unless leg strength is a very weak area. Masters riders or those with lower back issues should not include squats in their routine and should perform the leg press instead.

Squat - 2-3 sets of 8-12 repetitions

Leg press - 2-3 sets of 8-12 repetitions

Calf raise - 2-3 sets of 8-12 repetitions

Step-ups - 2-3 sets of 8-12 repetitions

Bench press - 2-3 sets of 8-12 repetitions

Lat pulldown - 2-3 sets of 8-12 repetitions

Push-ups - 2-3 sets of 25 repetitions

Sit-ups (crunches) - 2-3 sets of 25 repetitions

Back extensions - 2-3 sets of 25 repetitions

Descending

Descending ability, like any other skill, is best obtained and improved with practice. The more time you can spend on descending, the more confidence and speed you will be able to develop. The most important aspect of descending is relaxation. Anxiety can narrow your concentration and you may end up missing a dangerous aspect of the road ahead. Speed is obviously important but pushing your speed to the point of fear will not help your descending skills. Work on relaxation and speed will follow. Keep a slight bend in the arms and slide back in the saddle, keeping your hands on the drops of your bars. One important riding habit to develop is to look far enough in front of you to match the pace at which you are descending. During a faster descent you need to watch the road much further in front of the bike. Set up well in advance of a curve and do whatever braking needs to done before entering the turn. If you are riding in a group, spread out. This will allow each rider to take their preferred line through the corners; critical in that you may not have time to adjust once you commit. It also allows a greater margin if a rider needs to brake. For long descents you should use both brakes equally. Once in a turn any traction used for braking significantly reduces the traction available for cornering. In wet conditions the distance required to stop is extended. Lightly apply the brakes periodically on a wet descent to remove excess water from the rims. Compete only against yourself on a fast descent and exercise caution on unfamiliar roads by always being prepared for road debris or traffic around every blind corner. In many cases descents are followed by another climb; if so, try to spin the pedals as you approach the bottom so that you will be warmed up for the next section of riding. Take it easy, relax, concentrate on the road, and most importantly, practice descending, and you will find your skills improving.

Mental Training

As professional cyclist Chris Boardman once said "The best climbers do not suffer less, they just suffer faster". Climbing is painful, suffering the name of the game. That said there may also be some less conventional ways to improve your climbing ability. Developing mental focus to enable one to block out distractions, including physical discomfort, is another attribute of good climbers and should be included in your training regimen. All negative

Saturday morning climb in Vermont

Long views in Maine

thoughts must go during workouts or races. The minute you think you cannot make a climb is when you may get dropped. Many riders are dropped on climbs before they reach their physical breaking point simply because of negative thoughts.

Begin working on mental focus by clearing your mind entirely. This can be a difficult skill to master but can be developed in stretches during long rides. Be patient as it sometimes takes time to see progress. Once this skill is developed begin to think of a single thought or image. Try to keep this single thought or image in your mind for extended periods. Once you have developed this ability you will find it much easier to concentrate over a climb. Work on visualizing images of light or soaring objects as you work your way up the hill. These images can lower the perception of effort. Even if climbing times are similar the effect should be one of additional energy for the remainder of the race or ride. Remember, everyone suffers on a tough climb. Climbing can be as much a mental as physical challenge, so try not to let a lack of self-confidence affect your performance. Developing ways to deal mentally with the physical aspects of getting over tough hills should produce better results on the road.

Climbing Tactics

There are some specific strategies regarding climbing that can have dramatic results when it comes to better race finishes. First of all, as with the overall route, it pays to be very familiar with the climbs along the way, so scout major hills if at all possible, noting the position of flat or very steep sections, particularly those that are stage/race finishes. When many inexperienced riders come to a hill they simply go all out and feel tremendous pressure to reach the top. Unless it is the last climb of the day doing so results in spending enormous amounts of energy that could be saved for the finish. Until you are a great climber you should maintain your own pace. Trying to stay with the top climbers is not good strategy. Instead try to find the exact personal pace that will help you cut your losses. Never ride faster than you know you can go. If needed, as you get comfortable with the climb, see if you can pick up the pace over the last half so that by the top you can catch the original group with which you started. You may be surprised by how many riders you pass along the way. Ideally try to time the effort so that you catch the pack at the summit. Unless you are the first over the top, be careful not to slow down near summits that are not race finishes. As the leaders begin to accelerate on the descent each rider has to push harder over the top in order to hold the wheel in front of him. Shift into a bigger gear as you approach the summit and accelerate over the top. You can recover on the descent from the extra effort involved.

Riders who are good sprinters often come to a hill in or near the lead and then drift to the back of the pack during the climb. On the descent and any following flats they can often catch the lead group before the next climb. By doing this several times early in a ride/race you can save a lot of energy for the finish while also developing the confidence of knowing that you do not have to crest climbs near the front to be successful. If the climb is the last of the day, obviously your tactics will need to change. You may need to make an all out effort to catch the lead group such as when the finish is very close or if being with the group will save a lot of energy (long, flat section just ahead). As you gain experience and become more aware of group dynamics you will start to make better decisions earlier in a climb and save energy as well.

Once you become a good climber, attack on the hills. Use your strength to put time on your competitors as you may need it over the remainder of the race/ride. An early attack can keep pressure on those who may be stronger in other areas. Riders that push too hard trying to keep up with you on a hill early in the race may find themselves struggling on the last climb of the day. Steeper sections are often a good place to launch an attack as you can more quickly open a gap before other riders react. However, attacking early on a hilly stage is a risky decision as you will either ride to victory or go down in flames if the peloton swallows you up before the finish. Depending on the result your decision will be portrayed as courageous or foolish bravado so if you go make sure you are committed to the move. Many a cyclist has made a name for themselves breaking away on a monster climb and staying away so don't let a prior failed attempt keep you from trying again.

If the race finish is the hill crest obviously it is best to be out in front by a comfortable margin and cruise to victory up the final climb. However, until you are a super climber that situation may rarely present itself. Unless it is a very long climb get into the lead group as soon as possible. Once there, knowing when to attack is a crucial skill to master. Much of your decision will be based on how you are feeling that day and on race conditions and will become clearer with additional climbing/racing experience. The other contending riders may also come into play. If there is a sprinter in the lead group you may want to go early and take his legs out from under him. If so, take a measured approach. Launch an attack but not an all out effort. Even though part of the group may stay with you, the effort should drop a few riders. If you are feeling good continue the attack. If you are able to continue at a relatively high cadence you should drop all but the strongest climbers. Unless you have ridden all riders off of your wheel it will come down to your placement in the group and timing as the finish line draws near.

The first thing you must do is know where the finish line is. If you scouted the hill, even if the last section is twisty with obscured views you should have an advantage. Once you have a good idea of how far away the line is, positioning will be key. Draft off other riders as much as possible as you approach the summit. When the finish is in sight try to be the second or third wheel before the final sprint begins. Realize this is easier said than done and knowing how to position within the group will again come from experience. The time to start your finishing sprint will depend upon your sprinting ability. The greater your sprinting skills, the earlier you can launch your assault. Always be alert for the rider in front of you moving first. Come out of the saddle on the down stroke as you make your move. Once you pull away try to stay directly in front of the rest of the pack so they will have to move around you to pass. Don't look back as you power toward the line. All of these actions should be thought out well before the actual finishing stretch. Many of these tactical maneuvers come with experience so train with experienced riders to see how they approach climbs, or shadow a particular rider, noting how they adjust to different situations on the hill.

Summary

To get the most out of the time on your bike and to avoid overtraining refer to the below summary:

- Build a strong aerobic base before adding a lot of climbing mileage to your training rides
- Add climbing to your regular training rides
- Utilize interval training to improve climbing ability
- Build up the intensity of your training slowly

- Train consistently for best results
- Eat a balanced diet
- Try to get a minimum of eight hours sleep each night
- Set short, medium and long-term goals
- Use a training diary and review when needed
- Know yourself and adjust your workouts accordingly
- Don't forget to include easy days on the bike if you are including extensive climbing routines in your training
- Use mental techniques to develop positive thoughts during climbing
- Practice descending skills to round out your mountain training
- Don't forget the tactical side of climbing

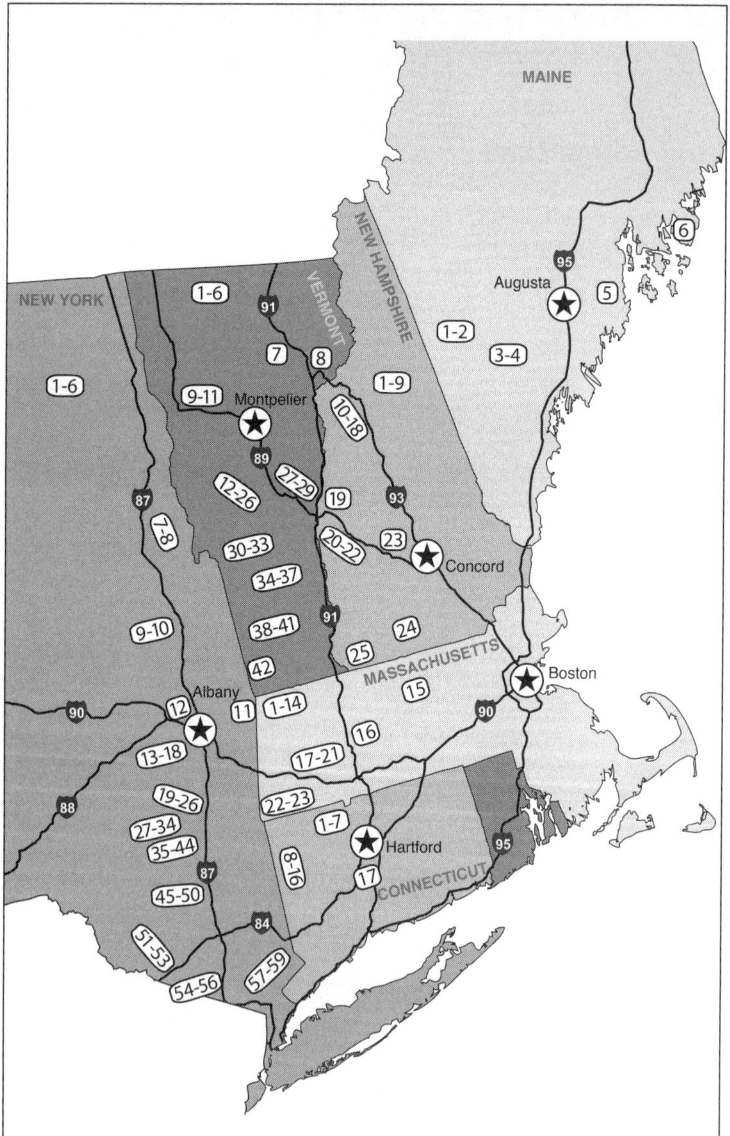
MAINE
NEW HAMPSHIRE
VERMONT
NEW YORK
MASSACHUSETTS
CONNECTICUT
Augusta
Montpelier
Concord
Boston
Albany
Hartford
95
91
89
93
87
90
88
84
1-6
7
8
9-11
12-26
27-29
30-33
34-37
38-41
42
1-2
3-4
5
6
1-9
10-18
19
20-22
23
24
25
1-6
7-8
9-10
11
12
13-18
19-26
27-34
35-44
45-50
51-53
54-56
57-59
1-14
15
16
17-21
22-23
1-7
8-16
17

Connecticut

Lost Acres Road

Total elevation - 582 ft | **Length - 3.0 miles**

Average Grade - 3.8% (12%) | **Rating - 0.21 (cat 3)**

Lost Acres Road is a popular climb quite close to the Massachusetts border in northern CT. It begins over shallow and then more challenging grade among some houses. The grade is rolling throughout with flats interspersed with more solid ramps. The houses recede eventually and you ride through thick woods. Near the summit the slope eases and the climb ends at the junction with Granville Road. You can turn left and climb quite shallowly for several miles up to East Hartland if you wish.

Directions - At the junction of Routes 539 and 189 in tiny North Granby, CT, head north on 189 for a short distance to Lost Acres Road on the left where the listed climb begins (see CT Map 1).

Mountain Road

Total elevation - 893 ft | **Length - 4.1 miles**

Average Grade - 4.1% (13%) | **Rating - 0.37 (cat 3)**

The work on this ascent comes fairly early and is a surprise for ascents in this area of the state. Leaving town you ride over gradually increasing grade. Soon you hit some double digit slope. Once this eases you ride over rolling grade which gradually lessens. At mile 3.7, turn right on Hartland Road (next climb) for 0.4 shallow miles up to a junction where the hill ends.

Directions - At the junction of Routes 539 and 189 in North Granby, CT, the climb begins by heading south on Route 539 (see CT Map 1).

Hartland Road

Total elevation - 828 ft	**Length - 4.8 miles**
Average Grade - 3.3% (7%)	**Rating - 0.27 (cat 3)**

Hartland Road is another popular area ascent over a shallow overall grade. It carries riders essentially due west to other climbing along with some traffic at times. As mentioned the grade for the entire hill is shallow to moderate as you ride through woods and among some residences here and there. Towards the top the slope gets very shallow and the listed hill ends at the junction with Route 179 in East Hartland.

Directions - In Granby, CT head west on Route 20 (West Granby Road) for several miles to where West Granby Road forks to the left. Continue straight to begin the listed climb (see CT Map 1).

North Hollow Road

Total elevation - 586 ft	**Length - 2.3 miles**
Average Grade - 4.8% (7%)	**Rating - 0.28 (cat 3)**

North Hollow Road is a short and scenic ascent in far northern Connecticut and is perhaps the most popular in the state. The grade is quite steady throughout and never gets steep as you ride along with little traffic most days. From the creek crossing, head south up the hill and somewhat narrow route under thick tree cover. The wooded setting makes for a pleasant ride and the climb ends at Balance Rock Road on the right as the slope flattens. Due to its mostly straight routing, North Hollow Road is a fairly quick and fun descent as well.

Directions - In East Hartland, CT at the junction of Routes 219 and 20, head north on Route 20 for 3.2 miles (descending the hill you will climb) to a creek crossing as the road makes a 90 degree turn to the left. Turn around to begin the listed ascent (see CT Map 1).

Morrison Hill Road

Total elevation - 749 ft | **Length - 2.9 miles**

Average Grade - 4.9% (8%) | **Rating - 0.37 (cat 3)**

The opposite side ascent of the previous hill, Morrison Hill Road also heads up the ridge under thick tree cover and over a mostly moderate grade. Soon it becomes stair step as you gain altitude. The road makes a right and then a left turn on the way up. Near the top you pop out of the trees and pass the entrance to the Granville State Forest on the right and the listed climb ends soon after as the grade flattens out.

Directions - See previous climb. At the creek crossing continue west for 0.5 miles to begin the ascent by continuing generally west up the hill (see CT Map 1).

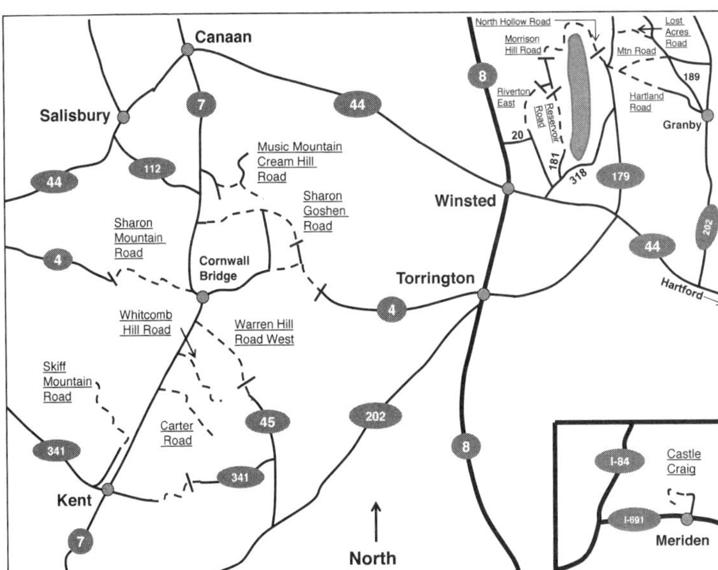

CT Map 1

Reservoir Climb

Total elevation - 724 ft	**Length - 5.1 miles**
Average Grade - 2.7% (11%)	**Rating - 0.42 (cat 3)**

Another very popular climb with area riders, the Reservoir Climb along Route 181 is a rolling ascent that carries cyclists due north. The road begins in thick woods and over moderate grade and carries little traffic most days. Soon you encounter a descent, one of several on the ascent which knock down its average grade. The pattern of up and down riding continues as you gain altitude. Near the top the pedaling gets easier one more time and the listed climb ends as the road descends at an unmarked but obvious top. The junction with Route 20 is 0.6 miles ahead.

Directions - At the junction of Routes 44 and 318 east of Winsted, CT, head east on 318 to Route 181 (breaks away to the left). Travel 181 north for 0.3 miles (grade change) to begin the listed climb (see CT Map 1).

Riverton East

Total elevation - 643 ft	**Length - 2.6 miles**
Average Grade - 4.7% (10%)	**Rating - 0.30 (cat 3)**

The climb of Riverton East begins over shallow grade as you head north out of the small town of Riverton. Soon you encounter the most challenging climbing on the hill. From that point you will pedal over stair step slope up the ridge with a few houses here and there. The grade eases up to the unmarked but obvious summit. Its junction with Route 181 is 0.2 miles ahead.

Directions - In Riverton, CT at the junction of Route 20 and East River Road, head north on 20 for 0.4 miles to begin the listed climb by continuing north on 20 (see CT Map 1).

Music Mountain/Cream Hill Road

Total elevation - 811 ft	**Length - 2.7 miles**
Average Grade - 5.7% (14%)	**Rating - 0.47 (cat 3)**

The hill begins on Music Mountain Road over solid grade generally to the north. Soon you hit a descent before the road turns to the right and resumes uphill, gradually getting challenging. Just less than one mile in and as the slope has eased, turn right on Cream Hill Road. This road is stair step up the hill and eventually includes the maximum grade. Soon after that the slope eases and then descends briefly. Climbing quickly resumes over shallow grade and stately trees and some views appear. The listed climb then ends as the road descends beyond.

Directions - On Route 7 in western Connecticut, just north of its junction with Route 112, head east on Lime Rock Station Road for 0.9 miles to Music Mountain Road on the left where the listed climb begins (see CT Map 1).

Sharon Mountain Road

Total elevation - 819 ft	**Length - 3.0 miles**
Average Grade - 5.2% (7%)	**Rating - 0.42 (cat 3)**

The ascent of Sharon Mountain Road along Route 4 is a solid hill that is popular with area riders. Through woods and over robust grade to begin, the slope eventually becomes stair step. A car or two may pass you on this hill but not enough to influence your ride. The grade then becomes more steady as you continue to gain altitude. Near the top the pedaling gets easier and the listed climb ends at Dunbar Road on the left.

Directions - At the junction of Routes 7 and 4 in Cornwall Bridge, CT head west on Route 4 (on the west side of the river) to begin the listed climb (see CT Map 1).

Sharon Goshen Road (Route 128)

Total elevation - 630 ft **Length - 3.5 miles**

Average Grade - 3.4% (8%) **Rating - 0.22 (cat 3)**

Another popular area ascent, Sharon Goshen Road is a variable grade hill that can lead to other riding/climbing nearby. It begins in town over solid grade. Soon it eases as you ride through thick woods. A flat is then found before climbing resumes in a stair step fashion. Where Route 125 goes straight, bear left to continue on Route 128. The climb soon ends where the road begins to descend down to Route 4.

Directions - At the junction of Routes 7 and 4 in Cornwall Bridge, CT head north on Route 7 for several miles to West Cornwall and Route 128 on the right. Head east on 128 (through the covered bridge) for a short distance to begin the listed climb (see CT Map 1).

Route 4 East

Total elevation - 692 ft **Length - 2.1 miles**

Average Grade - 6.2% (11%) **Rating - 0.44 (cat 3)**

The east side of Route 4 is a short but solid overall climb east of the town of Cornwall Bridge. An easy start soon gets more difficult as you encounter stout climbing for a time before things ease. Soon you pass the Mohawk Ski Area on the right just before you reach a 4 way stop (Route 128 to the left). Turn right to continue on Route 4 to find a descent and flat and then solid grade when climbing resumes. Another descent is then found before a final stretch of climbing up to a parking area on the right for the Mohawk State Forest where the listed climb ends.

Directions - At the junction of Routes 7 and 4 in Cornwall Bridge, CT head east on Route 4 for 3.3 miles (Route 125 on left) to begin the listed climb by continuing east on 4 (see CT Map 1).

Warren Hill Road West

Total elevation - 797 ft | **Length - 2.1 miles**

Average Grade - 7.2% (8%) | **Rating - 0.57 (cat 2/3)**

The west side of Warren Hill Road is a stout climb along Route 45 that carries some traffic at times. The road has a small shoulder for riding however. The grade is solid to start and then becomes stair step for the remainder of the ascent. Near the top the grades eases and the listed climb ends at Flat Rocks Road on the left. Due to its straight routing and average grade, Warren Hill Road West is a quick descent as well.

Directions - From the small town of Cornwall Bridge, CT, head south on Route 7 for several miles to Warren Hill Road on the left where the climb begins by heading east on Warren Hill Road (Route 45) (see CT Map 1).

Riders on Route 4 East in CT

Whitcomb Hill Road

Total elevation:	**740 ft**	**Length:**	**1.8 miles**
Top elevation:	**1,270 ft**	**Average grade:**	**7.8%**
Minimum grade:	**1%**	**Maximum grade:**	**18%**
Distance ≥ 5%:	**1.2 miles**	**Distance ≥ 10%:**	**0.5 miles**
Steepest mile:	**8.3%**	**Steepest 3 miles:**	**NA**
Traffic:	**1**	**Descent:**	**4**
Rating:	**0.61 (cat 2)**		

A climb more brutal than its statistics suggest, Whitcomb Hill Road may be the most difficult in the state of Connecticut as it contains severe grade in places. From the start at its junction with Route 7, be ready early as the slope is double digit to begin and just gets steeper. Soon you hit the maximum on the hill as you ride the narrow and deeply wooded track. Little traffic at least allows you to concentrate on the task at hand. After this shock to the system, pedaling eases but remains challenging before easing further to almost flat. Soon a guard rail appears on the right indicating the halfway point in the ascent.

The road curves to the left as you continue to gain altitude. A few houses then begin to appear and the grade slowly increases again. Keep turning the pedals as the slope soon ramps back up to double digit for the finishing stretch. Finally the woods part as you approach a red barn on the right and a white house on the left in somewhat open ground. Just beyond, the road goes flat where the listed hill ends. Is Whitcomb Hill Road the most difficult paved hill climb in Connecticut? There are many in contention for this honor so you decide. Its grade and tight routing make for a challenging descent as well.

Crux Stretch - The initial 0.3 miles are over impressive double digit grade (approaching 20% at one point) and are the key to a successful summit.

Directions - From the small town of Cornwall Bridge, CT, head south on Route 7 for several miles to Whitcomb Hill Road on the left where the climb begins (see CT Map 1).

Steeps on Whitcomb Hill Road

Whitcomb Hill Road, CT

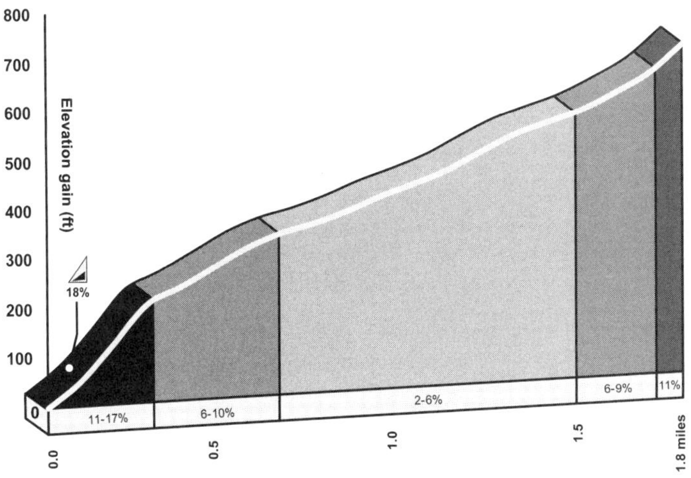

Carter Road

Total elevation - 670 ft | **Length - 1.7 miles**

Average Grade - 7.5% (20%) | **Rating - 0.54 (cat 2/3)**

Carter Road is similar to the previous ascent (Whitcomb Hill Road) in that it carries a stout overall and maximum grade although it contains even more grade variability. After a very challenging start the slope eases and then a descent is found. Climbing soon resumes over moderate grade before steepening again, including a short stretch of double digit pedaling. The slope eases greatly as you glide by a red barn but then soon goes to double digit again before easing up to an unmarked but obvious summit.

Directions - From the small town of Kent, CT, head north on Route 7 for several miles to Carter Road on the right and the climb begins at this junction (see CT Map 1).

Skiff Mountain Road

Total elevation - 748 ft | **Length - 1.8 miles**

Average Grade - 7.9% (13%) | **Rating - 0.60 (cat 2)**

Another contender for the most difficult climb in Connecticut, Skiff Mountain Road is an additional fairly short and stout test in the western part of the state. From climb start, the road dives into the woods over gradually increasing grade. Soon you are riding over stout grade on the dark road, including the climb maximum. From this point the slope generally eases the further you ride to the east. At mile 1.7, you pass Fuller Mountain Road on the left. Keep straight here for a very short distance and the listed climb ends as the route flattens on top.

Directions - In Kent, CT at the junction of Routes 341 and 7, head west on 341 for 0.4 miles to Skiff Mountain Road on the right. Travel Skiff Mountain for 1.0 miles to begin the climb as the road bears to the left and begins to ascend (see CT Map 1).

341 West

Total elevation - 766 ft | **Length - 2.8 miles**

Average Grade - 5.2% (8%) | **Rating - 0.52 (cat 2/3)**

The west side of Route 341 is a moderate sloped ascent fairly close to the New York border that does carry some traffic. The initial climbing is shallow to moderate with a few houses but mostly woods along the way. Soon you encounter a flat. Climbing then resumes over the most challenging grade on the hill before easing just before the listed climb end at Bald Hills Road on the left.

Directions - In Kent, CT at the junction of Routes 341 and 7, head east on 341 for 0.7 miles to begin the listed climb by continuing east on 341 (see CT Map 1).

Castle Craig

Total elevation - 552 ft | **Length - 1.3 miles**

Average Grade - 8.0% (14%) | **Rating - 0.46 (cat 3)**

The climb to Castle Craig may be the most challenging in the Bristol/ Meriden area of Connecticut. In thick woods for almost the entire ascent, you head west over solid grade to begin which gradually steepens up to a junction on the left and the slope eases. Keep straight here to soon find more challenging pedaling. Just before climbs end you find the maximum grade on the hill which is just before a small parking area at the end of the road. If you turn left at the junction, you have 0.4 miles of up and down pedaling to the actual Castle Craig. Stats for this version of the hill are the identical distance at 7.1% average grade.

Directions - In Meriden, CT on West Main Street at the stoplight for Hubbard Park, head into the park for 0.2 miles and then cross under Interstate 691. Continue north for 1.2 miles along a reservoir to its dam. Cross the dam (turn left) and travel into the woods for an additional 0.5 miles to a 90 degree left turn to begin (see CT Map 1).

6%
NEXT
3/4 MILE

Maine

Evans Notch North

Total elevation - 577 ft	**Length - 5.1 miles**
Average Grade - 2.1% (8%)	**Rating - 0.12 (cat 3/4)**

The north side of Evans Notch is a shallow grade hill close to the New Hampshire border. The road is quite narrow and the last mile carries more solid (but not steep) slope. It ends at the obvious notch in a pleasant setting.

Directions - In Gilead, Maine head west on Route 2 for a short distance to Route 113 (left). Head up 113 for ~3 miles to a crossing of Big Creek where the listed climb begins (see ME Map 1).

Evans Notch South

Total elevation - 844 ft	**Length - 2.1 miles**
Average Grade - 7.6% (11%)	**Rating - 0.64 (cat 2)**

One of the most scenic climbs in the Northeast, the south side of Evans Notch, located near the New Hampshire border, is also very isolated. The road is quite narrow and dark in places as it carries you up to the notch through a tunnel of trees and with little traffic most days. A fairly shallow start, the grade soon ramps up before you encounter a stretch of flat riding. Soon climbing resumes over moderate grade and the hill eventually enters deep woods and contains extended double digit grade toward the summit and can make you work for its scenic top. The summit is obvious and there are hiking possibilities at the notch as well.

Directions - In North Chatham, ME on Route 113, head north on 113 into New Hampshire and the state line is the listed climb start (continue north on 113) (see ME Map 1).

Streaked Mountain East

Total elevation - 778 ft **Length - 3.6 miles**

Average Grade - 4.1% (8%) **Rating - 0.32 (cat 3)**

One of the more difficult Maine climbs, the east side of Streaked Mountain along Route 117 is an interesting ascent located in the central section of the state that carries intermittent traffic. With an easy start, the grade is stair step up this hill with no real surprises along the way. Towards the top you will find a short descent which knocks down its average grade just a bit. The final climbing is over shallow grade and the listed climb ends at an unmarked top as the slope flattens out.

Directions - In the small town of Buckfield, Maine at the junction of Routes 117 and 140, head west on Route 117 for 1.0 miles to Sodom Road on the left to begin the listed climb by continuing west on 117 (see ME Map 1).

Streaked Mountain West

Total elevation - 814 ft **Length - 4.8 miles**

Average Grade - 3.2% (8%) **Rating - 0.26 (cat 3)**

The west side of Streaked Mountain is a similar if a bit longer and more shallow overall ascent compared with its east side. From the junction of Routes 117 and 19, head east over moderate grade which soon eases. At mile 1.7 you cross a creek but with little grade change. A short distance later the grade pops up to the most challenging on the hill. A stair step pattern then emerges as the route goes up and down as it gains altitude. Towards the top you find one more solid ramp through the trees up to the unmarked but obvious summit.

Directions - In Norway, ME at the junction of Routes 19 and 117, the climb begins by heading east on 117 (see ME Map 1).

Mount Battie

Total elevation - 595 ft | **Length - 1.7 miles**

Average Grade - 6.6% (14%) | **Rating - 0.39 (cat 3)**

The climb of Mount Battie is a short and sharp ascent on the Maine coast. A short stretch of moderate climbing up from Route 1 leads to flat ground and the toll booth. Turn left just beyond and soon the grade picks up as you ride through thick woods and little traffic most days. There are two ramps of steeper grade to negotiate, the 2nd of which contains the maximum on the hill. Near the top the slope eases up to a small parking area with excellent views of the coast and Atlantic Ocean.

Directions - In Camden, ME on Route 1 the climb begins at the entrance to Mount Battie State Park (see ME Map 1).

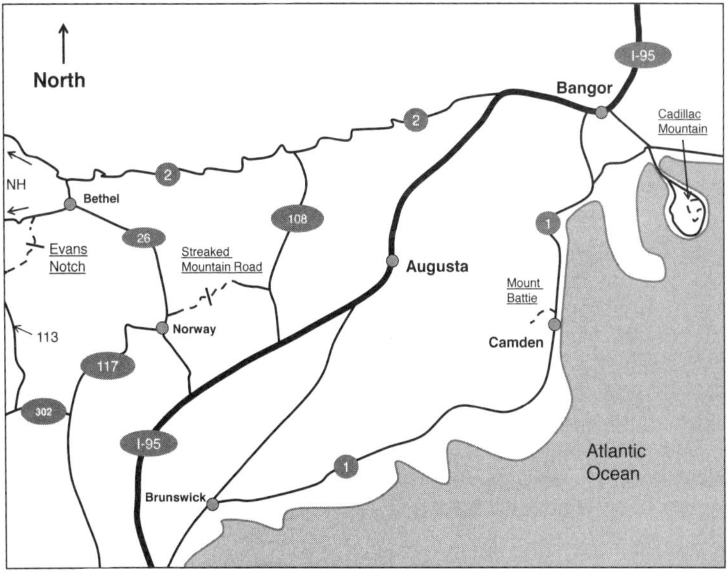

ME Map 1

Cadillac Mountain

Total elevation:	**1,404 ft**	**Length:**	**5.5 miles**
Top elevation:	**1,504 ft**	**Average grade:**	**4.8%**
Minimum grade:	**0%**	**Maximum grade:**	**8%**
Distance ≥ 5%:	**2.5 miles**	**Distance ≥ 10%:**	**0.0 miles**
Steepest mile:	**6.1%**	**Steepest 3 miles:**	**5.3%**
Traffic:	**4**	**Descent:**	**3**
Rating:	**0.68 (cat 2)**		

Located in Acadia National Park right on the picturesque Maine coast, Cadillac Mountain is a very scenic climb that rises from just above sea level and is very likely the most difficult ascent in the state. It is over mostly moderate and fairly steady grade along the majority of its route. The views on top are quite good and you will likely have some company (mostly auto traffic) on your way up but not so much that it ruins the climb.

From climb start at the junction of Routes 3 and 223 in Bar Harbor, head south on 223 over shallow grade. You then stair step up the hill which includes a small descent. The grade then gradually increases and at mile 1.1 bear right into the national park to find a short stretch of solid grade. At the junction turn left to find shallow grade. From this point you ride along up and down slope for one mile with some traffic most days. At mile 2.2, turn left to the summit into the woods and find the steepest sustained climbing on the hill. Soon very good views appear to your left as you ride along the ridgeline as the trees disappear. The grade eventually eases back and then when it ramps up again, more very good scenery is encountered. Towards the summit you find a short descent. Climbing then resumes over shallow grade and the hill ends at a parking area with hiking possibilities. The descent of Cadillac Mountain is mostly uncomplicated except perhaps for its intermittent traffic.

Crux Stretch - While there are no steeps on this hill, it may be the initial mile right after the final left turn that is the key to the summit.

Directions - At the junction of Routes 3 and 223 in Bar Harbor, ME, head south on 223 to begin (see ME Map 1).

Views from Cadillac Mountain

Cadillac Mountain, ME

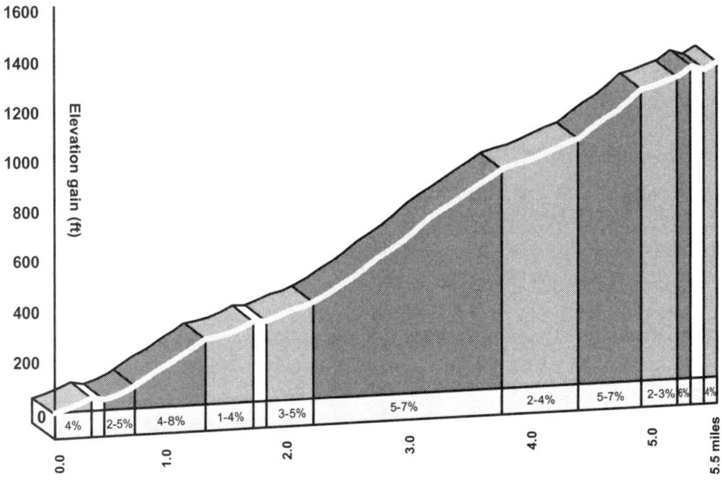

Massachusetts

Petersburgh Pass East

Total elevation - 1,226 ft	**Length - 4.0 miles**
Average Grade - 5.8% (7%)	**Rating - 0.71 (cat 2)**

The east side of Petersburgh Pass is a pleasant and steady grade ride towards New York State. Some views appear to the left as you gain altitude and there is usually little traffic on this road which becomes quite twisty in places but there are no surprises on this one. Near the top you enter New York and the summit is reached soon after (pullout on left).

Directions - In Williamstown, MA head south on Route 7 for a short distance to Route 2 on the right where the listed climb begins by heading west on Route 2 (see MA Map 1).

Mount Greylock South

Total elevation - 2,287 ft	**Length - 9.6 miles**
Average Grade - 4.5% (13%)	**Rating - 1.05 (cat 2)**

The south side of Mount Greylock is a bit longer but quite a bit less steep than its north side. A few solid ramps early on are interspersed with long stretches of shallow climbing over its middle core. At mile 8.7 you reach the junction of the north side approach (next climb) on your left but keep straight. Towards the top you will again find a bit more solid grade and long views on clear days. The climb soon ends as the road ends near the top of the mountain.

Directions - In Pittsfield, MA head north on Route 7 for several miles to the Mount Greylock State Reservation road on the right. The listed climb begins at this junction (see MA Map 1).

Mount Greylock North

Total elevation:	**2,780 ft**	**Length:**	**9.0 miles**
Top elevation:	**3,475 ft**	**Average grade:**	**5.9%**
Minimum grade:	**0%**	**Maximum grade:**	**17%**
Distance ≥ 5%:	**6.4 miles**	**Distance ≥ 10%:**	**0.5 miles**
Steepest mile:	**8.5%**	**Steepest 3 miles:**	**8.3%**
Traffic:	**3**	**Descent:**	**4**
Rating:	**1.82 (cat 1)**		

The northern approach to Mount Greylock is very likely the most difficult climb in Massachusetts and I want to apologize to MA riders for using an incorrect start for this hill in The Complete Guide to Climbing by Bike (nationwide guide). The hill is solid immediately as you pull away from State Street. Soon bear right on Reservoir Road and find continued double digit grade. This section quickly becomes quite variable with shallow riding interspersed with double digit ramps. At mile 2.3 turn left to continue as you enter the Mount Greylock State Reservation. The route heads into deep woods here and the road narrows and begins to twist up the hill.

The next several miles are solid overall and through multiple S bends that carry you higher up the mountain. Beyond this quite solid slope the grade eases a bit but the route remains tight and twisty. A nice view appears briefly to your right as you approach a junction. At that junction, turn left to continue over mild grade and with nice views to your right. Near the very top the road splits and the listed climb ends very near the top of the mountain at the top of the circle. The descent of the north side of Mount Greylock is a challenging one in places (closed in winter - Mount Greylock State Reservation - 413 499-4262).

Crux stretch - The initial mile may be the key on this hill as it contains several ramps of double digit grade or the 3 miles of > 8% grade that begin as you enter the state reservation.

Directions - In North Adams, MA at the intersection of Route 8 and State Street, head up State Street to begin (see MA Map 1).

Views along Mount Greylock

Mount Greylock North, MA

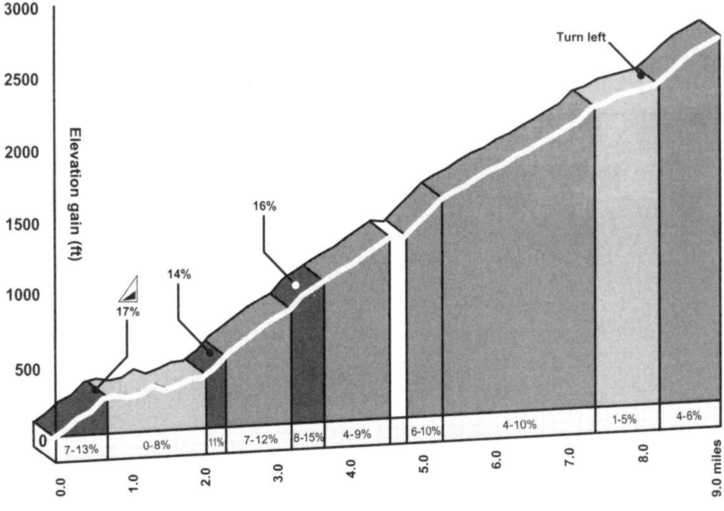

Mohawk Trail East

Total elevation - 1,589 ft	**Length - 7.4 miles**
Average Grade - 4.1% (8%)	**Rating - 0.65 (cat 2)**

The east side approach up Mohawk Trail is an interesting ascent with a bit of traffic at times. You find shallow grade as you climb alongside a creek within the drainage to begin. Several miles in, the slope ramps up and the route gets more twisty. Soon the grade eases again and you break out of the drainage. A bit further up the hill you will find a descent but climbing soon resumes over moderate grade which takes you up to the obvious summit.

Directions - In Charlemont, MA head west on Route 2 for several miles to the Mohawk Trail State Forest facility on the right where the listed climb begins (see MA Map 1).

Mohawk Trail West

Total elevation - 1,259 ft	**Length - 4.2 miles**
Average Grade - 5.7% (8%)	**Rating - 0.72 (cat 2)**

The west side of Route 2 is a steady grade climb with traffic from picturesque North Adams in western Massachusetts. An easy start in town soon leads to increased grade but there are no real surprises on this one. Eventually you encounter a big hairpin turn to the right as you ascend the ridgeline. Soon the grade eases up to the obvious summit. The traffic will be with you on this one most days but it is a worthwhile climb and a fast descent back into town except for the tight switchback and vehicles at times.

Directions - In North Adams, MA head east on Route 2 for a short distance to Miners Street on the right where the listed climb begins by continuing east on Route 2 (see MA Map 1).

Whitcomb Hill Road

Total elevation - 1,299 ft | **Length - 2.9 miles**

Average Grade - 8.5% (11%) | **Rating - 1.10 (cat 2)**

Whitcomb Hill Road is a steady and solid grade ascent away from the scenic Deerfield River toward Route 2 in western Massachusetts. Good scenery and a wide and lightly travelled road make for a pleasant ascent as long as the stout (but mostly steady) grade does not deter. There are also a few switchbacks along the way to spice things up. At mile 2.5 turn right on busier Route 2 to finish over more moderate grade at the obvious summit. Due to grade Whitcomb Hill Road is also a quick and somewhat challenging descent.

Directions - On Route 2 west of Charlemont, MA, take Zoar Road north (easy to miss). At the junction go left to stay on the river and in ~4.5 miles Whitcomb Hill Road appears on the left where the climb begins (see MA Map 1).

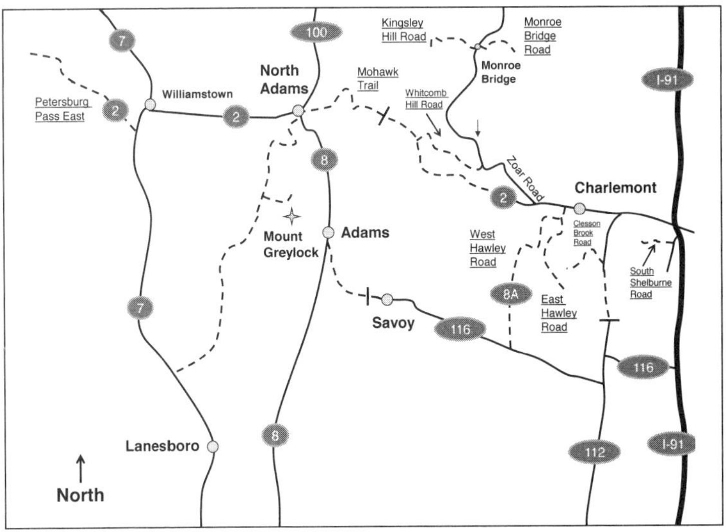

MA Map 1

Kingsley Hill Road

Total elevation:	**948 ft**	**Length:**	**1.4 miles**
Top elevation:	**2,045 ft**	**Average grade:**	**12.8%**
Minimum grade:	**1%**	**Maximum grade:**	**24%**
Distance ≥ 5%:	**1.1 miles**	**Distance ≥ 10%:**	**0.7 miles**
Steepest mile:	**14.1%**	**Steepest 3 miles:**	**NA**
Traffic:	**1**	**Descent:**	**4**
Rating:	**1.25 (cat 1)**		

Isolated Kingsley Hill Road. located in northwestern Massachusetts, is a severe and unique ascent on a very narrow road. The first half mile of this one is simply the steepest that I have found in the continental United States. Don't blink in the small town of Monroe Bridge or you will miss the turnoff. The rough surface adds to the difficulty along with a significant stretch of 20+% grade. If you survive the first half mile, keep going as the first mile of Kingsley Hill Road is also one of the steepest around.

The hill begins over solid grade which only gets steeper the further west you ride. Leaving town quickly, you enter thick woods as you encounter severe grade. Soon the slope hits 20% so just keep turning the pedals to make progress. At the half mile point the grade eases, giving you a chance to catch your breath.

The slope eases here but is still solid and soon you are again riding over double digit slope although not to the level of the previous section. The woods begin to thin a bit and a road appears on the left. Keep riding straight as the grade eases as a few houses appear. Turn left at the road junction for 0.1 miles to finish over moderate grade up to an unmarked top.

Crux stretch - The first half mile, which may be the steepest of this length in the United States, could end up terminating your attempt at this hill.

Directions - In the tiny town of Monroe Bridge, MA head west on Kingsley Hill Road from River Road right in the center of town (see MA Map 1).

The start of Kingsley Hill Road

Kingsley Hill Road, MA

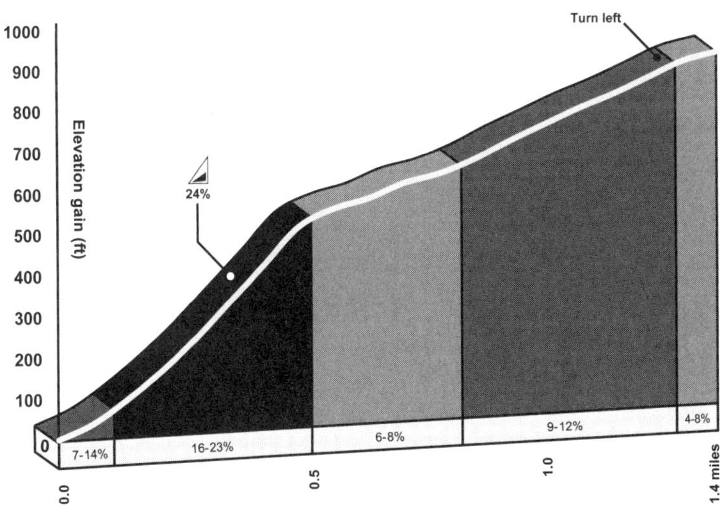

Monroe Hill Road

Total elevation - 812 ft	**Length - 1.3 miles**
Average Grade - 11.8% (18%)	**Rating - 0.96 (cat 2)**

Not quite as fearsome as nearby Kingsley Hill Road but no day at the park either, Monroe Hill Road is another short and very steep ascent near the scenic Deerfield River in northwestern Massachusetts. It is very interesting around the small dam that you must cross to get to its start (if coming from Monroe Bridge). Its steepest section near the bottom, you bear to the right about halfway up to find decreased grade and the listed climb ends at an unmarked but obvious top. This is also a very scenic climb that flows through thick woods over most of the route. Monroe Hill Road is a fast descent due to grade as well so watch the tight turn at the very bottom of the hill.

Directions - In Monroe Bridge, Massachusetts head east on Monroe Bridge Road. Cross the dam and the climb begins just beyond at an obvious grade change as the road pulls away from the river (see MA Map 1).

116 West

Total elevation - 859 ft	**Length - 2.9 miles**
Average Grade - 5.6% (8%)	**Rating - 0.48 (cat 3)**

The west side of Route 116 is a solid hill away from Adams, MA. Never steep, it does carry a fairly stout overall grade and some traffic but it does have a small shoulder for riding. The initial slope is quite variable and then you encounter 1.4 miles of more solid and steady grade. After that segment the pedaling gets easier again and you will find a descent. Climbing soon resumes over shallow grade up to the listed climb top (road descends beyond).

Directions - In Adams, MA at the junction of Routes 8 and 116, head east on 116 for 2.3 miles to Wells Road on the right to begin the climb by continuing east on 116 (see MA Map 1).

West Hawley Road

Total elevation - 1,016 ft	**Length - 6.6 miles**
Average Grade - 2.9% (9%)	**Rating - 0.30 (cat 3)**

West Hawley Road is a shallow overall ascent through pleasant surroundings. Over a shallow start, the route then stair steps up the hill through woods with a few residences here and there. After about 3 miles you find the most challenging sustained climbing on the hill. The hill eases at a small pond on the right as you enter Plainfield. From here the effort is shallow to moderate up to the top. At Route 16, turn either right or left for 0.1 miles to finish.

Directions - In Charlemont, MA head west on Route 2 for a short distance to Route 8A. Head south and then quickly turn right to remain on 8A/West Hawley Road. Travel 8A for 2.7 miles to begin the listed climb by continuing south on 8A/West Hawley Road (see MA Map 1).

East Hawley Road

Total elevation - 1,229 ft	**Length - 3.7 miles**
Average Grade - 6.3% (12%)	**Rating - 0.77 (cat 2)**

East Hawley Road is a solid climb located in the central mountains of the state. The route is twisty immediately as you enter the woods. You pass a few houses down low as the slope is stair step with shallow climbing interrupted by more solid ramps. A switchback to the right is found at mile 2.6 which introduces stout grade. Towards the summit the slope becomes variable and soon the grade eases up to its listed top at Grout Road on the left.

Directions - In Charlemont, MA head west on Route 2 for a short distance to Route 8A. Head south on 8A and then quickly take a left on South River Road for 0.2 miles to East Hawley Road on the right. Travel East Hawley south for 0.3 very shallow miles where the climb begins by continuing south (see MA Map 1).

Clesson Brook Road

Total elevation - 1,012 ft	**Length - 5.2 miles**
Average Grade - 3.7 (9%)	**Rating - 0.37 (cat 3)**

Clesson Brook Road is an isolated and mostly shallow ascent that takes riders west to other riding/climbing. Along a creek down low, you ride through woods and by some homes with easy pedaling. After two miles you will ride by a covered bridge on the left. Soon the route gets quite dark but the pedaling stays mostly moderate throughout. Over the 2nd half of the climb the grade gets stair step in nature and the ascent eventually ends as the slope eases up to Plainfield Road.

Directions - From Buckland, MA, head south on Route 112 for a short distance and Clesson Brook Road is on the right where the listed climb begins (see MA Map 1).

112 North

Total elevation - 501 ft	**Length - 1.6 miles**
Average Grade - 5.9% (7%)	**Rating - 0.30 (cat 3)**

The north side of Route 112 is a short and pleasant ascent you can use to link up with other riding/climbing in the area. The two lane road carries a bit of traffic at times but not enough to ruin the climb and there is a small shoulder for riding. From climb start the grade gradually increases up to solid as you ride through woods but there is no steep stuff on this hill. The listed climb ends after 1.6 miles as the slope goes flat. Its intersection with Route 116 is 0.6 miles further south.

Directions - From Buckland, MA, head south on Route 112 for a short distance to a pullout on the left where the listed climb begins as the grade changes dramatically (see MA Map 1).

South Shelburne Road

Total elevation - 565 ft | **Length - 1.9 miles**

Average Grade - 5.6% (8%) | **Rating - 0.32 (cat 3)**

South Shelburne Road is an isolated climb near Greenfield, MA. After an easy start you enter woods to find a bit more challenging grade including a right hand switchback. Soon the grade eases, goes back up and then you find a short descent. Climbing then resumes over gradually increasing grade through a right turn and the listed climb ends at an unmarked top just before another descent.

Directions - At the junction of Interstate 91 and Route 2A (Exit 26) in Greenfield, MA, head east on 2A for a very short distance to Newton Street. Head south on Newton and quickly bear left on Fairview. Head west on Fairview across I-91 to its end at South Shelburne Road where the climb begins (see MA Map 1)

Wachusett Mountain

Total elevation - 1,072 ft | **Length - 3.6 miles**

Average Grade - 5.6% (12%) | **Rating - 0.62 (cat 2)**

Wachusett Mountain is likely the most popular ascent of any meaningful length in Massachusetts as it lies quite close to the Boston metro area. It begins over solid grade and soon you enter woods. At mile 1.3, turn right into the State Reservation to continue. Here you encounter a flat/ descent before climbing resumes over shallow and then variable grade. Soon the road becomes one way at a flat. The next section has more challenging pedaling along with a descent. Where the road comes back together, turn left to find steeper grade for the final pitch up to the summit where the climb soon ends at a small parking area.

Directions - At the junction of Routes 2 and 140 in Westminster, MA, head south on 140 for several miles to Mile Hill Road (right). Travel this road for 0.5 miles to the Wachusett Mtn Ski Area (right) where the climb begins by continuing south on Mile Hill (see MA Map 2).

Mount Holyoke

Total elevation - 818 ft | **Length - 2.1 miles**

Average Grade - 7.4% (15%) | **Rating - 0.62 (cat 2)**

Mount Holyoke is a short and steep ascent within Skinner State Park that dead ends very close to the top of the mountain. Through dark woods for the most part, the hill begins over shallow and gradually increasing grade. As you swing 90 degrees to the left the slope picks up to double digit for a stretch. It then becomes variable, including a small descent, and the route twisty. Towards the top are several S bends to negotiate with a bit more stout grade. A final right hand turn leads to double digit grade and a small parking area and views. Keep riding beyond, right up to roads end for the full climb.

Directions - On Route 9 in Hadley, MA, head south on Route 47 for several miles to the road to Skinner State Park on the left where the climb begins (see MA Map 2).

A rider on Mount Holyoke

66 East

Total elevation - 851 ft | **Length - 4.2 miles**

Average Grade - 3.8% (10%) | **Rating - 0.35 (cat 3)**

The east side of Route 66 west of Northampton, MA is a fairly popular hill over mostly shallow to moderate grade. Heading essentially directly west, you begin with a shallow start through pleasant surroundings and with intermittent traffic which tends to thin the further you ride. The route then stair steps up the hill through some woods and with a few residences here and there. Just over 3 miles into the ascent you find the most challenging sustained climbing on the hill. It is fairly short and the grade then eases just before the unmarked summit which is short of the top of its west side (next climb).

Directions - In Northampton, MA head west on Route 66 for 5.7 miles to Loudville Road. 0.4 miles further west you cross a creek where the listed climb begins by continuing west on 66 (see MA Map 2).

66 West

Total elevation - 781 ft | **Length - 2.7 miles**

Average Grade - 5.5% (8%) | **Rating - 0.43 (cat 2/3)**

The west side of Route 66 is a shorter and more stout overall climb compared to its east side that begins from Route 112. It launches over solid grade as you quickly encounter woods along with a few houses. Two miles in find a flat and then soon after a short descent which knocks down the hill's average grade. Climbing then resumes over moderate grade which continues up to its listed top at Alan Coit Road on the right.

Directions - At the junction of Routes 20 and 112 in Huntington, MA, head north on 112 for 3.5 miles to Route 66 on the right where the listed climb begins by heading east on 66 (see MA Map 2).

Montgomery/Southampton Roads

Total elevation - 725 ft **Length - 2.2 miles**

Average Grade - 6.2% (14%) **Rating - 0.46 (cat 3)**

This combination of roads (really one road) Is a short and solid hill that is very popular with area riders as it carries folks from the Springfield/ Holyoke/Westfield areas towards more gravity challenging riding. From the junction you pull away over mostly moderate grade. The road becomes Southampton Road at some point as you gain altitude. About 2/3rds of the way up the hill you find a descent, knocking down the average grade. Soon climbing resumes over the most challenging grade on the mountain. Towards the very top the slope eases up to its listed top at the junction with the main road to the town of Montgomery. Stats for this hill are estimated.

Directions - From the junction of Routes 202 and 10 just west of Holyoke, MA, head west on North Road for several miles to Russellville Road on the right. Travel Russellville Road for 1.0 miles to Wyben Road where the climb begins by continuing straight on what is now Montgomery Road (see MA Map 2).

Russell Stage Road

Total elevation - 1,116 ft **Length - 3.9 miles**

Average Grade - 5.4% (11%) **Rating - 0.61 (cat 2)**

Russell Stage Road is a solid hill that parallels Interstate 90 in the western part of Massachusetts. It begins among houses and over shallow grade that soon gets a bit steeper. Higher up, you will ride through woods and over a stair step grade with the uphill ramps getting steeper as you go. At mile 4.5 you cross under Interstate 90 over solid slope. Soon the pedaling gets easier and at mile 3.8 you reach Route 23 in Blandford. Turn right for 0.1 miles to finish the listed hill at North Street on the right. Its steeper ramps make Russell Stage Road an interesting descent as well.

Directions - In Russell, MA the climb begins at the junction of Route 20 and Russell Stage Road (see MA Map 2).

Near the end of Wachusett Mountain

Riders near the finish of Wachusett Mountain (photo by Destination Cycling)

23 East

Total elevation - 1,109 ft **Length - 5.1 miles**

Average Grade - 4.1% (9%) **Rating - 0.46 (cat 3)**

The east side of Route 23 is an interesting ascent that parallels busy Interstate 90. From the junction with Route 20 you pull away to the west over solid grade and through woods. One mile in you will cross under the interstate. The slope then becomes somewhat rolling with easy pedaling interspersed with more solid ramps although you will not find steep climbing on this hill. Towards the summit you enter the town of Blandford and the slope eases up to the listed top at the junction with North Street on the right.

Directions - Just south of Russell, MA the climb begins at the junction of Routes 20 and 23 by heading west up 23 (see MA Map 2).

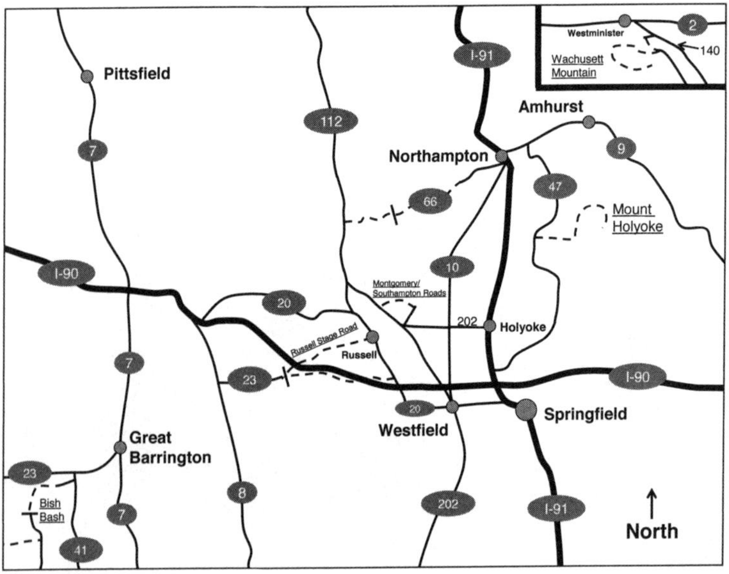

MA Map 2

Bish Bash East

Total elevation - 788 ft | **Length - 3.1 miles**

Average Grade - 4.8% (9%) | **Rating - 0.38 (cat 3)**

Bish Bash East is an isolated climb located in far western Massachusetts. Over a shallow start, the route quickly gets steeper and then rolls a bit as you ride through thick woods. Soon the road curves left as it follows the ridge over the steepest sustaining pedaling on the hill. You then go up and down for the remainder of the ascent. Further along views appear to the left. Beyond West Street on the right climb one more ramp up to a flat where the listed ascent ends.

Directions - From the junction of Routes 23 and 41 in Egremont, MA, head south on 41 for a very short distance to Mount Washington Road (may be unmarked) on the right. Travel Mount Washington Road for 1.7 miles to Jugg End Road (left) where the climb begins by continuing west on Mount Washington Road (see MA Map 2).

Bish Bash West

Total elevation - 1,017 ft | **Length - 4.8 miles**

Average Grade - 4.0% (13%) | **Rating - 0.41 (cat 3)**

Beginning in New York, the west side of Bish Bash is a dark in places and interesting ascent. From Taconic State Park, head east over moderate grade, soon entering Massachusetts. You pass several parking areas for Bish Bash Falls along the way as you ride over variable grade and with one more solid ramp. The slope then eases and at the stop sign, turn right to find a big S bend that contains the climb maximum. Soon, variable grade returns along with a few residences. At the next junction, turn left and ride for 0.2 shallow grade miles to finish at an unmarked top.

Directions - At the junction of Routes 22 and 344 in Copake Falls, NY, head east on 344 for 0.4 miles to begin the listed climb by continuing east on 344 (see MA Map 2).

17%
NEXT
2 MILES

New Hampshire

Crawford Notch South

Total elevation - 541 ft	**Length - 1.8 miles**
Average Grade - 5.7% (8%)	**Rating - 0.31 (cat 3)**

Crawford Notch is a short but solid hill located west of Mount Washington that does carry some traffic at times. It begins over shallow grade that gradually steepens as you ride northwest between steep mountain walls. Towards the top the slope eases and then there is one more short solid stretch up to the listed top. Crawford Notch is a quick descent as well.

Directions - In Bartlett, NH on Route 302, head west on 302 for ~15 rolling miles to begin the climb by continuing west at the final grade change (see NH Map 1).

Pinkham Notch South

Total elevation - 843 ft	**Length - 3.8 miles**
Average Grade - 4.2% (8%)	**Rating - 0.36 (cat 3)**

The south side of Pinkham Notch is a medium length and grade climb towards mighty Mount Washington. Begin by riding north on Route 16 over moderate slope and with traffic here and there. There are no surprises on this one and eventually you can see the big peaks of the White Mountains to your left. The climb ends as the road goes flat beyond. The Mount Washington Auto Road is several miles further north.

Directions - In Jackson, NH on Route 16, head north on 16 for several miles to begin the climb by continuing north on 16 (see NH Map 1).

Mount Washington

Total elevation:	**4,695 ft**	**Length:**	**7.5 miles**
Top elevation:	**6,258 ft**	**Average grade:**	**11.9%**
Minimum grade:	**2%**	**Maximum grade:**	**22%**
Distance ≥ 5%:	**7.3 miles**	**Distance ≥ 10%:**	**6.7 miles**
Steepest mile:	**13.3%**	**Steepest 3 miles:**	**12.4%**
Traffic:	**1**	**Descent:**	**5**
Rating:	**6.61 (hors)**		

In the universe of notable ascents, there are climbs and there are climbs so where does one begin for this one? Very likely the most difficult road bike hill climb in the United States and perhaps the World, the Mount Washington Auto Road is also one of the most spectacular alpine routes in the country. It is only open to bikes during annual hill climb races and at times for several hours for a practice ride shortly before those races. No concession to gradient was made on this hill as it starts out steep and never lets up all the way to its high elevation and wind swept summit. When you turn off of the main road you descend a bit down to the tollbooth. This stretch accounts for the frequent inaccurate listing that the climb of Mount Washington is 7.6 miles in length (the Mount Washington road is 7.6 miles in length while the portion of the road that is uphill is 7.5 miles long).

Begin just beyond the tollbooth where there is a brief shallow section and then the fun begins. A ramp of 12-14% grade smacks you in the face to let you know what is in store the rest of the way up the mountain. The route is tree covered early on as you continue uphill over very solid slope, the narrow roadway taking you through multiple curves and is rolling in places as you continue to gain altitude. You get a brief glance at the top of the mountain in this section before the trees close back in. Double digit grade climbing continues with only brief respite. Soon the trees begin to thin with some great views although it is difficult to appreciate them as you grind higher. Approximately 3.5 miles into the climb, the trees recede for good, revealing amazing views. A short distance later you round a bend and for the first time you see what is ahead of you (and it is not a pretty sight). The gradient then steepens through a section of multiple S bends.

At mile 4.4, the road turns to gravel for just less than one mile (as

Big views along Mount Washington

Mount Washington, NH

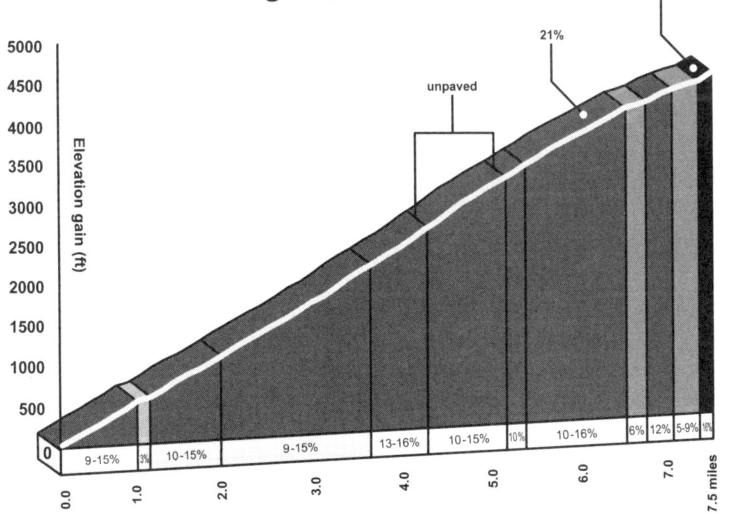

of 2015, 12% of this road is not paved, however, the unpaved section of the road is easily ridden as the route receives so much traffic that the dirt/gravel is packed tight and smooth, and frequent rain eliminates dust much of the time. There are plans to eventually pave the entire climb) with sustained grades of 11-16% along a spectacular and exposed ridgeline. Towards the end of the unpaved section the pedaling gets a bit easier just before the road makes a right hand turn. Pavement returns at mile 5.3 and the grade gradually steepens again. Big time exposure is present in places here and a very steep turn to the left contains 20% slope briefly. The grade then eases as you climb into a tundra-like setting with rolling and wide open rocky terrain. At mile 7.4 a parking lot appears on the left and the grade ramps up. Just beyond the lot the steepest part of the climb is encountered as you bear to the right but the end is in sight. The grade eases over the last few yards as you finish the climb at the brown souvenir hut (with newer facilities nearby). If you make it, congratulate yourself as you have conquered what is perhaps the most challenging paved hill in cycling. Some of the best views on earth greet you at the top of the hill on clear days. The descent of Mount Washington should be among the most difficult but of course, who really knows?

As mentioned, currently opportunities to legally ride this monster are limited as it is raced only twice a year but in a sense this only adds to its legend. Mount Washington is about the same length but considerably steeper than the famous Mortirolo in Italy and Angliru in Spain, and longer and steeper than the Zoncolan in Italy, generally considered among the hardest hill climbs used in European cycling tours (closed in winter - Mt. Washington Auto Road – (603) 466-3988 or www.mt-washington.com).

Crux stretch - Perhaps all but 6 or 8 pedal strokes but it may be the 0.9 miles of packed gravel that begins at mile 4.4 that is the key to the summit.

Directions - From Gorham, NH head south on Route 16 for approximately 8 miles to Glen House. The Mount Washington Auto Road is on your right. Head down this road 0.1 miles to begin the climb just beyond the toll booth (see NH Map 1).

The starting gate

The final stretch

Switchback Way

Total elevation - 1,050 ft | **Length - 2.1 miles**

Average Grade - 9.5% (15%) | **Rating - 1.02 (cat 2)**

Switchback Way is a steep test on a dead end road with two options near its end. It begins over stout grade within a mountain neighborhood, the grade gradually increasing. Soon you encounter several S turns and woods. Houses reappear higher up as the grade eases but soon you find the steepest sustained climbing on the hill. Continue straight at a four way stop to continue over double digit slope. At Washington Boulder on the left, the grade eases and soon you reach a junction. Turn right here to climb for 0.2 additional miles to a dead end. Turning left at the junction you find a slightly longer but less steep finish.

Directions - In Jackson, NH at the southern junction of Routes 16 and 16A, head north on 16A for 0.5 miles to Switchback Way on the right where the climb begins (see NH Map 1).

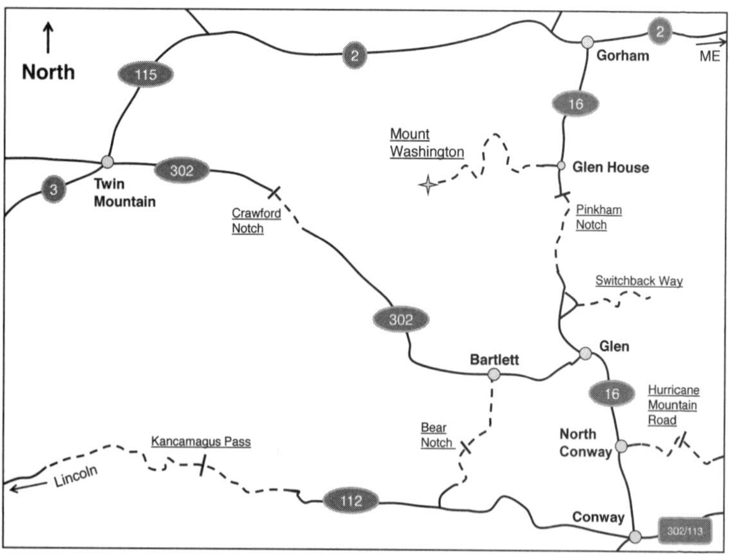

NH Map 1

Bear Notch North

Total elevation - 1,103 ft | **Length - 4.7 miles**

Average Grade - 4.5% (8%) | **Rating - 0.49 (cat 3)**

One of the most scenic climbs in this guide, the north side of Bear Notch is a shallow grade hill near North Conway, NH. You ride within woods and with little traffic for the entire ascent. There are no surprises on this one and the climb ends at an unmarked but obvious summit. The south side of Bear Notch is a similar but more shallow hill (3.9 miles at 2.5% average grade).

Directions - In Bartlett, NH at the junction of Route 302 and Albany Avenue, head south on Albany Avenue for 0.1 miles to begin the climb by continuing south (see NH Map 1).

Hurricane Mountain Road West

Total elevation - 973 ft | **Length - 1.7 miles**

Average Grade - 10.8% (21%) | **Rating - 1.16 (cat 2)**

The west side of Hurricane Mountain Road near North Conway is a famous area climb, even steeper than its east side (next climb) but just a bit shorter and also along a dark and narrow route. Although it has somewhat similar statistics this side seems to have a more ominous look and feel as you ride it. A variable grade will wear you down and the maximum is near the top just before a steep right hand turn. From this point the listed top is close and it is unmarked but obvious as the grade decreases dramatically. Due to its steep grade and narrow gauge it is also a difficult descent.

Directions - From North Conway, New Hampshire head north on Route 16 for a short distance. Hurricane Mountain Road will be on your right. Travel Hurricane Mountain Road east for 1.8 miles to the small bridge where the listed climb begins (see NH Map 1).

Hurricane Mountain Road East

Total elevation:	**1,193 ft**	**Length:**	**2.2 miles**
Top elevation:	**1,718 ft**	**Average grade:**	**10.3%**
Minimum grade:	**1%**	**Maximum grade:**	**22%**
Distance ≥ 5%:	**2.0 miles**	**Distance ≥ 10%:**	**1.4 miles**
Steepest mile:	**12.8%**	**Steepest 3 miles:**	**NA**
Traffic:	**1**	**Descent:**	**5**
Rating:	**1.32 (cat 2)**		

The east side of Hurricane Mountain Road can also be considered must do for the serious climber. Steep over much of its course, the route is also along a dark in places and always narrow road. A variable grade can make this route difficult but its relatively short length ensures most will get to its scenic top with its hiking possibilities.

The hill begins over moderate grade as you immediately dive into thick woods to start. The dark slope reaches double digit quickly before easing. Soon you are back up again; a pattern that continues over the entire route. One mile in, the gradient eases significantly for a stretch. Continuing to go up and down, at mile 1.7 you encounter the steepest sustained climbing on the hill, hitting and going beyond 20% briefly. The tree cover opens up here a bit as you approach the summit, perhaps signaling that the end is near. Towards the very top the slope eases for a final time and the listed climb soon ends as the grade goes flat. As mentioned, the east side of Hurricane Mountain Road is one of the steepest hills in New England. That grade produces a tricky descent as well so watch your speed on the way down.

Crux stretch - Perhaps the very steep 0.3 miles near the top that begins at mile 1.7 may be the key to a successful summit.

Directions - In tiny Fryeburg, Maine on Route 302 head north on River Street into New Hampshire. Shortly turn right on East Conway/Green Hill Road. Travel this road for several miles and Hurricane Mountain Road will be on your left where the listed climb begins (see NH Map 1).

The top of Hurricane Mountain East

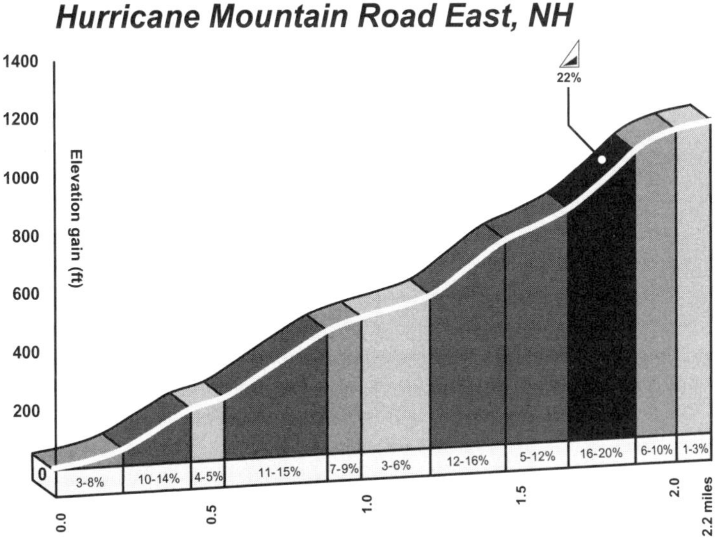

Kancamagus Pass East

Total elevation - 1,392 ft | **Length - 4.9 miles**

Average Grade - 5.4% (7%) | **Rating - 0.76 (cat 2)**

One of the most scenic climbs in this guide, the east side of Kancamagus Pass is a steady grade ascent through woods and with views in places. It is also one of the most popular in the Northeast. It begins as you ride west over moderate grade which eases as you approach a bridge about 0.5 miles in. Just beyond the bridge moderate grade returns as the road flows through graceful turns. The last 1.5 miles are just a bit steeper and then the grade eases as you approach the finish at the signed summit.

Directions - In Conway, NH head west on Route 112 to Bear Notch Road on the right. From that point, continue west on 112 for 4.8 additional miles to a 90 degree right turn to begin the listed climb (see NH Map 1).

Kancamagus Pass West

Total elevation - 1,689 ft | **Length - 7.8 miles**

Average Grade - 4.1% (8%) | **Rating - 0.70 (cat 2)**

Another popular area ascent, the west side of scenic Kancamagus Pass is a bit longer and less steep overall compared to the east side but is also a scenic ascent that does carry a bit of traffic at times. From Hancock Campground head east over shallow grade which gradually steepens. Soon the road flows through multiple curves as you gain altitude. The last 1.5 miles are the steepest sustained climbing on the hill and the climb ends at the signed summit in pleasant surroundings.

Directions - From Interstate 93 in Lincoln, NH, head east on Route 112 for 5.1 miles to begin the listed climb by continuing east (see NH Map 1).

3 Mile Hill

Total elevation - 909 ft | **Length - 2.1 miles**

Average Grade - 8.2% (13%) | **Rating - 0.75 (cat 2)**

While not quite 3 true miles in length, 3 Mile Hill is a solid climb along Route 18 located very close to Interstate 93 that leads to the Cannon Ski Area. From its unmarked start (grade change) head east over shallow grade which soon goes flat and then gradually increases. Eventually you enter Franconia Notch State Park over solid grade and usually little traffic. Towards the very top the slope eases and the climb ends at the parking lot for the ski area on the right.

Directions - In Franconia, NH at the junction of Routes 116 and 18, head east on 18 for 2.1 miles to begin the climb by continuing east on 18 (see NH Map 2).

The top of Kancamagus Pass

Kinsman Notch East

Total elevation - 911 ft	**Length - 3.4 miles**
Average Grade - 5.1% (8%)	**Rating - 0.46 (cat 3)**

The east side of Kinsman Notch is another popular area hill that carries riders west from the Lincoln, NH area over a road that sees little traffic most days. The first half mile is fairly shallow and then the grade picks up but is not steep. Soon more challenging pedaling arrives over a mostly straight section that takes you further up the mountain. The road again begins to curve a bit over the final segment up to the unmarked but obvious summit as the grade flattens out. The straight section makes for a fairly quick descent as well.

Directions - The climb begins at the junction of Routes 112 and 118 located just west of the small town of Lincoln, NH by heading west on 112 (see NH Map 2).

Kinsman Notch West

Total elevation - 555 ft	**Length - 1.9 miles**
Average Grade - 5.5% (7%)	**Rating - 0.31 (cat 3)**

The west side of Kinsman is a bit shorter than its east side but with similar overall grade. A shallow start gradually gets more challenging as you head east. A rock wall soon appears to your right which adds a somewhat alpine feel to the scenery of the climb which is quite good already. Near the top the slope eases back and the listed climb ends at an unmarked top as the grade flattens out with a small lake to your right.

Directions - From the junction of Routes 116 and 112, head east on 112 for 2.6 shallow and rolling miles to begin the listed climb by continuing east (see NH Map 2).

Along the west side of Kinsman Notch

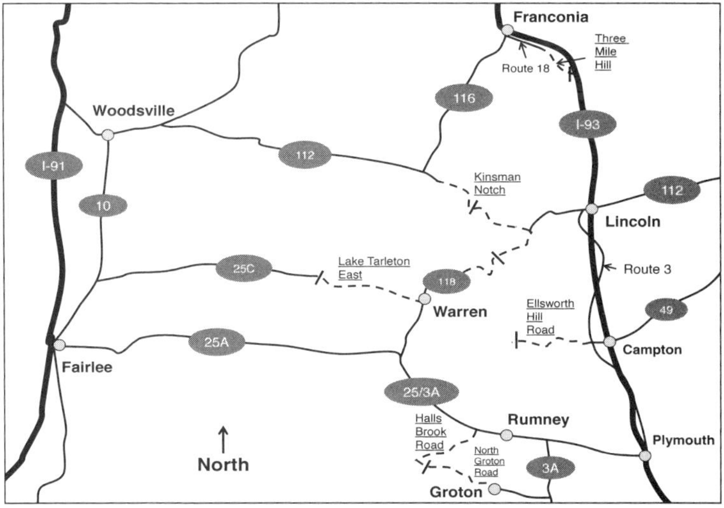

NH Map 2

118 North

Total elevation - 1,574 ft	**Length - 5.5 miles**
Average Grade - 5.4% (9%)	**Rating - 0.86 (cat 2)**

The north side of Route 118 is one of the most scenic climbs in this guide. Beginning over shallow grade, you also dive into deep woods near the start. The grade is stair step for most of its length, with some steeper ramps to negotiate in places but there are no real surprises (and little traffic) on this popular hill. At one spot near the top the trees part to reveal long views to your left. It is brief however and the thick woods quickly close in again and take you up to its unmarked but obvious summit.

Directions - The climb begins at the junction of Routes 112 and 118 just west of the small town of Lincoln, NH by heading south on 118 (see NH Map 2).

118 South

Total elevation - 1,303 ft	**Length - 3.8 miles**
Average Grade - 6.5% (8%)	**Rating - 0.86 (cat 2)**

The south side of 118 is a bit shorter and steeper overall but similar to its north side the road on which you ride carries little traffic much of the time. It begins over shallow grade which goes up and down early on and you pass a few houses along the semi wooded road. The slope gradually increases so that the middle of the climb contains the most challenging pedaling on the mountain. As you approach the top the grade eases just a bit overall and the climb ends at an unmarked summit within thick cover.

Directions - From the junction of Routes 25 and 118 just north of Warren, NH, head north on 118 for 3.5 miles to begin the climb by continuing north (see NH Map 2).

Lake Tarleton East

Total elevation - 776 ft	**Length - 2.3 miles**
Average Grade - 6.4% (13%)	**Rating - 0.50 (cat 2/3)**

The east side of Lake Tarleton along Route 25C is a short and stout hill that carries riders west from Route 25. You enter woods to begin over moderate grade that soon gets more challenging. Near the end of its first mile you encounter steeper pedaling which last for over a half mile. The slope then becomes stair step up the hill. Near the top you find the steepest ramp on the ascent which eases as you cross under some power lines. The end is near here and the climb soon ends as the grade flattens out. Due to grade and routing, 25C is a pretty quick descent as well.

Directions - In Warren, NH at the junction of Routes 25 and 25C, head west on 25C for 1.2 shallow grade miles to begin the climb by continuing west (see NH Map 2).

Ellsworth Hill Road

Total elevation - 830 ft	**Length - 2.6 miles**
Average Grade - 6.1% (14%)	**Rating - 0.50 (cat 2/3)**

Ellsworth Hill Road is another short and solid ascent near Interstate 93 in central New Hampshire. The hill begins over solid grade which becomes stair step. Early on you encounter a short descent but climbing quickly resumes as you continue west through woods and with a few homes along the way. Near the top you find the steepest ramp on the hill. The grade then eases and goes flat a short distance later at an unmarked top.

Directions - At the junction of Interstate 93 and Route 49 in Campton, NH, head west on 49 for a short distance to its junction with Route 3. At that junction, just to your left, is Dan Webb Road where the climb begins (Ellsworth Hill Road is a very short distance ahead on the right) (see NH Map 2).

Halls Brook Road North

Total elevation - 998 ft	**Length - 4.6 miles**
Average Grade - 4.1% (12%)	**Rating - 0.41 (cat 3)**

Halls Brook Road is a twisty and variable grade climb near the small town of Rumney, NH. From Route 25, pull away to the south over gradually increasing grade. The road is quite twisty as you find steep ramps interspersed with a descent. Just over two miles in, another descent announces the beginning of a flatter overall stretch. Soon you cross beneath some power lines which open up the thick woods you have been riding within. At mile 3.7 you reach the junction with North Groton Road. Turn left here to finish over mostly moderate grade up to an unmarked top.

Directions - In Rumney, NH on Route 25, head west on 25 for a short distance to Halls Brook Road on the left where the climb begins (see NH Map 2).

North Groton Road (Groton Dump)

Total elevation - 897 ft	**Length - 3.5 miles**
Average Grade - 4.9% (14%)	**Rating - 0.44 (cat 3)**

The climb of North Groton Road (Groton Dump to many) is a popular ascent with solid ramps. From the town of Groton, begin over shallow grade which soon turns more challenging. You pass a few houses along the narrow and somewhat dark road as you continue to gain altitude along the rolling route. A steep ramp then takes riders up to the dump as the grade eases but keep climbing for another 0.7 miles up to the unmarked but obvious summit (identical top to previous climb).

Directions - In Groton, NH, head north on North Groton Road for 0.1 miles to begin the listed climb by continuing north on North Groton Road (see NH Map 2).

The top of solid Lake Tarleton East

Double digit grade on Pack Monadnock

King Road

Total elevation - 641 ft **Length - 1.3 miles**

Average Grade - 9.4% (15%) **Rating - 0.60 (cat 2)**

King Road is very likely the most popular climb in the Hanover/Lebanon area that includes Dartmouth College. Short and sweet, it leaves the small community of Etna over solid grade which quickly gets steeper. The slope then becomes stair step as you ride towards the east through thick woods and past a few nice homes. Near the top is the steepest ramp on the hill and the climb quickly ends just beyond at Laramie Road on the right (road turns to gravel ahead).

Directions - In the small community of Etna just east of Hanover, NH, the climb begins at the junction of King Road and Etna Road by heading east on King Road (see NH Map 3).

Eastman Hill Road North

Total elevation - 566 ft **Length - 1.1 miles**

Average Grade - 9.7% (15%) **Rating - 0.55 (cat 2/3)**

Another area short and steep ascent, Eastman Hill Road carries riders south from Route 4 towards Interstate 89. It begins over solid grade which quickly gets steeper as you enter deep woods. At mile 0.4 there is a right hand turn that occurs just before the steepest grade on the route is encountered. Halfway through the climb you find a small flat which really reduces the average grade of this steep hill. You finish over more moderate grade up to the unmarked but obvious summit. From here you descend a short distance down to I-89.

Directions - At the junction of Interstate 89 and Route 4 in Lebanon, NH, head east on Route 4 for a short distance to Eastman Hill Road on the right where the listed climb begins (see NH Map 3).

Methodist Hill Road North

Total elevation - 676 ft	**Length - 1.3 miles**
Average Grade - 9.8% (14%)	**Rating - 0.67 (cat 2)**

Another short and steep area ascent, the north side of Methodist Hill Road can be combined into quite a hilly route if needed. The first section of climbing is the crux stretch as it is over mostly double digit slope but the road carries little traffic most days. After a half mile things ease off and then the route gradually gets steeper again. The worst is over however and the climb soon comes to an end at an unmarked but obvious summit.

Directions - On Interstate 89 just south of Lebanon, NH, exit to Eastman Hill Road (Exit 16). At the junction go east on Methodist Hill Road for 0.3 miles to begin the climb by continuing east up the hill (see NH Map 3).

Methodist Hill Road South

Total elevation - 804 ft	**Length - 1.9 miles**
Average Grade - 8.0% (15%)	**Rating - 0.64 (cat 2)**

The south side of Methodist Hill Road, while somewhat similar, is a bit longer and less steep overall compared to its north side. It begins by pulling away just east of Route 120 with little traffic over solid grade and then you encounter a flat. Climbing quickly resumes over the steepest grade on the ascent as you continue to gain altitude. The grade then eases up to a junction. Turn left to continue over first moderate and then solid slope which remains right up to climb's ends at an unmarked top.

Directions - In Lebanon, NH at the junction of Routes 4 and 120, head south on 120 for 4.9 miles to Methodist Hill Road on the left where the climb begins (see NH Map 3).

Kearsarge Mountain Road

Total elevation - 1,458 ft | **Length - 3.4 miles**

Average Grade - 8.1% (14%) | **Rating - 1.21 (cat 2)**

Kearsarge Mountain Road is a solid dead end climb located in central New Hampshire within Rollins State Park. Very narrow and twisty, it is also through a dark tunnel of trees over its lower end. It carries a stout and variable grade over much of its route and is double digit in places. Towards the top the trees thin in spots which provide views on clear days. The grade eases a bit as well over the 2nd half and the ascent ends at a parking lot. Because of its characteristics it is a somewhat difficult but fun descent.

Directions - From Main Street in Warner, New Hampshire head north on Kearsarge Mountain Road for ~5 miles to the toll gate where the climb begins. This approach road is a shallow, rolling climb with a short, steep pitch just before the toll booth and a nice warm up ride for the main climb (see NH Map 3).

Pack Monadnock

Total elevation - 774 ft | **Length - 1.3 miles**

Average Grade - 11.3% (23%) | **Rating - 0.94 (cat 2)**

Pack Monadnock is a short and very steep hill in southern New Hampshire that is often used by those training for Mount Washington as it contains severe stretches of grade in places. Begin beyond the toll booth as you dive into woods on the narrow road. Soon double digit grade arrives and a switchback to the left contains the climb maximum. Beyond the road goes flat in places and a few views appear. The final stretch is again severe and the climb dead ends at a parking area very close to the top of the mountain.

Directions - From Wilton, NH on Route 101 head west on 101 for ~8.5 miles to Miller State Park on the right. The climb begins just beyond the tollbooth (see NH Map 3).

Leviathan (Route 63)

Total elevation - 883 ft	**Length - 3.9 miles**
Average Grade - 4.3% (9%)	**Rating - 0.38 (cat 3)**

The climb of Leviathan (Route 63) is a nice hill near the Massachusetts and Vermont borders of New Hampshire. Quite popular with area riders, it carries cyclists and a few vehicles north along a moderate grade and towards other riding. The grade goes up and down on this one but there are no real surprises. There is one final stretch of more solid slope before the listed climb ends at an unmarked top after 3.9 miles.

Directions - At the junction of Routes 119 and 63 in Hinsdale, NH, head north on 63 to begin the climb (see NH Map 3).

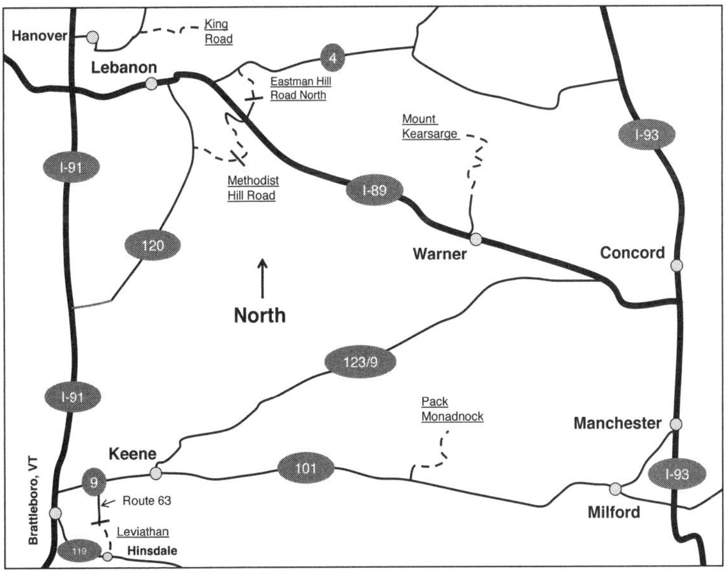

NH Map 3

NEXT
4 MILES
USE LOW
GEAR
END
40

New York

Gillispie Drive

Total elevation - 636 ft	**Length - 2.4 miles**
Average Grade - 5.0% (9%)	**Rating - 0.32 (cat 3)**

The climb begins over shallow grade as you head east among trees. Just over a mile in you find a steeper ramp which soon eases. Just beyond you encounter a descent. Climbing quickly resumes over shallow grade up to an unmarked top (road descends from here to Route 431).

Directions - In Franklin Falls, NY head east on Route 48 for 1.3 miles where you bear right to stay on Route 48. 0.7 miles further, bear left on Gillispie Drive. Continue east on Gillispie for ~1.0 miles to begin the listed climb by continuing east (see NY Map 1).

Styles Brook Road

Total elevation - 766 ft	**Length - 1.8 miles**
Average Grade - 8.1% (20%)	**Rating - 0.63 (cat 2)**

The climb of Styles Brook Road, while a dead end, is a classic ascent. Short but stout, you begin over shallow grade which soon becomes double digit as you enter thick woods. The slope from this point becomes stair step and includes a very steep stretch along with a short flat and descent which really lowers the average grade. Towards the top the grade eases and the trees part and the climb ends at an interesting stone house and barn.

Directions - In Keene, NY, head north on Route 9N for several miles to Styles Brook Road on the right where the climb begins (see NY Map 1).

Whiteface Mountain

Total elevation:	**3,566 ft**	**Length:**	**7.9 miles**
Top elevation:	**4,606 ft**	**Average grade:**	**8.6%**
Minimum grade:	**1%**	**Maximum grade:**	**12%**
Distance ≥ 5%:	**7.4 miles**	**Distance ≥ 10%:**	**1.2 miles**
Steepest mile:	**10.1%**	**Steepest 3 miles:**	**9.7%**
Traffic:	**1**	**Descent:**	**2**
Rating:	**3.13 (hors/cat 1)**		

One of the big American climbs, Whiteface Mountain is located in the majestic Adirondack Mountains of upper New York State. Somewhat isolated, the grade is shallow early but quickly becomes sturdy, including some double digit slope as you ride through mostly wooded scenery and little development (Santa's Workshop not withstanding). Just over three miles into the ascent the grade eases a bit and you come to a toll booth ($6 for bikes).

The difficulty picks up beyond the toll booth as the next three miles average just under 10% grade. The roadway here, while steep, is also fairly steady which seems to abate its severe slope somewhat. The trees thicken a bit as well and the road picks up a somewhat isolated, mountain feel. Closer to the summit the slope finally eases and a few graceful turns lead you higher on the mountain over mostly moderate grade. When the summit is in sight, a narrow and elongated parking lot soon appears as the grade eases further as the ascent winds down. The end is near and the listed climb ends where the road dead-ends at the upper end of the parking lot at the castle like visitors center (restrooms and water).

The climb of Whiteface Mountain is almost identical in length and grade to the famous Tour de France climb of l'Alpe d'Huez. It is also one of the fastest descents in the U.S. and there is an annual race on its slopes (closed in winter - Whiteface Mountain Memorial Highway - 518 946-2223).

Crux stretch - The 3 mile stretch of ~10% grade from mile 3.3.

Directions - In Wilmington, NY the climb begins at the junction of Routes 86 and 431 by heading west up 431 (see NY Map 1).

The start of mighty Whiteface Mountain

Whiteface Mountain, NY

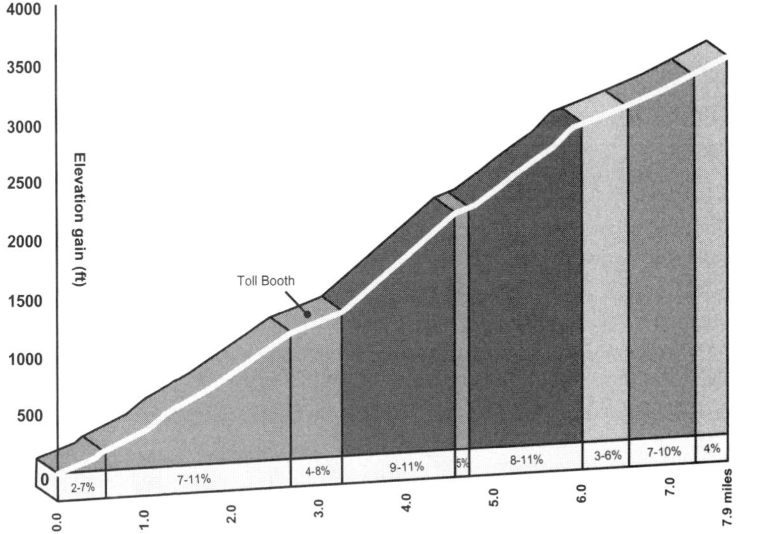

73 East

Total elevation - 1,196 ft	**Length - 4.3 miles**
Average Grade - 5.3% (8%)	**Rating - 0.63 (cat 2)**

The climb of 73 East is a solid ascent from the small town of Keene that leads towards Lake Placid along with some traffic at times. The grade is solid to start as you pull away from the small town of Keene. It then becomes stair step as the road heads through a sweeping left turn. The grade then eases for the remainder of the climb. Towards the top the route becomes quite scenic. A rock wall signals the summit is near and the listed climb's unmarked top occurs as a lake appears on the left. Beyond, the road continues to climb intermittently but shallowly as significant climbing has ended.

Directions - At the northern junction of routes 73 and 9N in the small town of Keene, NY, head west on Route 73 for 0.3 miles to begin the climb (see NY Map 1).

Hurricane Road

Total elevation - 843 ft	**Length - 1.8 miles**
Average Grade - 8.9% (14%)	**Rating - 0.75 (cat 2)**

Hurricane Road is an interesting ascent from the small town of Keene that leads into a hill side neighborhood. Short and steep, the grade is quite variable as you ride the scenic road. The route twists away from Route 73 over moderate grade and passes multiple residences along the way. The grade is stair step over the initial mile and then becomes more steady over the final stretch which leads to the listed climb's unmarked top after 1.8 miles. Beyond, the road continues to climb but intermittently (significant climbing has ended). If you continue east on Hurricane Road you reach Route 9N.

Directions - At the junction of Route 73 and Hurricane Road in Keene, NY, head east on Hurricane Road to begin (see NY Map 1).

9N West

Total elevation - 595 ft **Length - 1.9 miles**

Average Grade - 5.9% (8%) **Rating - 0.35 (cat 3)**

The west side on Route 9N is a short and solid hill that is popular with area climbers. A shallow start soon turns to more solid climbing as you head directly east with your target in front of you. Soon two lanes uphill appear giving you more room although traffic is generally light on this road. The slope eases before a final solid section takes you to its unmarked top. The end of Hurricane Road (previous ascent) is a short distance ahead on the left. Due to its straight routing, 9N West is a fast descent.

Directions - At the junction of Route 73 and 9N just south of Keene, NY, head east on 9N to begin the climb (see NY Map 1).

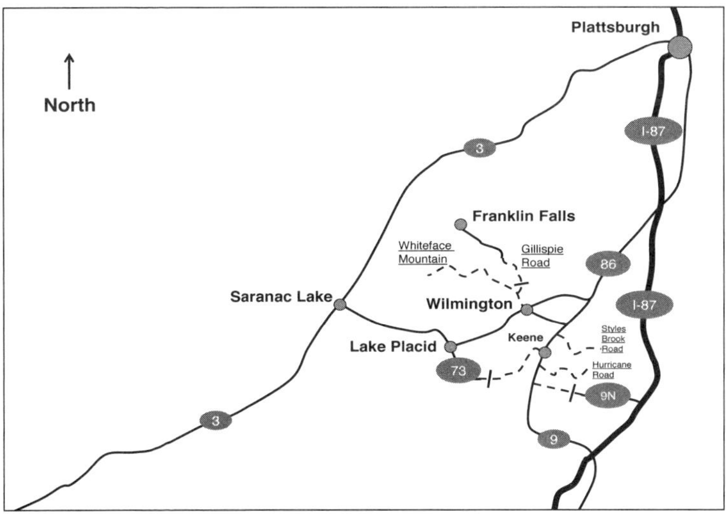

NY Map 1

Iron Mountain

Total elevation - 908 ft | **Length - 2.5 miles**

Average Grade - 6.9% (8%) | **Rating - 0.63 (cat 2)**

Iron Mountain along Route 74 us a short and solid ascent located close to the Vermont border. The climb begins as the road expands to two lanes uphill and is over a stout and steady grade as you ride to the west. There can be a few cars along the way but the road is wide so plenty of room for riding. At mile 2.0 there is a short descent and then climbing resumes over more moderate grade up to the unmarked summit just before the road reduces back to one lane each way. Due to grade and routing Iron Mountain is a quick descent as well.

Directions - At the junction of Routes 9N and 74 in Ticondergoa, NY, head west on 74 for 0.9 miles (grade change) to begin the climb by continuing west (see NY Map 2).

Graphite Mountain East

Total elevation - 1,351 ft | **Length - 5.1 miles**

Average Grade - 5.0% (10%) | **Rating - 0.68 (cat 2)**

The east side of Graphite Mountain along Route 8 is another solid New York hill near picturesque Lake George. In town to begin, you head west over initially shallow grade. Quickly leaving town, you then encounter stair step slope as the road begins to twist up the mountain and traffic thins. 1.5 miles in you find the most challenging climbing on the hill which lasts for over one mile. The grade then eases and you find a descent. Climbing quickly resumes over shallow grade up the summit.

Directions - From the junction of Routes 9N and 8 in Hague, NY on the shores of upper Lake George, the climb begins by heading west on Route 8 (see NY Map 2).

Grade on Petersburgh Pass

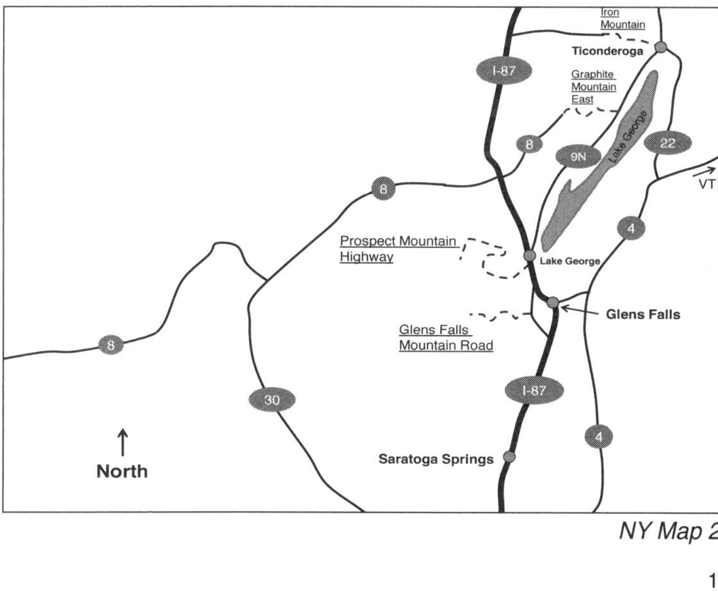

NY Map 2

Prospect Mountain Highway

Total elevation - 1,604 ft	**Length - 5.7 miles**
Average Grade - 5.3% (9%)	**Rating - 0.86 (cat 2)**

Prospect Highway is a steady grade ascent away from scenic Lake George to altitude. From the road junction begin the climb over solid grade. Soon it eases as you cross over Interstate 87. At mile 0.8 you pass the road's toll house ($2 for bikes; the road closes at 5 PM). From here the route stair steps up the hill; shallow at first and then you hit the first ramp of solid grade as the trees close in which part in places for nice views. At mile 5.3 you reach a large parking area on the right (all vehicles except motorcycles and shuttle buses must stop here). The final stretch is over moderate grade and takes you up to the dead end top (closed in winter - (518) 668-5198).

Directions - In the small town of Lake George, NY the climb begins at the junction of Prospect Mountain Highway and Route 9 by heading up Prospect Highway (see NY Map 2).

Glens Falls Mountain Road East

Total elevation - 696 ft	**Length - 1.3 miles**
Average Grade - 10.1% (15%)	**Rating - 0.71 (cat 2)**

The east side of Glens Falls Mountain Road is a short and steep test just west of the town of Glens Falls. An easy start soon turns tough as the grade quickly ramps up and then soon you enter the trees. This section is over a tight and twisty route and includes a few S bends that include the maximum grade. The slope eases a bit as you pass Tuthill Road on the right but then quickly gets back up to double digit and the top comes quickly (descent beyond).

Directions - In Glens Falls, NY take Luzern Road west to its junction with West Mountain Road. Continue straight on what is now Glens Falls Mountain Road to begin the climb (see NY Map 2).

Petersburgh Pass West

Total elevation - 1,297 ft	**Length - 4.0 miles**
Average Grade - 6.1% (7%)	**Rating - 0.80 (cat 2)**

The west side of Petersburgh Pass is a solid ascent that takes riders towards the state of Massachusetts. An easy start as you ride east soon leads to more solid and steady grade. The road twists a bit up the ridgeline as you ride with little traffic most of the time. The last mile is over the most challenging grade and the climb ends at the big pullout on the right. Massachusetts is just a short distance further east.

Directions - At the junction of Routes 2 and 22 in Petersburgh, NY, head east on Route 2 for 1.4 miles to begin the climb by continuing east (see NY Map 3).

Crawford Road

Total elevation - 1,049 ft	**Length - 2.4 miles**
Average Grade - 8.3% (16%)	**Rating - 0.87 (cat 2)**

Crawford Road is a solid hill away from the Mohawk River that is very popular with local riders. From Route 5S, head south along Lower Gregg Road over shallow grade for a short distance, passing over rail road tracks and then under Interstate 90. After 0.3 miles, bear right on Crawford Road to find more solid slope. Soon find quite challenging pedaling along with a few houses as you ride generally south. The grade goes up and down through this stretch but remains solid overall. Near the top the slope eases and the climb ends at an unmarked but obvious summit with views to the south as the road descends beyond (see NY Map 3).

Directions - From Exit 1 on Interstate 890 in Schenectady, NY, head west on Route 5S for a short distance to Lower Gregg Road on the left where the listed climb begins (see NY Map 3).

85/157

Total elevation - 797 ft **Length - 3.4 miles**

Average Grade - 4.4% (7%) **Rating - 0.35 (cat 3)**

This is the first of 3 climbs up a ridgeline a short distance southwest of Albany. It begins over solid grade in the small town of New Salem along Route 85. After a sweeping turn to the left, at mile 1.1 turn right on Route 157 to continue. At this point the grade decreases as you ride along a ridgeline. It remains quite moderate as you head generally north towards John Boyd Thatcher State Park. The listed climb ends after 3.4 miles as the road flattens at a camping/parking area for the park on the left.

Directions - In New Salem, NY the climb begins at the junction of Routes 85 and 85A by heading west on Route 85 (see NY Map 3).

Pinnacle Climb

Total elevation - 1,171 ft **Length - 3.7 miles**

Average Grade - 6.0% (16%) **Rating - 0.72 (cat 2)**

The steepest of the 3 climbs up this ridge and likely the most popular, after the solid start and turn onto Route 157 (see previous ascent), at mile 1.9, turn left onto Beaver Dam Road to continue. This road has an S bend within it to start, introducing more stout grade. After that feature is negotiated, you encounter a stair step route with easy pedaling mixing with double digit slope. At mile 2.7 turn left on Route 303 to find the most challenging pedaling on the hill. Double digit grade greets you here as you climb straight up the hill. Near the top the slope eases and the climb ends as the road flatten out at a camp area.

Directions - In New Salem, NY the climb begins at the junction of Routes 85 and 85A by heading west on Route 85 (see NY Map 3).

85/Wolf Hill Road

Total elevation - 1,185 ft	**Length - 4.9 miles**
Average Grade - 4.6% (13%)	**Rating - 0.54 (cat 2/3)**

The longest of the 3 climbs, after the solid start and turn onto Route 157 (see previous two ascent), at mile 1.2, turn left onto Wolf Hill Road (unmarked as of 2014). The initial 0.7 miles contain some of the most challenging grade on the hill over a twisty road, followed by a short descent. Climbing soon resumes over variable slope and among a few residences, including another short descent before more stout grade is found. At mile 3.8, turn right on Route 303 to continue. This finishing stretch is over moderate grade and the climb ends at an unmarked top as the grade flattens out (the end of the previous climb is 1.3 miles further north).

Directions - In New Salem, NY the climb begins at the junction of Routes 85 and 85A by heading west on Route 85 (see NY Map 3).

10 North

Total elevation - 1,153 ft	**Length - 4.0 miles**
Average Grade - 5.5% (9%)	**Rating - 0.63 (cat 2)**

The north side of Route 10 is a pleasant ascent along an open road that carries a little traffic but not enough to ruin the ride. The grade gradually increases as you pull away from Route 7 with two lanes uphill and then becomes quite steady. After 2 miles, the extra lane disappears and then the slope becomes more variable. A descent is eventually encountered towards the top, climbing then resumes over shallow and then more solid slope and the hill ends at a pullout to the left. Due to its mostly straight routing 10 North is a fast descent.

Directions - From the junction of Route 10 and Interstate 88 west of Albany, travel Route 10 south for 0.1 miles to its junction with Route 7 to begin the climb by continuing south on 10 (see NY Map 3).

4 North

Total elevation - 880 ft | **Length - 2.0 miles**

Average Grade - 8.3% (13%) | **Rating - 0.73 (cat 2)**

The north side of Route 4 is a steep test in the hilly country southwest of Albany. It begins over solid grade and among a few houses as you quickly leave town, soon pedaling over double digit slope. The route then opens up as you pass two silos on the left. The road flattens briefly soon after but then quickly gets stout again as you continue to gain altitude. From here the grade goes up and down before finally easing for the last time shortly before the climb ends at an unmarked top in an open field.

Directions - In Warnerville NY at the junction of Routes 7 and 4 just north of Interstate 88, head south on Route 4 (West Fulton Road) for 0.6 miles to begin the climb as Route 4 bears to the right and pulls away from I-88 (see NY Map 3).

Cotton Hill Road West

Total elevation - 1,143 ft | **Length - 2.6 miles**

Average Grade - 8.3% (14%) | **Rating - 0.95 (cat 2)**

Cotton Hill Road is another steep area ascent. Shallow grade at climb start soon leads to more stout and rolling climbing, passing a few houses and eventually entering thick woods in places. Just under one mile in, you will find a short descent. Climbing then resumes over gradually increasing slope before Cotton Hill State Forest appears on the left. Continue to ascend for another mile over mostly solid grade before the slope eases and the listed climb ends soon after as the road flattens. The east side of Cotton Hill Road is a less steep and well defined climb.

Directions - In Middleburgh, NY the climb begins at the junction of Route 145 and Cotton Hill Road by heading east on Cotton Hill Road up the hill (see NY Map 3).

Potter Mountain Road

Total elevation - 1,082 ft | **Length - 3.1 miles**

Average Grade - 6.6% (14%) | **Rating - 0.72 (cat 2)**

Potter Mountain Road is one of several area climbs heading west into the northern fringes of the Catskills. From the old school house, head west on moderate grade which in due course becomes more solid, the most challenging slope on the hill. Eventually the pedaling gets easier and some views and a few houses appear as you continue to gain altitude. A short flat is found near the top and then climbing resumes over somewhat shallow grade up to listed climb top at Good Fellow Lane on the right.

Directions - Just north of Durham, NY at the junction of Route 145 and 81, head west on 81 (Potters Hollow Road) for 1.2 miles to creek crossing (and Potters School house on the right) to begin the climb by continuing west on what is now Potter Mountain Road (see NY Map 3).

22/20

Total elevation - 1,370 ft | **Length - 4.2 miles**

Average Grade - 6.2% (15%) | **Rating - 0.87 (cat 2)**

The combination of Routes 22 and 20 (mostly Route 20) is another solid area hill to altitude. It begins over solid grade which quickly eases and within 0.2 miles Route 22 goes to left. Continue straight to stay on Route 20 over gradually increasing slope which soon becomes stair step. After several miles you enter fields with views of the mountains to the left. At mile 3.6 find a flat and a left turn onto Route 10 to continue. Route 10 quickly gets back up to solid and then becomes stair step. After 0.6 miles on Route 10, find a final flat with long views to the left to end the listed climb.

Directions - In Durham, NY at the junction of Routes 145 and 22, head west on 22 to begin the climb (see NY Map 3).

Cunningham Road

Total elevation - 1,158 ft	**Length - 2.8 miles**
Average Grade - 7.8% (14%)	**Rating - 0.91 (cat 2)**

Cunningham Road is another stout area hill and perhaps the most isolated. The grade is solid right away as you pull away from the stop sign at climb start. Soon you enter trees. Beyond, the grade increases and views appear to your right after you exit the woods. From here the slope becomes stair step with one ramp in particular carrying quite solid grade, including the climb maximum. Near the top the pedaling eases and the listed climb ends with its junction with Route 10.

Directions - In Durham, NY at the junction of Routes 145 and 22, head west on 22 for a short distance to Route 20. Turn left on Route 20 and travel 0.8 miles to Cochrane Road. Turn right on Cochrane and Cunningham Road will appear shortly on the left where the climb begins (see NY Map 3).

23 East

Total elevation - 1,082 ft	**Length - 5.4 miles**
Average Grade - 3.8% (8%)	**Rating - 0.41 (cat 3)**

The east side of Route 23 is a shallow grade hill that has some traffic at times. It is perhaps the easiest way to climb to the west in the area. Carrying two lanes uphill, it is over a shallow to moderate grade all the way up and ends at an unmarked but obvious top as the road descends beyond. Climbing from Route 145 creates a climb of 9.5 miles at 3.0% average grade.

Directions - In Cairo, NY at the junction of Routes 145 and 23, head west on 23 for 4.1 rolling miles to where the road expands to two lanes uphill to begin the listed climb by continuing west on Route 23 (see NY Map 3).

Kaaterskill Falls (23A)

Total elevation - 1,360 ft | **Length - 4.6 miles**

Average Grade - 5.6% (8%) | **Rating - 0.76 (cat 2)**

From the stoplight in Palenville, climb west on Route 23A in town to begin over shallow grade and with intermittent traffic. Soon you hit a small descent and then more solid ascending. Another descent is then encountered and once it passes you are uphill the remainder of the way. At mile 3.2 you pass the waterfall on your right as the road gets twisty. Above the falls is the most challenging climbing on the hill over a narrow and tortuous road that hugs a drainage. Towards the top, two lanes uphill appear and the listed climb ends soon after at the Mountain Top Historical Society on the right.

Directions - At the junction of Routes 23A and 32A in tiny Palenville, NY, head west on 23A to begin the climb (see NY Map 3).

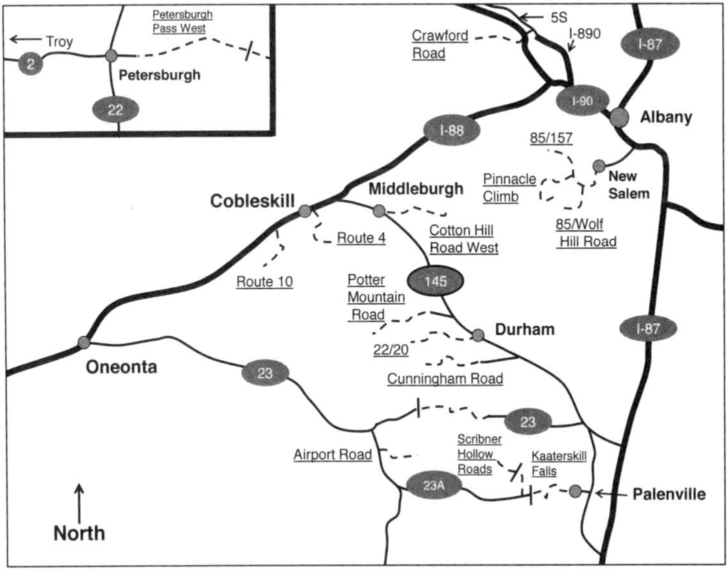

NY Map 3

Scribner Hollow Road North

Total elevation - 487 ft	Length - 1.1 miles
Average Grade - 8.4% (12%)	**Rating - 0.41 (cat 3)**

The north side of Scribner Hollow Road is a shot but stout hill that connects to other riding/climbing. From the creek crossing, you will head south up the hill over stair step grade. Steep ramps are interspersed with shallow sections in a rural setting with little traffic. Near the top a steeper ramp contains double digit slope. The last 0.3 miles are shallow and the listed climb ends at an unmarked top as the grade flattens out within woods.

Directions - At the junction of Routes 23C and 296 just north of the small town of South Jewett, head east on 23C for a short distance to Scribner Hollow Road on the right. Travel Scribner Hollow Road for 0.3 miles to begin the listed climb (see NY Map 4).

Scribner Hollow Road South

Total elevation - 594 ft	Length - 2.0 miles
Average Grade - 5.6% (13%)	**Rating - 0.34 (cat 3)**

The south side of Scribner Hollow Road is another short and steep area ascent that is quite popular with local climbers. From Route 23A, ride north over stout grade to begin as you leave town. Quickly the slope eases and becomes rolling and stair step for the remainder of the hill. You pass woods and several homes along the way as the grade goes up and down but is solid overall. The last stretch eases and the listed climb ends at the sign 'Town of Jewett' in a wooded setting.

Directions - In Hunter, NY the climb begins at the junction of Route 23A and Scribner Hollow Road by heading north on Scribner Hollow Road (see NY Map 4).

Airport Road

Total elevation - 882 ft | **Length - 2.1 miles**

Average Grade - 8.0% (22%) | **Rating - 0.72 (cat 2)**

Airport Road is a classic; a short and stout climb that is a member of the exclusive 20% grade club. The hill begins by entering woods over moderate grade that quickly gets steep and then eases. Soon a vicious ramp of double digit slope arrives which includes the climb maximum. This section gradually eases and then becomes quite shallow as you break out of the trees into fields. As you continue east, the pedaling gets more challenging and then stair step including a short flat. Climbing quickly resumes up to an unmarked top as the road descends beyond.

Directions - Just south of the junction of Routes 23 and 23A, the climb begins at the junction of Routes 23A and 23C (Airport Road) by heading east on Airport Road (see NY Map 4).

Near the top of Airport Road

206 North

Total elevation - 1,061 ft | **Length - 2.7 miles**

Average Grade - 7.4% (9%) | **Rating - 0.79 (cat 2)**

The north side of Route 206 is a short and solid grade ascent just south of Walton, NY. A short shallow section at climb start as you leave town soon yields to stout pedaling. The route heads up a ridgeline and the road carries intermittent traffic. About halfway up you encounter a short flat and then you are back up to solid slope. Near the top the grade eases and the climb ends under a flashing light. Due to grade and a fairly straight routing, 206 North is a fast descent as well.

Directions - In Walton, NY at the junction of Routes 10 and 206, head south on Route 206 for 0.1 miles to begin the listed climb (see NY Map 4).

206 South

Total elevation - 1,140 ft | **Length - 5.2 miles**

Average Grade - 4.2% (8%) | **Rating - 0.47 (cat 3)**

The south side of Route 206 is a longer and less steep overall hill compared to its north side. From Downsville, you pull out of town over shallow and gradually increasing slope. Soon you are riding along a ridgeline and within woods in places as well as among a few vehicles here and there. Several miles in you find the steepest sustained climbing on the hill. The solid climbing continues up to the listed top at a large pullout on the left. After a flat the road then continues to climb intermittently and over very shallow slope but significant climbing has ended.

Directions - In Downsville, NY at the junction of Routes 30 and 206, head north on Route 206 to begin (see NY Map 4).

206 South/Wilson HLW Road

Total elevation - 976 ft **Length - 5.2 miles**

Average Grade - 3.6% (8%) **Rating - 0.35 (cat 3)**

This hill shares its start with that of 206 South (previous ascent). After 2.5 shallow to moderate grade miles on Route 206, turn right on little used Wilson HLW Road. The first 1.2 miles of Wilson HLW Road are over mostly shallow grade as you ride through woods and a small farm. The final mile is over more stout slope and there is a house and red barn near the unmarked but obvious summit in a pleasant setting.

Directions - In Downsville, NY at the junction of Routes 30 and 206, head north on Route 206 to begin (see NY Map 4).

Colchester Mountain Road

Total elevation - 942 ft **Length - 2.2 miles**

Average Grade - 8.1% (15%) **Rating - 0.79 (cat 2)**

The north side of the previous ascent, Colchester Mountain Road is a solid hill mostly through thick woods and the top climb in the immediate area in the author's opinion. From East River Road, head south up the hill into the trees and over stout grade. Soon the slope eases a bit and you break out of the trees. After 0.5 miles of moderate pedaling, the steepest sustained climbing on the hill is found over double digit grade. This challenging section eases but then quickly ramps back up to finish over double digit slope at an obvious top.

Directions - In Walton, NY at the junction of Routes 10 and 206, head south on Route 206 for 0.1 miles to East River Road on the left. Travel East River Road east for 2.7 miles to Colchester Mountain Road on the right where the climb begins (see NY Map 4).

26 North

Total elevation - 943 ft | **Length - 2.4 miles**

Average Grade - 7.4% (12%) | **Rating - 0.71 (cat 2)**

The north side of isolated Route 26 is another area short and stout ascent that is not climbed often. From hill start you head south over shallow and then gradually increasing grade. Within a half mile you enter the trees which recede further up the mountain. The final mile is over stout grade and includes a right hand turn with views. The solid pedaling continues right up to climb top at an unmarked but obvious summit.

Directions - In tiny Hawleys, NY on Route 10, head south on Hawleys/Downsville Road (Route 26) for a short distance to a 90 degree turn to the left (straight becomes East River Road) to begin the climb by continuing south on 26 (see NY Map 4).

26 South

Total elevation - 509 ft | **Length - 1.4 miles**

Average Grade - 6.9% (12%) | **Rating - 0.35 (cat 3)**

The south side of Route 26 is a similar ascent compared to its north side. From the brown house the hill begins over moderate grade which quickly gets steeper as you pull away to the north. Soon another grade increase is encountered as you continue to gain altitude up the mountain. Towards the very top the pedaling eases up to the unmarked but obvious top. The descent of 26 South is a quick one as well. You can begin the climb in the town of Downsville but if so the first few miles are very shallow.

Directions - In Downsville, NY on Route 30, head north on Knox Avenue (becomes Route 26) for 3.6 rolling and mostly shallow grade miles (brown House on right) to begin the listed climb by continuing north on 26 (see NY Map 4).

Berkaboom Road

Total elevation - 1,005 ft | **Length - 3.9 miles**

Average Grade - 4.9% (11%) | **Rating - 0.49 (cat 3)**

Berkaboom Road is an isolated and pleasant climb in the western portion of the Catskills Mountains. It begins over shallow grade which soon gets steeper as you plunge into thick woods. There is a flat early on and the grade is up and down from this point. You pass a waterfall along the way as well. Towards the top find a half mile of solid grade which yields to a small descent. Climbing then resumes over gradually steepening grade including a short section that is double digit. Near the very end the slope eases and the climb ends at Mountain Lake Road (dirt) on the left. The other side of this one (Big Pond Road) is a smaller hill (2.1 miles at 5.0%).

Directions - At the junction of Routes 28 and 30, head west on 30 for 8.1 miles. Just after you cross the lake, take a left on an unmarked (as of 2014) road. Travel this road for 1.9 miles to begin the climb on what is now Berkaboom Road (see NY Map 4).

Beech Hill Road North

Total elevation - 1,025 ft | **Length - 3.5 miles**

Average Grade - 5.6% (13%) | **Rating - 0.57 (cat 2/3)**

The north side of Beech Hill Road is a dark climb up from the Pepacton Reservoir. The opening pedaling is quite easy as you ride through woods and soon cross a creek. Just over a mile in you find a descent and a red barn. The woods then open a bit and the grade increases. Soon you are on quite stout slope and working a bit. The grade eases just before the top at an octagonal house on the right. The south side of Beech is a more shallow hill (2.9 miles at 4.4%).

Directions - Follow the previous directions to the lake crossing. Instead of turning left, continue on Route 30 for a short distance to Beech Hill Road (left) where the climb begins (see NY Map 4).

Devils Kitchen

Total elevation:	**1,149 ft**	**Length:**	**1.9 miles**
Top elevation:	**1,826 ft**	**Average grade:**	**11.5%**
Minimum grade:	**0%**	**Maximum grade:**	**22%**
Distance ≥ 5%:	**1.6 miles**	**Distance ≥ 10%:**	**1.2 miles**
Steepest mile:	**12.8%**	**Steepest 3 miles:**	**NA**
Traffic:	**2**	**Descent:**	**5**
Rating:	**1.42 (cat 1/2)**		

Devils Kitchen is one of the steepest climbs in the Northeast and the entire United States. Even though incredibly steep, the grade is stair step up the hill in places with very short, shallow sections to give you a chance to catch your breath (perhaps).

Be ready early on as you encounter double digit grade as soon as you head up the hill, leaving the town behind. Quickly a shallow section follows but the slope ramps right back to double digit quite quickly. This pattern repeats itself as you gain altitude, with the steepest sections generally getting steeper the higher you climb, eventually hitting 20%+ grade in two different places. Be on the lookout for the rock wall on the right which announces the steepest grade on the hill. It is short and as you glide to the right (views left) and then to the left the pedaling gets a little easier. Quickly however, you are back up to more challenging riding. Keep pushing the pedals if you can as the worst is over at this point as the last section is over moderate grade which tends to decrease as you ride generally west. The listed climb ends at a pullout on the left as the slope descends slightly beyond.

You can continue to ascend but much of the remainder of Platte Clove Road is over mostly shallow and up and down terrain (see the next climb for one solid route however). Devils Kitchen is a challenging descent as well.

Crux stretch - It may be the short stretch at mile 1.1 just after the rock wall appears on the right that contains 20%+ grade.

Directions - In West Saugerties, NY head north on Platte Clove Road to Becker Road (left) where the listed climb begins (see NY Map 4).

Near the start of severe Devils Kitchen

Devils Kitchen, NY

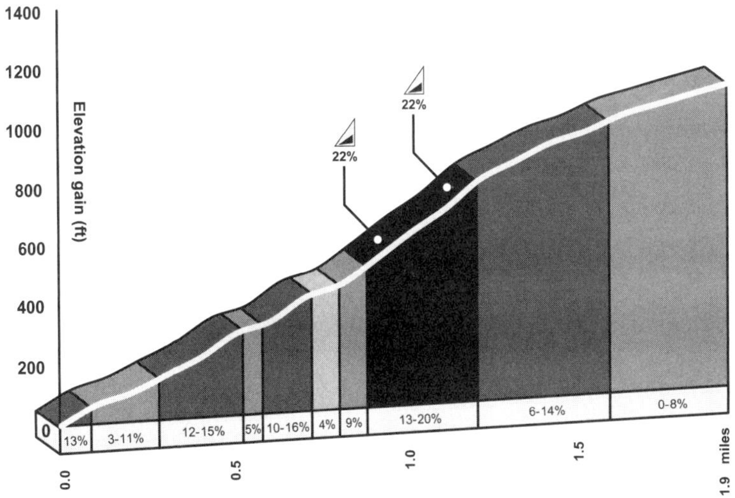

Devils Kitchen/Josh Road

Total elevation - 1,629 ft	**Length - 3.2 miles**
Average Grade - 9.6% (22%)	**Rating - 1.74 (cat 1)**

This is a continuation of the prior ascent up to a dead end with added solid grade. After the horrors of Devils Kitchen, continue west on Platte Clove Road to find a short descent. Climbing then resumes over moderate grade and at mile 2.3 turn right on Josh Road to again find double digit slope. The route is stair step from here with quite steep ramps including one that includes just under 20% grade. Towards the top the slope eases a bit and the road dead ends within thick woods. Josh Road is a very quick descent as well.

Directions - In tiny West Saugerties, New York head north on Platte Clove Road to Becker Road (on the left) where the listed climb begins (see NY Map 4).

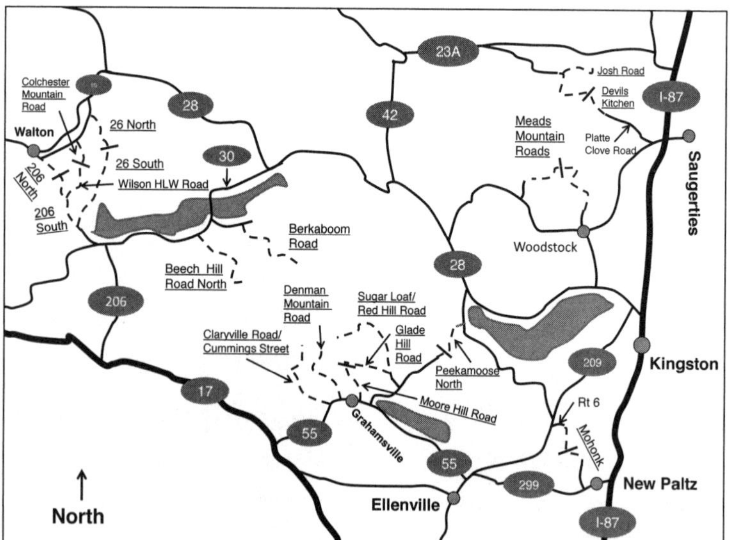

NY Map 4

Meads Mountain Road East

Total elevation - 1,116 ft	**Length - 1.9 miles**
Average Grade - 11.1% (16%)	**Rating - 1.24 (cat 2)**

The east side of Meads Mountain Road is another short and very steep Catskills climb that is among the steepest in the region. Along a dark and narrow road, there are a few houses down low but traffic should always be light on this one. Steep almost all the way up, the climb ends at a parking area for a trailhead on the right on top. Due to severe grade the east side of Meads Mountain Road is a quick descent as well.

Directions - In the center of Woodstock, NY on Route 212 head north on Rock City Road (Route 33). Go straight at the 4 way stop sign (road becomes Meads Mountain Road) and the listed climb soon begins at Hickory Hollow on the right (see NY Map 4).

Meads Mountain Road West

Total elevation - 807 ft	**Length - 2.4 miles**
Average Grade - 6.4% (13%)	**Rating - 0.51 (cat 2/3)**

The west side of Meads Mountain Road is a more moderate ascent than its east side but still carries sections of quite solid grade. The initial climbing is stair step and through a neighborhood and tree cover. Several of the ramps carry short sections of double digit grade and there is also a descent. Towards the top you find the steepest sustained climbing on the hill as the road opens a bit. The grade then eases up to the obvious top.

Directions - From Woodstock, NY on Route 212, head north on 212 for several miles to Reynolds Road on the right. Travel Reynolds for a short distance to MacDaniel Road on the right. Travel MacDaniel for a very short distance to cross a creek where the climb begins by continuing east (see NY Map 4).

Peekamoose Road North

Total elevation - 1,011 ft	**Length - 5.0 miles**
Average Grade - 3.8% (12%)	**Rating - 0.39 (cat 3)**

The north side of Peakamoose Road is a very scenic ride along a narrow road with little traffic. The overall grade is quite shallow but it does include a solid section along the way. It begins beside a creek and easy pedaling which then goes up and down. 3 miles in you find stout grade which gradually eases up to the unmarked summit. The south side of Peekamoose is a very shallow but scenic hill.

Directions - At the junction of Routes 28A and 42 in tiny West Shokan, NY, head south on Route 42 for 1.0 shallow miles to a creek crossing to begin the listed climb by continuing south on 42 (see NY Map 4).

Sugar Loaf/Red Hill Road

Total elevation - 1,596 ft	**Length - 4.2 miles**
Average Grade - 7.2% (13%)	**Rating - 1.15 (cat 2)**

Sugar Loaf/Red Hill Road is another solid Empire State climb that includes a double digit grade half mile within its lower half. The slope is variable overall and via a pleasant wooded route within a country neighborhood and with little traffic. At mile 3.5 turn left on Red Hill Road to continue. The grade eases as you approach the unmarked but obvious top (driveway on right) as the grade flattens and the road is a fun descent.

Directions - In Grahamsville, NY head east on Route 55 for a short distance and then merge left onto Route 55A. Shortly keep straight on Route 153 and then almost immediately turn left on Sugar Loaf Road. Glade Hill Road will appear on your left in 0.5 miles where the listed climb begins by continuing straight on Sugar Loaf Road (see NY Map 4).

Claryville Road/Cummings Road

Total elevation - 693 ft	**Length - 2.2 miles**
Average Grade - 6.0% (11%)	**Rating - 0.41 (cat 3)**

Claryville Road is a short but solid ascent from the small town of Grahamsville, NY. The start is stout as you soon head up the hill over the steepest sustained climbing on the hill along with a car or two here and there. At mile 1.4 turn right on Cummings Road as Claryville Road flattens out. Cummings Road begins as shallow but gradually increases in grade, passing a few homes within woods. Towards the very top the slope eases considerably and the climb ends as the pavement ends.

Directions - In Grahamsville, NY on Route 55, the climb begins at its junction with Claryville Road right in town (see NY Map 4).

The start of Bear Mountain

Glade Hill Road

Total elevation:	**1,251 ft**	**Length:**	**1.9 miles**
Top elevation:	**2,179 ft**	**Average grade:**	**12.5%**
Minimum grade:	**3%**	**Maximum grade:**	**23%**
Distance ≥ 5%:	**1.8 miles**	**Distance ≥ 10%:**	**1.7 miles**
Steepest mile:	**13.8%**	**Steepest 3 miles:**	**NA**
Traffic:	**1**	**Descent:**	**5**
Rating:	**1.68 (cat 1)**		

One of the steepest hills in the Northeast as well as the entire United States, Glade Hill Road is a severe ascent located within the scenic Catskills Mountains. A moderate start soon gets very steep as you encounter an S bend with severe grade. On top, the torture continues as you gain altitude on the isolated road. A field and farmhouse soon appear. The double digit grade eventually eases just before the roadway crosses quite closely between 2 farm buildings. Severe pedaling quickly returns however but then eases slightly as the road now heads along a ridge with a drop off (and views) to the left. You then head into the woods for a time as slightly more challenging pedaling returns.

Continuing uphill as the trees thin a bit, you quickly encounter the maximum grade on the hill through a semi right hand turn. As you approach a shelf the grade eases but remains double digit. It then gradually increases as the road straightens up the hill. Towards the very top the slope finally eases and the climb ends at its junction with Moore Hill Road (subsequent climb). Needless to say, Glade Hill Road is a quick and challenging descent (it may be better to descend Moore Hill Road instead).

Crux stretch - It may be the S bend and section just beyond that you encounter at mile 0.15 that is 14-17% grade.

Directions - In Grahamsville, NY head east on Route 55 for a short distance and merge left onto Route 55A. Shortly, keep straight for Route 153 and then almost immediately turn left on Sugar Loaf Road. From this point, Glade Hill Road will appear on your left in 0.5 miles where the climb begins (see NY Map 4).

The innocuous start of severe Glade Hill Road

Glade Hill Road, NY

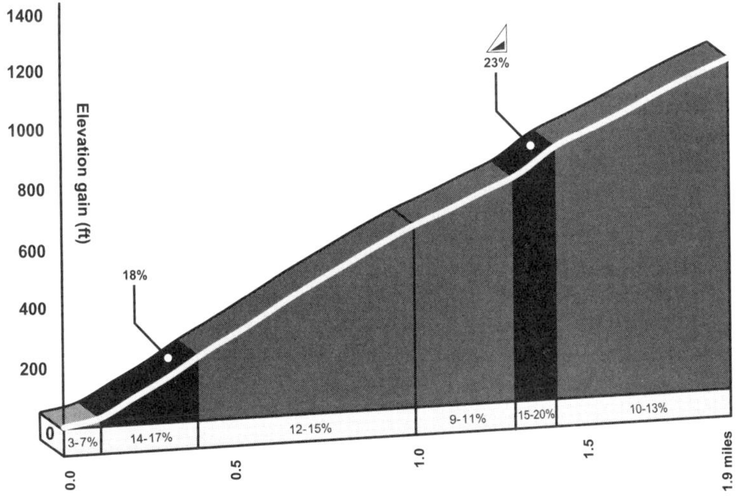

Moore Hill Road

Total elevation - 1,247 ft	**Length - 3.0 miles**
Average Grade - 7.9% (14%)	**Rating - 0.98 (cat 2)**

Moore Hill Road is a pleasant Catskills ascent with a grade that will make you work for its dead end top that it shares with Glade Hill Road (previous climb). A fairly variable grade that includes double digit sections will wear on you and most of the ascent is through thick woods with a somewhat isolated feel. The grade eases as you approach the obvious top. Moore Hill Road is a bit of an easier descent than very steep Glade Hill Road as well.

Directions - In Grahamsville, NY head east on Route 55 for a short distance to Moore Hill Road on your left. Head up Moore Hill Road for 0.1 miles to begin the listed climb (see NY Map 4).

Denman Mountain Road

Total elevation - 1,085 ft	**Length - 2.5 miles**
Average Grade - 8.2% (23%)	**Rating - 0.91 (cat 2)**

Denman Mountain Road is an interesting climb that carries little traffic (dead end of a sort). It carries a solid grade that includes a short stretch above the rarified air of 20%. From Route 55 you hit solid slope immediately to begin among a few residences. From this point the grade is stair step up the hill. At mile 1.5 the road reduces to a true single lane, disappearing into thick woods. Eventually you break out into a field as the grade flattens. Soon the route turns to the left to finish and it is here that you encounter severe double digit slope and poor pavement (as of 2014). Towards the very top the grade eases and the listed climb ends as the pavement ends. You can follow the path to your right for a short distance to break out onto Moore Hill Road (previous).

Directions - In Grahamsville, NY on Route 55, the climb begins at its junction with Denman Mountain Road in town (see NY Map 4).

Single lane on Denman Mountain Road

Near the start of Mohonk East

Mohonk East

Total elevation - 854 ft	**Length - 2.2 miles**
Average Grade - 7.3% (9%)	**Rating - 0.63 (cat 2)**

The east side Mohonk is short and solid hill that sees quite a few riders. From Buttersville Road head up the hill over shallow to moderate grade and a few vehicles at times. There are a few houses along this stretch as well. Soon more challenging pedaling arrives as you gain altitude. As the grade eases you ride through fields and as it picks back up you approach a golf course. Towards the very end the slope eases as congestion from the golf course increases and the climb top is obvious at a short one lane section under a walkway.

Directions - From New Paltz, NY head west on Route 299 for a short distance to Springtown Road on the right. Travel Springtown for 0.5 miles to Mountain Rest Road on the left. Travel Mountain Rest for just over one mile to Butterville Road on the left where the climb begins by continuing straight up the hill (see NY Map 4).

Mohonk West

Total elevation - 721 ft	**Length - 2.1 miles**
Average Grade - 6.5% (13%)	**Rating - 0.47 (cat 3)**

The west side climb of Mohonk carries a bit less grade and traffic compared to its east side. There is a short stretch of severe grade at climb start and then you pedal over easy slope. At mile 0.3 turn right to stay on Route 6 to continue over gradually increasing grade. This point is the start of the climb for many locals. Soon the road swings through a turn to the left with increasing grade. This is the steepest sustained climbing on the hill and continues for a while. Near the summit the slope eases a bit and the climb ends at an obvious top.

Directions - Just north of tiny Accord, NY at the junction of Routes 209 and 1, head north on Route 1 for a short distance to Route 6. Turn right on Route 6 and travel it for 2.4 miles to begin the listed climb by continuing east on Route 6 (see NY Map 4).

52 East

Total elevation - 889 ft | **Length - 2.8 miles**

Average Grade - 6.0% (8%) | **Rating - 0.54 (cat 2/3)**

The climb up the east side of Route 52 is over fairly steady grade and with a few vehicles at times. An easy start in town soon leads out of town to the west and to more challenging pedaling with shade in places. The road leads you through mostly gentle curves over its route and there are no real surprises on this one. Although the slope eventually eases slightly, it is solid right up to the unmarked but obvious summit.

Directions - In the small town of Walker Valley on Route 52 in the southern part of the state, the climb begins at the fire house by heading west on 52 (see NY Map 5).

52 West

Total elevation - 1,184 ft | **Length - 4.2 miles**

Average Grade - 5.4% (9%) | **Rating - 0.63 (cat 2)**

The west side of Route 52 begins over moderate grade in the town of Ellenville and carries intermittent traffic. Quickly leaving town, the road narrows and steepens as it passes some houses early on the route. It then swings to the right as you leave town to head up along a ridgeline and the pedaling gets easier. Soon, very good views appear to your right and the road contains a shoulder for a bit more room for riding (the road carries some intermittent traffic). The grade goes up and down on this section right up to the unmarked but obvious summit.

Directions - In Ellenville, NY at the junction of Routes 209 and 52, head east on 52 for 0.5 miles to begin the climb at Tow Path on the right by continuing east on 52 (see NY Map 5).

South Gully Road

Total elevation - 1,539 ft | **Length - 3.9 miles**

Average Grade - 7.5% (14%) | **Rating - 1.18 (cat 2)**

The climb of South Gully Road shares its start with 52 West (previous ascent). After 0.7 miles on Route 52, turn left (suddenly) on South Gully Road and find double digit grade which includes the hill maximum. This is over a fairly straight stretch of road which you need to watch if you descend the route (quick). The grade goes up and down as you continue, including short ramps of double digit climbing. At mile 3.0 turn right and then left to continue to the unmarked top just beyond a red barn on the left.

Directions - In Ellenville, NY at the junction of Routes 209 and 52, head east on 52 for 0.5 miles to begin the climb at Tow Path on the right by continuing east on 52 (see NY Map 5).

South Gully Road/Mount Meenagha

Total elevation - 1,483 ft | **Length - 3.1 miles**

Average Grade - 8.5% (19%) | **Rating - 1.29 (cat 2)**

One of the most difficult climbs in the state of New York, South Gully Road/Mount Meenagha follows the previous ascent's moderate and then solid grade until mile 1.6 when you turn left from South Gully to Mount Meenagha and almost immediately find the maximum grade on the hill. The challenging pedaling soon eases slightly just before a sharp turn to the right as a few houses appear but double digit slope then returns. Towards the very top the grade finally eases for good and the climb ends as the road comes to an end at a cul-de-sac within a wooded setting.

Directions - In Ellenville, NY at the junction of Routes 209 and 52, head east on 52 for 0.5 miles to begin the climb at Tow Path on the right by continuing east on 52 (see NY Map 5).

Steep grade on South Gully Road

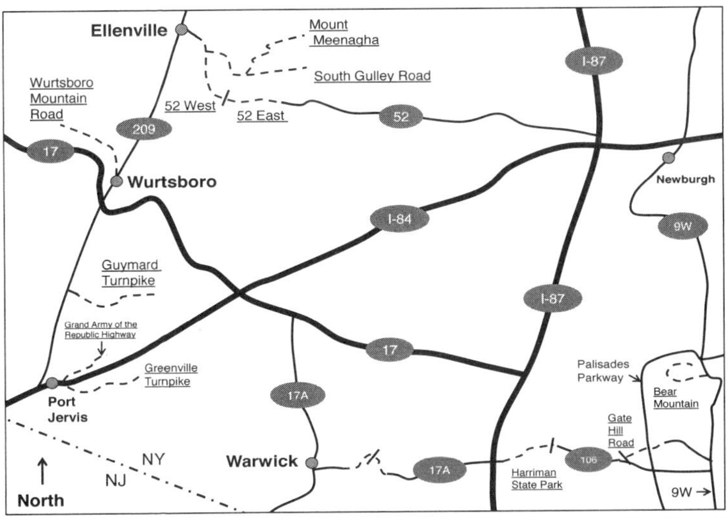

NY Map 5

Wurtsboro Mountain Road

Total elevation - 947 ft	**Length - 5.0 miles**
Average Grade - 3.6% (7%)	**Rating - 0.34 (cat 3)**

A straighter climb you may not find, Wurtsboro Mountain Road begins over shallow grade and gradually steepens as you ride due west with some traffic most days. This is the very definition of a stair step hill as well as each more solid ramp is followed by a shallow one. Just over 4 miles into the ascent, you find a descent. Some may choose to end the climb here but in another 0.4 miles you can climb one final ramp to end the listed climb before the road descends for good down to Route 17.

Directions - In Wurtsboro, NY at the junction of Route 209 and Wurtsboro Mountain Road (Route 172), head west on Wurtsboro Mountain Road to begin (see NY Map 5).

Guymard Turnpike West

Total elevation - 716 ft	**Length - 2.4 miles**
Average Grade - 5.7% (8%)	**Rating - 0.41 (cat 3)**

The west side of Guymard Turnpike is a short and fairly solid ascent in the southern part of the state. You enter woods at the start over solid slope. In less than a mile the road picks up a center stripe. Just beyond is a flat and then climbing resumes briefly before a longer flat that begins at a rail road crossing. Climbing then resumes over the steepest sustained climbing on the hill and a switchback to the right. Soon the grade eases again before another short flat and then the listed climb ends at a 3 way stop.

Directions - In Godeffroy, NY on Route 209, head east on Guymard Turnpike (unmarked as of 2014) for 1.1 miles to a left turn where the climb begins by continuing east (see NY Map 5).

Grand Army of the Republic Highway

Total elevation - 779 ft	**Length - 3.4 miles**
Average Grade - 4.3% (7%)	**Rating - 0.34 (cat 3)**

The Grand Army of the Republic Highway is a steady grade hill from Port Jervis that parallels Interstate 84. The hill begins in town along quite shallow grade and some vehicles and congestion. The pedaling gradually gets more difficult (and the vehicles ease) as you ride east but is never challenging on this ascent. The road gently twists up the hill just to the north of Interstate 84 before ending at an unmarked but obvious top.

Directions - In Port Jervis, NY the climb begins at the junction of Routes 6 and 15 (the road that heads under Interstate 84 and into New Jersey, turning into Route 23 once there) by heading east on Route 6 (see NY Map 5).

Greenville Turnpike

Total elevation - 836 ft	**Length - 2.5 miles**
Average Grade - 6.3% (9%)	**Rating - 0.53 (cat 2/3)**

Greenville Turnpike is a solid grade climb right along the New Jersey border. It begins as quite shallow and gradually steepens as it parallels Interstate 84. Just over one mile in, the road enters a neighborhood and picks up a center stripe. It becomes more twisty here as well and you find the steepest sustained climbing on the hill. Towards the end the slope eases and the climb ends at Nelson Drive on the right.

Directions - In Port Jervis, NY at the junction of Routes 6 and 15, head south on 15 under Interstate 84. Greenville Turnpike is the first road on your left and the climb begins at the junction (unmarked as of 2014) by heading east on Greenville Turnpike (see NY Map 5).

17A East

Total elevation - 493 ft	**Length - 1.7 miles**
Average Grade - 5.5% (8%)	**Rating - 0.27 (cat 3)**

The east side of Route 17A is a short and fairly popular climb over one of the multiple north/south running escarpments of southern New York. Carrying intermittent traffic, the ascent begins over solid and steady grade as you head west up the wooded ridge. After 0.7 miles the slope eases and from there becomes stair step. The last stretch is again over stout slope and the climb ends as the grade flattens on top.

Directions - At the junction of Routes 17 and 17A just west of Interstate 87, head west on 17A for several miles to Benjamin Meadows Road on the right where the climb begins by continuing west on 17A (see NY Map 5).

17A West

Total elevation - 645 ft	**Length - 2.1 miles**
Average Grade - 5.8% (9%)	**Rating - 0.38 (cat 3)**

Another popular and somewhat stout hill in southern NY, an easy start soon leads to solid grade as the somewhat narrow road with intermittent traffic heads into woods. The route then heads uphill in a stair step fashion which includes a short descent. Towards the top the pedaling gets easier and the climb ends at an unmarked but obvious top as the road descends beyond. Parallel (just to the north of 17A) Kain Road is a steeper approach (0.8 mi at 12% average grade) to this same point.

Directions - In Greenwood Lake, NY the climb begins at the junction of Route 17A and Fernwood Drive (on the right) by heading east on 17A (see NY Map 5).

Popular Gate Hill Road

A rider in Harriman State Park

Harriman State Park West

Total elevation - 542 ft | **Length - 3.1 miles**

Average Grade - 3.3% (6%) | **Rating - 0.18 (cat 3/4)**

While not a difficult ascent, the western approach into scenic Harriman State Park on Route 106 is a very popular route for local riders. It begins as shallow which gradually increases as you ride east including the steepest ascending (although not steep) on the hill. Just over one mile in, you come to a lake and the grade eases and then the road descends. From here you ride over shallow grade that includes another descent and a flat. The listed climb ends at a descent that leads down to a traffic circle.

Directions - At the junction of Routes 17 and 17A just west of Interstate 87, head east from the junction (under Interstate 87) on what is now Route 106 for 0.1 miles to begin the climb by continuing east into Harriman State Park (see NY Map 5).

Gate Hill Road

Total elevation - 463 ft | **Length - 1.5 miles**

Average Grade - 5.8% (8%) | **Rating - 0.27 (cat 3)**

Gate Hill Road is a short and very popular ascent that leads riders into Harriman State Park and other pleasant riding in the area. Most traffic is local as many use close by and 4 lane Palisade Parkway. It is over somewhat steady grade and heads through a small neighborhood that includes a very large residence. The grade eases near the top and the listed climb ends as the road comes to an end at a junction within the state park.

Directions - Take Exit 14 on Palisade Parkway for Gate Hill Road. The listed climb begins at Zackary Taylor on the left by heading south on Gate Hill Road (see NY Map 5).

Bear Mountain

Total elevation - 1,267 ft	Length - 4.5 miles
Average Grade - 5.3% (8%)	Rating - 0.68 (cat 2)

The biggest climb in the New York City area and one of the most popular in the state, Bear Mountain carries a solid grade up to very good views of the Hudson River valley. The route begins over moderate grade as you enter woods. Just over one half mile in, you encounter a traffic circle where the grade eases. Quickly a switchback to the left introduces more stout slope. Soon the route becomes stair step and views appear to your left. At mile 2.4, bear to the right to continue uphill over more solid grade. After a mile within the trees, views appear again to the left. Towards the top the road heads inland and the climb ends at a parking area at the very top of the mountain with long views.

Directions - The climb begins at the junction of Route 9W and the entrance road to Bear Mountain State Park, just south of the junction of Routes 9W and 6 on the Hudson River (see NY Map 5)

Along Bear Mountain

NEXT
2 MILES
USE LOW
GEAR

Vermont

105 East

Total elevation - 1,022 ft | **Length - 3.0 miles**

Average Grade - 6.5% (9%) | **Rating - 0.66 (cat 2)**

The east side of Route 105 is a bit shorter but more stout overall hill compared to its west side. You ride up stair step grade on this one but there are no real surprises along the way. The final stretch is more stout and consistent (and scenic) and the climb ends at an obvious top with a big pullout on the right. It is a pretty quick descent as well.

Directions - At the junction of Routes 101 and 105 just north of Jay, VT, head west on 105 for 2.1 miles to begin the listed climb by continuing west (see VT Map 1).

105 West

Total elevation - 1,599 ft | **Length - 7.1 miles**

Average Grade - 4.3% (8%) | **Rating - 0.68 (cat 2)**

The west side of Route 105 is a fairly long and pleasant ascent that runs very close to the Canadian border in places. It begins over solid grade as you pull away from the junction at climb start into woods. The slope then goes up and down and includes a flat and a descent on the route. The last 2.8 miles are more steady and solid as you ride through some gentle curves. Towards the very top the grade eases and the climb ends at an obvious summit.

Directions - In Richford, VT head north on Route 105 for a short distance to its junction with Route 105A where the climb begins by heading east on 105 (see VT Map 1).

Blue House Hill North

Total elevation - 700 ft | **Length - 3.1 miles**

Average Grade - 4.3% (10%) | **Rating - 0.31 (cat 3)**

The north side of Blue House Hill is a pleasant climb over variable terrain that typically carries little traffic. From Route 105 you climb through the small town of Richford to begin. You find the most challenging pedaling early on and then the route eases as you leave the town behind. The remainder of the route is through fields and woods over up and down terrain but no particularly challenging pedaling. Towards the end the grade eases further and the climb terminates at an unmarked top.

Directions - The climb begins just east of Richford, VT at the junction of Route 105 and South Richford Road by heading south on South Richford Road (see VT Map 1).

Blue House Hill South

Total elevation - 678 ft | **Length - 3.7 miles**

Average Grade - 3.5% (14%) | **Rating - 0.25 (cat 3)**

The south side of Blue House Hill, while having similar stats, is a somewhat different ascent compared with its north side. From the covered bridge, head north by a few homes and over gradually increasing grade which soon hits double digit briefly. A descent is then encountered and then another which knocks down the average grade. Soon you find the most challenging half mile of pedaling on the hill that includes another segment of double digit slope. The grade then eases over the final stretch up to an unmarked top as the road goes flat.

Directions - In tiny Montgomery, VT on Route 118, head north on Fuller Bridge Road for 0.1 miles (just beyond the covered bridge) to begin the climb by continuing north (see VT Map 1).

A rider on Route 105

Looking down Blue House Hill

Jay Peak North

Total elevation - 1,328 ft	**Length - 5.0 miles**
Average Grade - 5.0% (12%)	**Rating - 0.70 (cat 2)**

The north side of Jay Peak is a solid hill located close to the Canadian border. From the small town of Jay, head west and then generally south over shallow grade to begin. The pedaling gradually gets more difficult and the road more twisty. After easing back, the grade gets steeper again as you pass the Jay Peak Ski Area on the right with the sharp peaked mountain right in front of you. The grade then eases, goes back up and then a descent is found. Although you may think this is the top, keep going as climbing resumes one last time over the steepest slope on the hill before easing up to the listed top at a small parking area.

Directions - From the junction of Routes 101 and 242 just east of Jay, VT, head west on 242 for 1.4 miles to begin the listed climb by continuing west on 242 (see VT Map 1).

Jay Peak South

Total elevation - 1,714 ft	**Length - 6.3 miles**
Average Grade - 5.2% (11%)	**Rating - 0.91 (cat 2)**

The south side ascent to Jay Peak is also a solid and variable grade hill and a bit longer compared to its north side. It quickly leaves the tiny town of Montgomery Center to begin over rolling grade with a few sharper ramps. Most of the route ascends in stair step fashion as you ride north through fields and woods. Towards the top you find the steepest sustained grade on the hill and the climb ends at a small parking area (hiking).

Directions - The climb begins at the junction of Routes 118 and 242 in picturesque Montgomery Center, VT by heading north on 242 (see VT Map 1).

122 North

Total elevation - 660 ft	**Length - 2.6 miles**
Average Grade - 4.8% (9%)	**Rating - 0.32 (cat 3)**

122 North is a pleasant ascent in eastern Vermont that carries little traffic most of the time. From Route 16, pull away up the hill on a narrow road and over solid grade. Soon the pedaling is over stair step slope and among some woods and a few houses. Just beyond the halfway point you find the most challenging riding on the hill. Towards the summit the grade eases and the climb ends at an unmarked but obvious top.

Directions - From Glover, VT on Route 16, head south on 16 for a short distance to Route 122 on the left where the climb begins (see VT Map 1).

Riders approaching Jay Peak

Burke Mountain

Total elevation:	**2,381 ft**	**Length:**	**4.7 miles**
Top elevation:	**3,211 ft**	**Average grade:**	**9.6%**
Minimum grade:	**0%**	**Maximum grade:**	**24%**
Distance ≥ 5%:	**4.0 miles**	**Distance ≥ 10%:**	**2.7 miles**
Steepest mile:	**15.6%**	**Steepest 3 miles:**	**13.0%**
Traffic:	**1**	**Descent:**	**5**
Rating:	**2.92 (hors/cat 1)**		

Burke Mountain is a difficult and severe climb located in northeast Vermont. You begin in town over shallow grade. At mile 0.2 turn right on Mountain Road. The grade picks up here as you head east and then goes up and down, touching double digit briefly. It then eases before gradually increasing back to steep.

At mile 2.4, bear left onto Campground Road and it is here that you realize that your pleasant ride is over for the day. 14-16% grade smacks you in the face as you soon head into thick woods on the narrow road to begin one of the steepest miles in the U.S. After 0.5 miles you get a short break and then you must negotiate the steepest half mile on the route. The slope then eases but only slightly and soon you begin to wind through a few fairly tight switchbacks.

The thick woods eventually thin and there are a few views in places where the ski lift climbs the hill. The grade eases just a bit over the 2nd half of the upper section but keep in mind sustained climbing at 10-14% grade can still be challenging. Multiple switchbacks carry you up the hill and the listed ascent ends at the small parking area on the right. You can stop and admire the views or keep left to ride the narrow path to get to the very top of the pavement and another very short section of 20% grade (upper section closed in winter - East Burke Sports - 802 626-3215). There is an annual race on Burke Mountain's slopes and the upper section is a difficult descent as well.

Crux stretch - The initial mile of Campground Road is one of the steepest in the U.S. and a real key to the summit.

Directions - In East Burke, VT on Route 114 the climb begins just beyond the bridge just east of East Burke Sports (see VT Map 1).

On upper Burke Mountain

Burke Mountain, VT

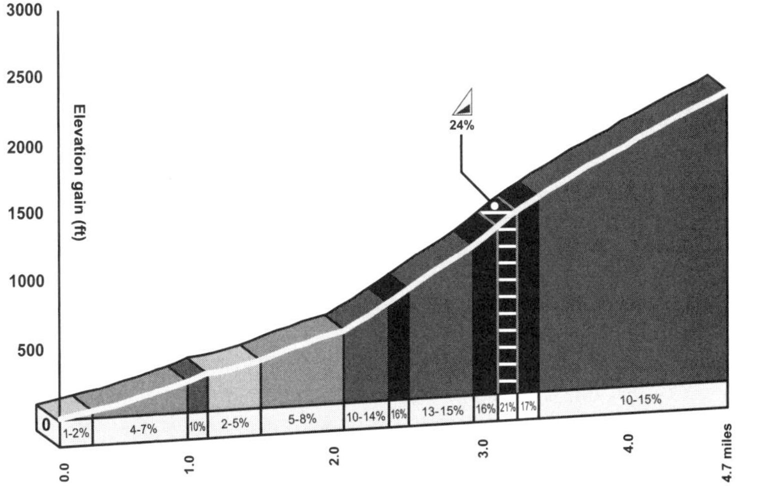

Smugglers Notch East

Total elevation - 1,221 ft **Length - 4.5 miles**

Average Grade - 5.1% (20%) **Rating - 0.64 (cat 2)**

The east side of Smugglers Notch is a very popular ascent west of Stowe with a real punch at this end. The hill begins over solid grade among a small amount of congestion. Just over a mile in, the slope levels out and includes several small descents. Eventually you leave traffic behind as you continue west as the grade begins to undulate. With less than a mile remaining your pleasant ride is over for the day as the grade picks up to double digit as the road reduces to a wide single lane. Short stretches of 20% are encountered and the ascent soon ends at an obvious top within interesting surroundings.

Directions - From Stowe, VT at the junction of Routes 100 and 108, head west on Route 108 for just under 5 miles to begin the listed climb by continuing west on 108 (see VT Map 1).

Smugglers Notch West

Total elevation - 1,120 ft **Length - 3.1 miles**

Average Grade - 6.8% (11%) **Rating - 0.77 (cat 2)**

The west side of Smugglers North is a more steady grade hill and while it does not include the severe grade of the finishing stretch of its east side, may be more difficult overall. Quite popular with area riders, the somewhat narrow road carries some intermittent traffic at times but not enough to ruin the ride. Towards the top you find slightly increased grade and the climb ends soon after at the obvious notch.

Directions - At the junction of Routes 15 and 108 just east of tiny Cambridge, VT, head east on 108 for a short distance to the Smugglers Resort. The listed climb begins just beyond the resort by continuing east on 108 (see VT Map 1).

Bolton Mountain

Total elevation - 1,787 ft | **Length - 4.2 miles**

Average Grade - 8.1% (16%) | **Rating - 1.48 (cat 1/2)**

Bolton Mountain is a solid climb that leads to a ski area located a short distance east of Burlington, VT. A warning sign greets riders at its innocuous beginning. Soon the few houses located at the start fade as you head up the mountain, shortly hitting a section of double digit grade before easing. From here to the summit the grade is variable with multiple double digit sections and the road has plenty of room for riding. There is a short flat section near the halfway point followed soon after by an almost half mile long section which carries the steepest extended grade and could be considered the crux stretch on this hill. Near the top the slope eases a bit, the trees part and the climb dead ends at a ski resort near the top of the mountain.

Directions - In Bolton, Vermont on Route 2 head east on 2 for a short distance (just north of Interstate 89) and turn left on Bolton Mountain Road. The climb begins just beyond the junction (see VT Map 1).

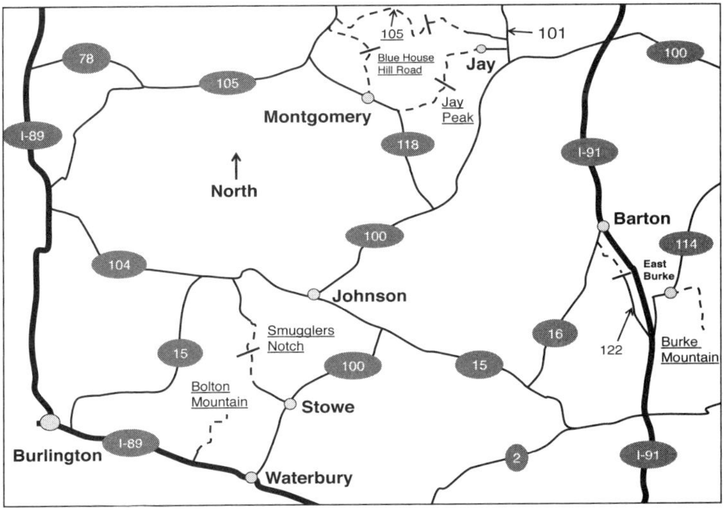

VT Map 1

Appalachian Gap East

Total elevation - 1,332 ft	**Length - 2.7 miles**
Average Grade - 9.3% (13%)	**Rating - 1.25 (cat 2)**

The east side of Appalachian Gap in scenic central Vermont might surprise you. Its grade is fairly steady (steep) over much of its length which belies its overall steep nature. The road is somewhat narrow and does not carry a lot of traffic most of the time. It begins as stout grade, eases a bit for a short stretch and then steepens again, a pattern that is repeated as you ascend west. The steepest section on this hill is toward the top and the grade only eases over the last 0.2 miles of the route. The view at the obvious top (looking west) is one of the best in Vermont. The annual race on its slopes runs the full length of the hill which includes a shallow start (stats for the entire hill - 6.2 miles at 4.9% average grade).

Directions - At the junction of Routes 100 and 17 just south of Waitsfield, VT, head west on Route 17 for 3.4 slightly uphill miles to begin the listed climb at the grade change (see VT Map 2).

Appalachian Gap West

Total elevation - 1,224 ft	**Length - 2.7 miles**
Average Grade - 8.6% (17%)	**Rating - 1.08 (cat 2)**

The west side of Appalachian Gap is another solid Northeast ascent. The initial climbing is over moderate slope which goes up a bit and then reduces down to a creek crossing. From there the slope is up and down with several short sections of double digit grade. The last stretch contains the most challenging sustained climbing on the hill and the very end can test you up to its obvious summit. Great views from the top await on clear days and part of the descent is a burner

Directions - From South Starksboro on Route 17, head east on 17. The listed climb begins 1.0 miles beyond Gore Road (left) just after you cross a creek (see VT Map 2).

Sugarbush

Total elevation - 620 ft	Length - 1.9 miles
Average Grade - 6.2% (13%)	Rating - 0.38 (cat 3)

The climb of Sugarbush leads to a ski area is a short but fairly stout hill near many other area ascents in central Vermont. Within woods for much of its length, the route heads up the mountain through mostly gentle curves. The grade is variable with steep ramps interspersed with more moderate climbing. The final stretch is over more shallow slope and the climb dead ends at a parking lot for the resort.

Directions - From Route 100 just north of Warren, VT, the climb begins at its junction with the Sugarbush Resort Access Road by heading towards the resort (see VT Map 2)..

Lincoln Gap West

Total elevation - 1,385 ft	Length - 3.5 miles
Average Grade - 7.5% (20%)	Rating - 1.07 (cat 2)

One of the few climbs listed with some unpaved sections, the west side of Lincoln Gap is a somewhat isolated hill with a real challenge at its end. The grade is variable with steep ramps interspersed with more shallow to moderate climbing as you ride through woods for much of its length. The final stretch is paved and over vicious grade (last half mile is ~16% average grade), hitting 20% briefly. Just before the top the pedaling gets easier and the climb ends at the marked summit and a parking area with hiking possibilities (Long Trail).

Directions - In tiny Lincoln, VT, head south on East River Road for a short distance to Lincoln Gap Road on the left where the listed climb begins by heading east on Lincoln Gap Road (see VT Map 2).

Lincoln Gap East

Total elevation:	**1,098 ft**	**Length:**	**1.5 miles**
Top elevation:	**2,424 ft**	**Average grade:**	**13.9%**
Minimum grade:	**3%**	**Maximum grade:**	**21%**
Distance ≥ 5%:	**1.4 miles**	**Distance ≥ 10%:**	**1.3 miles**
Steepest mile:	**15.9%**	**Steepest 3 miles:**	**NA**
Traffic:	**1**	**Descent:**	**4**
Rating:	**1.58 (cat 1/2)**		

This is a short but severe climb up the east side of scenic Lincoln Gap in the Green Mountains of central Vermont. Its claim to fame is its steepest mile, one of the steepest in the U.S.

From a somewhat shallow start at the beginning of the pavement, the road bends to the right and trees close in, creating a dark tunnel through which to ride. Quickly the grade increases to double digit and soon you encounter the maximum grade on the hill but you hardly notice as the slope is oppressive and stays that way until just before the top. Nothing to do here but keep turning the pedals on the narrow, dark road as this section is simply extremely steep, with a mile near the top averaging just under 16%, one of the steepest paved miles of climbing in the United States.

Just before the top the grade eases and the trees part. Soon a small parking area comes into view and then the signed summit which may be a welcome sight. There are hiking possibilities at climbs' end as well. The east side of Lincoln Gap is a must do ride for the serious hill climber. Make sure you are sufficiently warmed up for this one as you do not want to underestimate its difficulty over a relatively short length (closed in winter - Green Mountain National Forest - 802 767-4261).

Crux stretch - The mile from 0.4 to 1.4 miles which is one of the steepest in the U.S. is the key to the summit.

Directions - On Route 100 just south of Warren, VT turn west on Lincoln Road. Head west for 2.5 miles, going from pavement to gravel in the process and the listed climb begins where the pavement reappears (see VT Map 2).

The start of Lincoln Gap East

Lincoln Gap East, VT

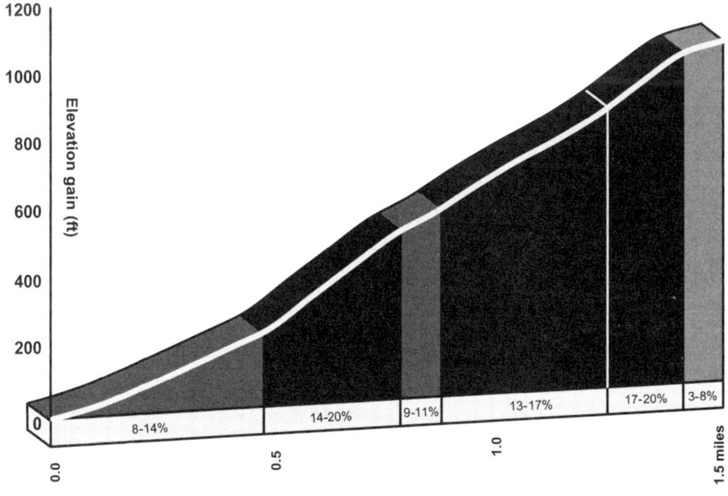

Roxbury Gap East

Total elevation - 1,409 ft | **Length - 3.5 miles**

Average Grade - 7.6% (13%) | **Rating - 1.08 (cat 2)**

I don't typically include climbs with a large amount of unpaved routing but the two listed on this page warrant inclusion as both sides of Roxbury Gap are stout hills and the unpaved sections are easily ridden on a road bike unless very churned up or wet. The east side begins over shallow grade which quickly gets steep. The slope then eases and after 1.5 miles the pavement ends (as of 2014). The grade picks up here and then goes up and down before a stout finish up to the obvious summit.

Directions - In Roxbury, VT the climb begins at the junction of Route 12A and Warren Mountain Road by heading west on Warren Mountain Road (see VT Map 2).

Roxbury Gap West

Total elevation - 1,466 ft | **Length - 4.5 miles**

Average Grade - 6.2% (13%) | **Rating - 0.91 (cat 2)**

The west side of Roxbury Gap is a longer and more shallow overall ascent compared to its east side but similarly its finish is stout. The first 2 miles are paved and go up and down as you leave the small town of Warren. The last 1.9 miles, which go from pavement to dirt, back to pavement and then a dirt finish, are the most challenging sustained climbing on the hill. The final stretch is over double digit grade which lasts right up to the obvious summit.

Directions - In Warren, VT at the junction of Route 100 and Main Street, head east on Main into Warren, turning left on Brook Road, for 0.3 miles to begin the climb by continuing east (see VT Map 2).

Middlebury Gap East

Total elevation - 1,250 ft **Length - 6.0 miles**

Average Grade - 3.9% (13%) **Rating - 0.49 (cat 3)**

The east side of Middlebury Gap is a scenic ascent that sees quite a few area riders and no more than intermittent traffic most days. It is over a quite variable grade that contains some challenging climbing on its slopes, including a difficult finish. Easy pedaling to begin gradually gets more demanding as you ride west although there is also a flat section along the way. 4.5 miles in, you find a double digit grade half mile to negotiate. The slope then eases briefly before more solid grade returns. The final half mile is again over double digit pedaling and the climb ends at Middlebury Gap.

Directions - In Hancock, VT at the junction of Routes 100 and 125, the climb begins by heading west on 125 (see VT Map 2).

Middlebury Gap West

Total elevation - 1,612 ft **Length - 8.3 miles**

Average Grade - 3.7% (12%) **Rating - 0.59 (cat 2/3)**

The west side of Middlebury Gap is a longer and more shallow ascent compared to its east side and it may contain even more grade variability. From the bridge over the creek the listed hill begins over stout grade which soon becomes moderate. It then goes up and down through the mountainous terrain with a few flats thrown in, reducing its average grade considerably. The final 1.3 miles are the most challenging sustained climbing on the hill and the summit is obvious at the gap.

Directions - At the junction of Routes 116 and 125 east of Middlebury, VT, head east on 125 for 1.0 miles to a creek crossing to begin the listed climb (see VT Map 2).

Brandon Gap East

Total elevation - 1,366 ft | **Length - 5.3 miles**

Average Grade - 4.2% (11%) | **Rating - 0.50 (cat 2/3)**

The east side of Brandon Gap over Route 73 through the scenic Green Mountains of Vermont is another area grade variable ascent and traffic is typically light on the hill as well. The first miles are mostly shallow to moderate with a short flat or two thrown in (along with short steeper ramps). The last segment is up and down as well but a bit steeper overall and the hill ends at obvious and scenic Brandon Gap.

Directions - At the junction of Routes 100 and 73, head west on 73 for just under 4 to Bingo Road on the right to begin the listed climb by continuing west on 73 (see VT Map 2).

Brandon Gap West

Total elevation - 1,591 ft | **Length - 4.9 miles**

Average Grade - 6.2% (13%) | **Rating - 0.98 (cat 2)**

The west side of Brandon Gap, while similar in some respects, has a bit more bite compared to its east side. It begins over mostly shallow grade with a flat and a steeper ramp eventually thrown in. The slope generally gets steeper the further west you ride the somewhat twisty road. A final flat is eventually encountered and then the last mile of the ascent contains the most challenging pedaling on the hill (over mostly double digit grade). The climb then ends at the obvious gap in a scenic setting.

Directions - At the junction of Routes 53 and 73 just east of tiny Brandon, VT, the listed climb begins by heading east on 73 (see VT Map 2).

Stout grade on Brandon Gap

The start of Jay Peak South

Rochester Gap East

Total elevation - 1,557 ft | **Length - 5.6 miles**

Average Grade - 5.3% (13%) | **Rating - 0.82 (cat 2)**

The east side of Rochester Gap is a solid ascent along variable grade. Begin by heading west from Route 12 over shallow grade along a creek and into woods. There are several descents along the way as well which reduces its average grade. The road is quite twisty and carries little traffic most of the time. With two miles left the grade increases dramatically overall and a few houses appear. The slope goes up and down but remains solid as you continue to gain altitude. Near the top a rock wall appears on the right where the listed climb ends as the road flattens out.

Directions - In Bethel, VT head north on Route 12 for 2 miles to Camp Brook Road (umarked as of 2014 and becomes Rochester Mountain Road) on the left where the climb begins by heading west on Camp Brook Road (see VT Map 2).

Rochester Gap West

Total elevation - 1,273 ft | **Length - 3.8 miles**

Average Grade - 6.4% (10%) | **Rating - 0.81 (cat 2)**

The west side of Rochester Gap is a bit shorter and steeper overall compared to its east side. From town, head east over gradually increasing grade. Just beyond 2 miles in, turn right to remain on Bethel Mountain Road. The slope increases here before quickly easing and then you encounter a descent. Beyond, you find the steepest sustained climbing on the hill. The grade eases just before the listed top which is well short of the east side summit.

Directions - In Rochester, VT on Route 100, head east on Bethel Mountain Road for 0.1 miles to begin the climb by continuing east (see VT Map 2).

North Road

Total elevation - 971 ft **Length - 4.4 miles**

Average Grade - 4.2% (12%) **Rating - 0.41 (cat 3)**

North Road is a very variable grade ascent in central Vermont that is quite popular with area riders. It begins to the south over moderate grade which quickly gets steeper, the steepest sustained climbing on the hill. From here, the slope goes up and down including multiple descents as you ride through farmland and small homes. Towards the top the overall grade levels off (ups and downs) and the listed climb ends at a somewhat sharp descent (although you see more climbing ahead you have reached the true high point) with a red house on the right.

Directions - In Bethel, VT at the junction of Routes 107 and 12, head south on 12 for a short distance to North Road on the left where the listed climb begins (see VT Map 2).

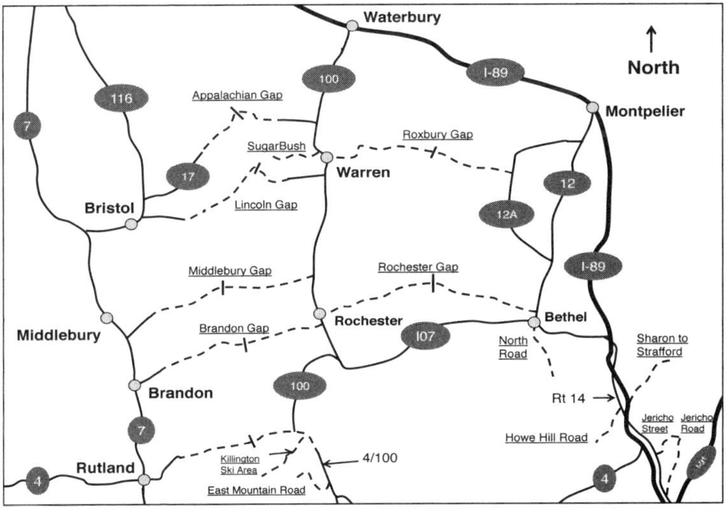

VT Map 2

Sharon to Strafford

Total elevation - 1,052 ft	**Length - 4.0 miles**
Average Grade - 5.0% (13%)	**Rating - 0.52 (cat 2/3)**

Sharon to Strafford along Route 132 is a solid hill that is one of many in the area. It begins by pulling away from Interstate 89 into a rainage over gradually increasing grade with a mile near hill start being the steepest sustained climbing on the hill. You then find a short descent and then more moderate pedaling. The final mile is again more challenging and the climb ends at an unmarked summit at a gap. The other side is a shorter but still interesting hill (2 miles at 6% average grade) west from the town of Strafford.

Directions - On Interstate 89 just north of White River Junction, VT, take Exit 2 (Route 132). The climb begins at the bottom of the exit by heading north on 132 (see VT Map 2).

Howe Hill Road

Total elevation - 900 ft	**Length - 3.2 miles**
Average Grade - 5.3% (14%)	**Rating - 0.48 (cat 3)**

Howe Hill Road is a popular area climb that heads directly south. Over variable grade, the start is solid as you pull away from the river. You ride mostly through woods with a few breaks for views along the way. Just over a mile in you find a descent and flat. Climbing then resumes over stout grade which then eases up to the listed top (unmarked) with a descent beyond.

Directions - On Interstate 89 just north of White River Junction, VT, take Exit 2 (Route 132). Turn left at the bottom of the exit and travel 0.2 miles to Route 14. Turn right on 14 and travel 0.3 miles and turn left across the bridge on The River Road. Travel this road for 0.5 miles to Howe Hill Road on the left where the climb begins (see VT Map 2).

Jericho Street

Total elevation - 706 ft | **Length - 1.7 miles**

Average Grade - 7.9% (12%) | **Rating - 0.56 (cat 2/3)**

Jericho Street (not to be confused with nearby Jericho Road - next climb) is a short and steep ascent that is very popular with area cyclists. Taking riders up the ridge from the White River, from Route 14 head uphill and quickly take a right to continue. Soon you cross a wooden bridge and from here the slope is stair step with some solid ramps and views to the left (initial mile is the steepest climbing). The slope then eases overall and near the top is one more stout ramp and the listed climb ends at a red barn. Continue for a short distance to Jericho Road on the right.

Directions - At the junction of Routes 5 and 14 in White River Junction, VT, head west on 14 for 4.8 miles to Jericho Street on the right where the climb begins (see VT Map 2).

Jericho Road

Total elevation - 766 ft | **Length - 2.4 miles**

Average Grade - 6.1% (14%) | **Rating - 0.46 (cat 3)**

Nearby Jericho Road is another solid hill that ends up in the same place as Jericho Street. It has a stout start as you dive into woods from Route 14. The grade then eases and becomes stair step for much of the remainder of the ascent. Near the top you break out into the open and then find one more steeper ramp of climbing before the listed ascent ends soon after at Miller Road on the left. Both of these roads are interesting and quick descents (careful of entering Route 14 at the bottom of each).

Directions - At the junction of Routes 5 and 14 in White River Junction, VT, head west on 14 for 2.1 miles to Jericho Road on the right where the climb begins (see VT Map 2).

4 East

Total elevation - 942 ft	**Length - 3.6 miles**
Average Grade - 5.0% (9%)	**Rating - 0.47 (cat 3)**

The east side of Route 4 in central Vermont begins over solid and steady grade as you head west with two lanes uphill usually along with some vehicle traffic. As you gain altitude the grade eases, first slightly and then markedly when you reach the junction of Route 100 on the right. From this point keep straight on Route 4 through some congestion. Once beyond it the grade picks back up to quite solid all the way up to the unmarked but obvious summit. The last section of 4 East is a quick descent.

Directions - At the southern junction of Routes 100 and 4, head north on 100/4 for several miles until the obvious grade change (lumber store on right) to begin by continuing west up the hill on 4 (see VT Map 3).

4 West

Total elevation - 1,055 ft	**Length - 5.0 miles**
Average Grade - 4.0% (8%)	**Rating - 0.42 (cat 3)**

The west side of Route 4 is a longer and less steep hill overall compared to its east side. From climb start, head east up the hill, likely with some traffic, to find a pattern of stair step grade. The steeper ramps are over moderate slope however so there are no surprises on this one. Near the top you pass the Pico Mountain Ski Area and the climb soon ends after one last solid ramp up to an unmarked summit.

Directions - In Rutland, VT head east on Route 4 for several miles to Medway Road on the left where the listed climb begins by continuing east on Route 4 (see VT Map 3).

Killington Ski Area

Total elevation - 1,289ft **Length - 5.1 miles**

Average Grade - 4.8% (17%) **Rating - 0.64 (cat 2)**

The climb to Killington shares its start with 4 East (previous) and contains some of the steepest grade in the state. After 0.9 steady grade miles on Route 4, turn left on West Hill Road. Quickly you slam into severe double digit slope, finding the climb maximum very early. The double digit slope lasts for 0.5 miles and then eases up to the junction with Killington Road. Turn left here to find a fairly long descent. Climbing then resumes over shallow and then more variable grade. The final segment up to the ski gondola is over gradually increasing and solid slope and the listed climb ends at the gondola area as the road ends.

Directions - At the southern junction of Routes 100 and 4, head north on 100/4 for several miles until the obvious grade change (lumber store on right) to begin by continuing west on 4 (see VT Map 3).

East Mountain Road

Total elevation - 993 ft **Length - 2.1 miles**

Average Grade - 9.0% (14%) **Rating - 0.89 (cat 2)**

East Mountain Road is a steep climb that leads into the Killington Resort from the east. After an easy start, the grade on this one gradually ramps up as you ride initially to the south. Soon a big turn to the right is encountered that heads riders north to find the most challenging pedaling on the hill. Towards the top the slope eases for a stretch and then you have one more solid ramp which takes you up to the listed climb top. Stats for this hill are estimated.

Directions - At the southern junction of Routes 100 and 4, head north on 100/4 for a short distance to East Mountain Road on the left. Travel west on East Mountain Road a short distance to begin the listed climb (see VT Map 3).

Tyson Road East

Total elevation - 1,204 ft | **Length - 5.8 miles**

Average Grade - 3.9% (8%) | **Rating - 0.47 (cat 3)**

The east side of Tyson Road is a fairly long ascent located in central Vermont that carries little traffic but is popular with area riders. From Route 106 in tiny Felchville, VT, head west to begin over first shallow and then more solid grade. Quickly however, the slope eases overall and remains that way for almost 3 miles. Just beyond 3 miles in you find more challenging pedaling but you will not find steep grade on this one. The slope then eases once more before increasing again up to the unmarked summit.

Directions - In Felchville, VT at the junction of Route 106 and Tyson Road, head west on Tyson Road to for a short distance begin (see VT Map 3).

Tyson Road West

Total elevation - 896 ft | **Length - 3.8 miles**

Average Grade - 4.5% (9%) | **Rating - 0.40 (cat 3)**

The west side of Tyson Road is shorter and a bit steeper compared to its east side. It begins among a few residences over fairly shallow grade as you head east. Soon you enter woods and encounter steeper (but not steep) grade. The trees then pull back in places and the slope eases. Two miles into the ascent you find a fairly long flat section with some descent which lowers the climb's average grade. Climbing then resumes over the final mile up to the unmarked summit (descent beyond).

Directions - In the small town of Tyson, VT at the junction of Route 100 and Kingdom Road, head east on Kingdom Road to begin (see VT Map 3).

Riders near the start of Jay Peak North

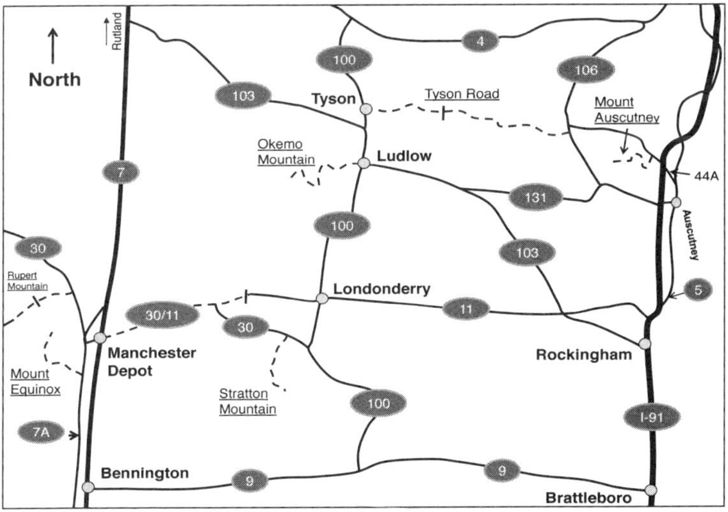

VT Map 3

Mount Auscutney

Total elevation:	**2.250 ft**	**Length:**	**3.7 miles**
Top elevation:	**2,771 ft**	**Average grade:**	**11.5%**
Minimum grade:	**0%**	**Maximum grade:**	**18%**
Distance ≥ 5%:	**3.2 miles**	**Distance ≥ 10%:**	**2.7 miles**
Steepest mile:	**12.5%**	**Steepest 3 miles:**	**11.6%**
Traffic:	**1**	**Descent:**	**5**
Rating:	**2.74 (cat 1)**		

Another legendary New England ascent, Mount Auscutney is an extremely steep and difficult climb located in eastern Vermont near the New Hampshire border. There are extended ramps of 15% grade and except for a stretch early within its second half the entire climb is steep.

You will hardly get a break over the first 2.5 miles as you ride multiple steep ramps linked by tight switchbacks. You are also moving within a thick tunnel of trees which seems to add to the sense of foreboding. Just beyond this steep initial stretch you can catch your breath as the grade eases and rolls a bit and you break out of the trees as the road opens up somewhat. The grade actually goes flat in several places briefly and then gradually increases. The torture soon returns as another double digit section greets riders just before the summit and the climb then ends at a parking area near the top of the mountain.

As mentioned, this is one of steepest ascents in the U.S. There is an annual race on Mount Auscutney and due to grade and turns it is a difficult descent (closed in winter - Mount Auscutney State Park - 802 674-2060; 800 299-3071 from Jan-April).

Crux stretch - Survive the first 2 miles (> 12% average grade) and you should make the top.

Directions - From the small town of Auscutney, VT head north on Route 5. After several miles turn left on Route 44A. The entrance to Auscutney State Park will appear on your left after 1.1 miles. Turn in and begin the climb just beyond the toll booth ($3 per car/bike as of 2015) (see VT Map 3).

A warning near the top of Auscutney

Mount Auscutney, VT

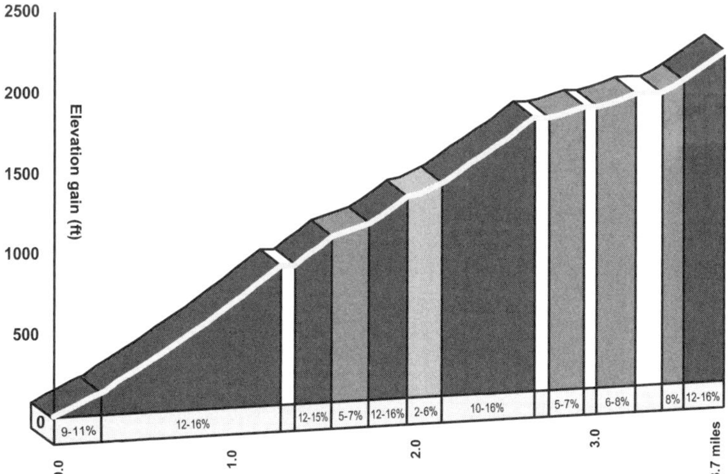

Okemo Mountain

Total elevation:	**2,099 ft**	**Length:**	**3.8 miles**
Top elevation:	**3,144 ft**	**Average grade:**	**10.5%**
Minimum grade:	**1%**	**Maximum grade:**	**17%**
Distance ≥ 5%:	**3.2 miles**	**Distance ≥ 10%:**	**2.7 miles**
Steepest mile:	**12.3%**	**Steepest 3 miles:**	**11.6%**
Traffic:	**1**	**Descent:**	**4**
Rating:	**2.40 (cat 1)**		

Another Northeast classic, this tough climb is routed through a ski area and heads towards the top of Okemo Mountain in scenic central Vermont. A steep mile (and very steep half mile) in the middle of the climb will test you although a majority of the hill is along double digit grade. Steep at the very start as you leave the village of Ludlow, the slope on this hill soon eases back as you pass through the lower reaches of a ski area. Once beyond, the grade picks up again quickly and you soon are riding over the steepest sustained roadway on the wooded mountain.

The climb soon becomes more isolated as you pull away from a bit of clutter down low and enter thick woods quickly followed by several switchbacks to carry you higher up the hill. The grade is variable over its second half but only in that it is either stout or steep. There is a bit of an isolated feel to the upper half of the hill although you can almost always see some piece of the ski operation nearby. Towards the summit the grade does not ease except at the very end and the listed climb ends where the pavement ends near the very top of the mountain.

Okemo Mountain is one of the steepest climbs in the Northeast. As you might imagine, its descent is challenging in places particularly in its upper half. There is an annual race on this hill as well.

Crux stretch - The half mile that begins around mile 0.8 is the steepest on this very steep hill.

Directions - In Ludlow, VT the climb begins at the junction of Okemo Mountain Road and Route 100 right in the middle of town (see VT Map 3).

Steep slope on Okemo Mountain

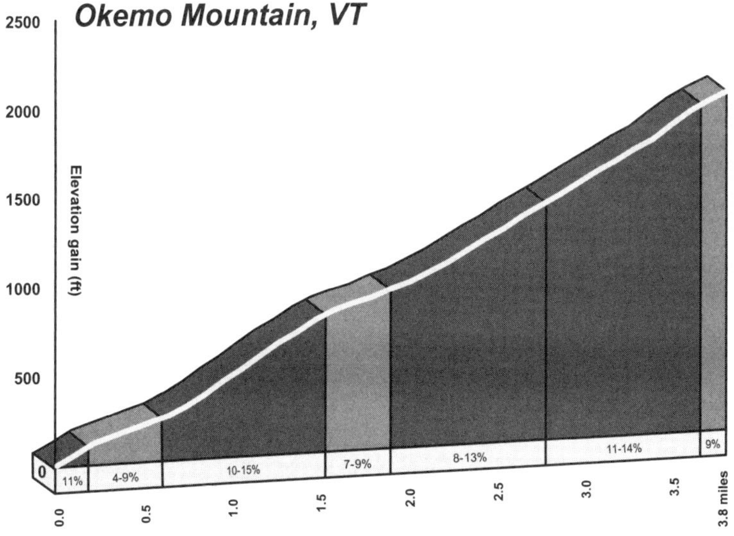

Rupert Mountain East

Total elevation - 861 ft | **Length - 2.0 miles**

Average Grade - 8.2% (10%) | **Rating - 0.70 (cat 2)**

The east side of Rupert Mountain is a short and stout hill along a somewhat narrow road that carries little traffic. From the red house, head up the hill over initially shallow and then gradually increasing grade. The road heads into the woods along the way and you will pass a few residences on the mountain as well. The slope goes up and down as you ride but not dramatically and is mostly steady. The very last segment is quite solid up to the unmarked but obvious summit.

Directions - In Dorset, VT at the junction of Routes 30 and 315, head west on 315 for 0.4 miles (red house on right) to begin the listed climb (see VT Map 3).

Rupert Mountain West

Total elevation - 630 ft | **Length - 1.7 miles**

Average Grade - 7.5% (13%) | **Rating - 0.48 (cat 3)**

More grade variable than its east side, the west side of Rupert Mountain Road is another short and solid climb with scenery that begins quite close to the New York border. The beginning is fairly solid and in open surroundings and with only intermittent traffic most days. Once you cross a bride over a small creek the pedaling gets more difficult. Eventually you enter woods in places and the last segment of climbing is over double digit grade up to the unmarked top. Due to grade the west side of Rupert Mountain is a quick descent as well.

Directions - In Rupert, VT head east on Route 315 for several miles to begin the listed climb by continuing east (see VT Map 3).

30/11 West

Total elevation - 1,337 ft **Length - 5.9 miles**

Average Grade - 4.3% (8%) **Rating - 0.58 (cat 2/3)**

The climb of Route 30/11 West is a stair step affair that carries riders towards Stratton Mountain and Route 100. From Manchester Center, head east over shallow grade and some traffic. The grade gradually increases but then becomes predominantly stair step with no particularly steep ramps. At mile 4.9 you pass the junction with Route 30 (to Stratton Mountain) on the right. Keep straight to remain on Route 11 to climb for one more mile over shallow to moderate grade past the Bromley Ski Area up to the listed summit (unmarked - grade flattens out).

Directions - In Manchester Center, VT the climb begins at the junction of Routes 30 and 7 by heading east up the hill on 30 (see VT Map 3).

Stratton Mountain

Total elevation - 824 ft **Length - 3.8 miles**

Average Grade - 4.1% (9%) **Rating - 0.34 (cat 3)**

The climb to Stratton Mountain is along a variable grade route located in southern Vermont. From Route 30 you climb south along solid slope to begin. Quickly a descent is encountered before climbing resumes along stout grade and among some homes. This pattern is repeated several times with the multiple descents really reducing the hill's average grade. The last climbing section takes you into the ski village and the listed climb ends at the Mountain Watch building on the right.

Directions - On Route 30 just east of tiny Bondville, VT, the climb begins at the junction of Route 30 and Stratton Mountain Access Road (see VT Map 3).

Mount Equinox

Total elevation:	**3,157 ft**	**Length:**	**5.2 miles**
Top elevation:	**3,811 ft**	**Average grade:**	**11.5%**
Minimum grade:	**0%**	**Maximum grade:**	**17%**
Distance ≥ 5%:	**4.9 miles**	**Distance ≥ 10%:**	**4.6 miles**
Steepest mile:	**13.3%**	**Steepest 3 miles:**	**12.2%**
Traffic:	**1**	**Descent:**	**5**
Rating:	**3.89 (hors)**		

Mount Equinox, located in southwest Vermont near the border with New York, is one of the most difficult climbs, not only in the Northeast but the entire United States. In addition, it is one of the steepest ascents of length in the paved road bike World and unfortunately is open to bikes only during the annual race on its slopes. The ascent includes multiple tight hairpin turns and is composed of extended climbing at double digit grade over a large portion of its route. There are spacious views on clear days when you reach a saddle as you approach the summit as well. This hill is simply one of the steepest sustained uphill routes one can find and a must do for serious climbers.

Steep right from the start, multiple ramps of 9-12% greet you as you head up the somewhat narrow roadway which quickly becomes enclosed by trees. One half mile in you get a short break with grade but double digit pedaling quickly returns. Within its 2nd mile however you encounter a short flat and then a small descent arrives to let you catch your breath. There are a few houses along this lower section as well which somehow seem out of place on this mountain road. Unfortunately you pay for the descent as just beyond you will suddenly encounter the steepest climbing segment along the route. This section was fairly recently repaved (2009) and is quite smooth and eventually extends through several tight switchbacks. The repaving took out the infamous 28% inside corner on a tight right hand turn. It is still plenty steep however and remains the crux stretch on this hill as the turn still contains the maximum grade on this severe climb.

At the beginning of the crux stretch, power up the steep wall and you soon encounter the right hand bend mentioned above. At the

The final stretch on Mount Equinox

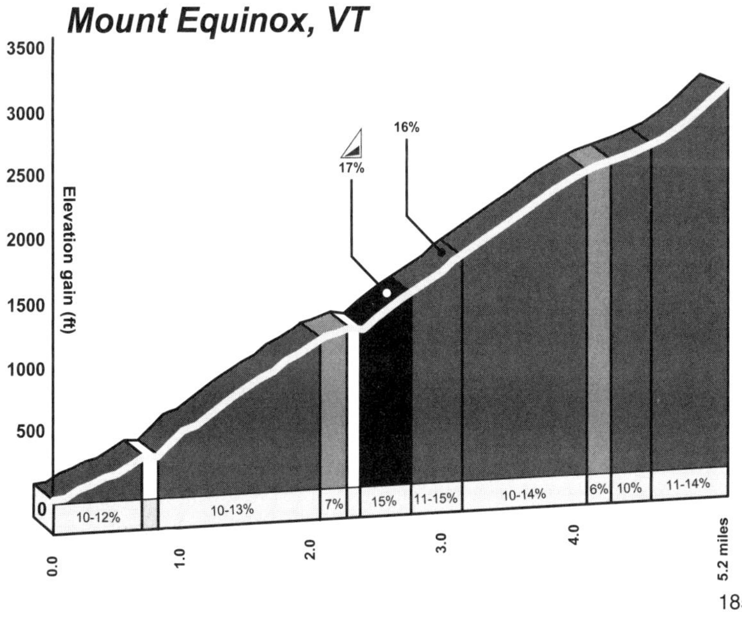

upper end of the bend the grade eases (but not by much) and you eventually encounter several other tight switchbacks. After the final switchback the route steepens a bit as you leave its upper end and the road straightens as you ride north. At 4.2 miles the grade eases considerably and the trees part as the road widens for a short segment as it begins to travel along an exposed saddle with excellent views ahead and both right and left down into the valleys on clear days. At this point you can finally see your objective just in front of you so just keep turning the pedals. Your work is not over however as the slope gradually gets steeper as you gain altitude along the exposed ridgeline and soon double digit grade pedaling returns along with the last few tight switchback turns and a bit more tree cover. A final straight and steep section finally leads to the dead end summit within a small parking area with long views of the surrounding countryside. When you reach the summit, enjoy it as you will have certainly earned it.

Mount Equinox is one of the great American climbs and as mentioned is among the steepest in the World at this length. Although just a bit shorter, it resembles several famous European climbs including Angliru in Spain and the Mortirolo in Italy, both of which have played havoc with professional pelotons, although it is steeper overall than both of those hills. It is perhaps most similar to the mighty Zoncolan (from Ovaro) in Italy (although lacking that climb's vicious middle section) that is used at times within the Giro d'Italia. As mentioned, it is only open to bikes for the annual climbing race on its slopes which is unfortunate but only adds to its mystique perhaps. The tollbooth on this road is manned from 9AM - 8PM ET (closed in winter - Mount Equinox Scenic Drive - 802 362-1114). Due to steep grade and routing, it's descent must be quite fast in places and challenging through its tight switchbacks but of course who really knows?

Crux stretch - The 1.5 mile stretch right after the short descent/ flat that is 12-16% grade for almost its entire length is a key to a successful summit.

Directions - From picturesque Manchester, VT head south on Route 7A for several miles. The Mount Equinox toll road will then appear on your right and the listed climb begins just beyond the toll gate (see VT Map 3).

A warning on Mount Equinox

Long views south on Equinox

Selected Hill Climb Races

Mount Greylock Hill Climb Time Trial (MA) - This race climbs the north side of category 1 Mount Greylock in western Massachusetts. For details go to www.greylocktt.nohobikeclub.org

Wachusett Mountain Hill Climb (MA) - A climbing race up the most popular route on Wachusett Mountain. For details go to www.destinationcycling.com/wachusetts-mountain-hill-climb/.

Mount Washington Hill Climb (NH) - The most difficult hill climb race in the U.S. and perhaps the world, the Mount Washington Hill Climb takes place each August. For additional details go to www.tinmtn.org/hillclimb.

Newton's Revenge (NH) - Another chance to ride mighty Mount Washington, a rare treat! For more details go to www.newtonsrevenge.com.

Kancamagus Bicycle Hillclimb Time Trial (NH) - Ride beautiful Kancamagus Highway in New Hampshire. For details go to www.nebikes.com.

Mount Kearsarge Hill Climb (NH) - Race difficult Mount Kearsarge in central NH. For details go to www.mtkearsargehillclimb.com.

Whiteface Mountain (NY) - A race climb up America's Alp d'Huez (see climb description). For details go to www.

whitefaceregion.com/events/whiteface-mountain-uphill-bikerace.

Mount Auscutney Hill Climb (VT) - Ride one of the steepest roads in the U.S. (see climb description). For details go to www.destinationcycling.com/mount-auscutney-hill-climb/.

Burke Mountain (VT) - A race up super steep Burke Mountain in northern Vermont. For details go to www.burkemountainbikerace.com.

Okemo Bike Climb (VT) - A race up double digit grade Okemo Mountain near Ludlow, VT. For details go to www.okemobikeclimb.com.

Gear Up for Lyme Mount Equinox Hill Climb (VT) - A very difficult race up Mt. Equinox and currently the only legal way to ride the hill. For additional details go to www.gearupforlyme.com.

Allen Clark Hill Climb (VT) - A climbing race up the tough east side of scenic Appalachian Gap in Vermont. For details go to www.achillclimb.org.

Bike Up the Mountain Point Series (BUMPS) - The BUMPS Series is a points series of multiple races on Northeast mountains. It awards a winners jersey for men and women based on points accumulated in up to five climbs. If a rider enters more than 5, the best five scores are counted. The series includes almost all of the above races and is a great supporter of climbing by bike in the Northeast. For details go to www.hillclimbseries.com.

50 Most Difficult Climbs
(Author Rating; Major Tour Rating)

1. Mount Washington, NH (6.61; hors)
2. Mount Equinox, VT (3.79; hors)
3. Whiteface Mountain, NY (3.13; hors/cat 1)
4. Burke Mountain, VT (2.92; hors/cat 1)
5. Mount Auscutney, VT (2.75; cat 1)
6. Okemo Mountain, VT (2.40; cat 1)
7. Mount Greylock North, MA (1.82; cat 1)
8. Devils Kitchen/Josh Road, NY (1.74; cat 1)
9. Glade Hill Road, NY (1.68; cat 1)
10. Lincoln Gap East, VT (1.58; cat 1/2)
11. Bolton Mountain Road, VT (1.48; cat 1/2)
12. Devils Kitchen, NY (1.42; cat 1/2)
13. Hurricane Mountain Road East, NH (1.32; cat 2)
14. South Gully/Mount Meenagha, NY, (1.29; cat 2)
15. Kingsley Hill Road, MA (1.25; cat 2)
16. Appalachian Gap East, VT (1.25; cat 2)
17. Meads Mountain Road East, NY (1.24; cat 2)
18. Mount Kearsarge, NH (1.21; cat 2)
19. South Gully Road, NY (1.18; cat 2)
20. Hurricane Mountain Road West, NH (1.16; cat 2)
21. Sugar Loaf/Red Hill Road, NY (1.15; cat 2)
22. Whitcomb Hill Road, MA (1.10; cat 2)
23. Roxbury Gap East, VT (1.08; cat 2)
24. Appalachian Gap West, VT (1.08; cat 2)
25. Mount Greylock South, MA (1.05; cat 2)

50 Most Difficult Climbs
(Author Rating; Major Tour Rating)

26. Switchback Way, NH (1.02; cat 2)
27. Brandon Gap West, VT (0.98; cat 2)
28. Moore Hill Road, NY (0.98; cat 2)
29. Monroe Bridge Road, MA (0.96; cat 2)
30. Cotton Hill Road West, NY (0.95; cat 2)
31. Pack Monadnock, NH (0.94; cat 2)
32. Denman Mountain Road, NY (0.91; cat 2)
33. Cunningham Road, NY (0.91; cat 2)
34. Roxbury Gap West, VT (0.91; cat 2)
35. Jay Peak South, VT (0.91; cat 2)
36. East Mountain Road, VT (0.89; cat 2)
37. 22/20, NY (0.87; cat 2)
38. Crawford Road, NY (0.87; cat 2)
39. 118 North, NH (0.86; cat 2)
40. Prospect Mountain, NY (0.86; cat 2)
41. 118 South, NH (0.86; cat 2)
42. Rochester Gap East, VT (0.82; cat 2)
43. Rochester Gap West, VT (0.81; cat 2)
44. Petersburgh Pass West, NY (0.80; cat 2)
45. 206 North, NY (0.79; cat 2)
46. Colchester Mountain Road North, NY (0.79; cat 2)
47. East Hawley Road, MA (0.77; cat 2)
48. Smugglers Notch West, VT (0.77; cat 2)
49. Kaaterskill Falls (23A), NY (0.76; cat 2)
50. Kancamagus Pass East, NH (0.76; cat 2)

Most Difficult Climbs by State

Connecticut:

1. Whitcomb Hill Road
2. Skiff Mountain Road
3. Warren Hill Road West
4. Carter Road
5. Music Mountain/Cream Hill Road

Maine:

1. Cadillac Mountain
2. Evans Notch South
3. Mount Battie
4. Streaked Mountain East
5. Streaked Mountain West

Massachusetts:

1. Mount Greylock North
2. Kingsley Hill Road
3. Whitcomb Hill Road
4. Mount Greylock South
5. Monroe Bridge Road

Most Difficult Climbs by State

New Hampshire:

1. Mount Washington
2. Hurricane Mountain Road East
3. Mount Kearsarge
4. Hurricane Mountain Road West
5. Switchback Way

New York:

1. Whiteface Mountain
2. Devils Kitchen/Josh Road
3. Glade Hill Road
4. Devils Kitchen
5. South Gully Road/Mount Meenagha

Vermont:

1. Mount Equinox
2. Burke Mountain
3. Mount Auscutney
4. Okemo Mountain
5. Lincoln Gap East

Additional Climbing Categories

Greatest Elevation Gain Climbs

1.	Mount Washington, NH	- 4,695 ft
2.	Whiteface Mountain, NY	- 3,566 ft
3.	Mount Equinox, VT	- 3,157 ft
4.	Mount Greylock North, MA	- 2,811 ft
5.	Burke Mountain, VT	- 2,381 ft
6.	Mount Greylock South, MA	- 2,287 ft
7.	Mount Auscutney, VT	- 2,250 ft
8.	Okemo Mountain, VT	- 2,099 ft
9.	Bolton Mountain, VT	- 1,787 ft
10.	Kancamagus Pass West, NH	- 1,689 ft

Highest Elevation Attained Climbs

1.	Mount Washington, NH	- 6,258 ft
2.	Whiteface Mountain, NY	- 4,606 ft
3.	Mount Equinox, VT	- 3,811 ft
4.	Mount Greylock, MA	- 3,475 ft
5.	Burke Mountain, VT	- 3,221 ft
6.	Okemo Mountain, VT	- 3,144 ft
7.	Mount Auscutney, VT	- 2,771 ft
8.	Mount Kearsarge, NH	- 2,610 ft
9.	118, NH	- 2,534 ft
10.	Sugar Loaf/Red Hill Road, NY	- 2,524 ft

Additional Climbing Categories

Steepest Climbs (min 1.3 miles)

1. Lincoln Gap East, VT - 13.9%
2. Kingsley Hill Road, MA - 12.8%
3. Glade Hill Road, NY - 12.5%
4. Mount Washington, NH - 11.9%
5. Monroe Bridge Road, MA - 11.8%
6. Mount Auscutney, VT - 11.5%
7. Mount Equinox, VT - 11.5%
8. Devils Kitchen, NY - 11.5%
9. Pack Monadnock, NH - 11.3%
10. Meads Mountain Road East, NY - 11.1%

Greatest Length of 10% Grade

1. Mount Washington, NH - 6.7 miles
2. Mount Equinox, VT - 4.6 miles
3. Burke Mountain, VT - 2.7 miles
4. Okemo Mountain, VT - 2.7 miles
5. Mount Auscutney, VT - 2.4 miles
6. Devils Kitchen/Josh Road, NY - 1.7 miles
7. Glade Hill Road, NY - 1.7 miles
8. Meads Mountain Road East, NY - 1.6 miles
9. Hurricane Mountain Road East, NH - 1.4 miles
10. Bolton Mountain, VT - 1.4 miles

Riders race on Mount Washington (photo by Leo Kenney Photography)

Lone struggle on the mountain (photo by Leo Kenney Photography)

Additional Climbing Categories

Most Technical Descents

1. Mount Washington, NH
2. Burke Mountain, VT
3. Hurricane Mountain Road West, NH
4. Glade Hill Road, NY
5. Mount Equinox, VT
6. Mount Auscutney, VT
7. Devils Kitchen/Josh Road, NY
8. Mount Greylock North, MA
9. Pack Monadnock, NH
10. Kingsley Hill Road, MA

Fastest Descents

1. Whiteface Mountain, NY
2. 105 East, VT
3. Prospect Mountain Highway, NY
4. Kancamagus Pass East, NH
5. Whitcomb Hill Road, MA
6. Colchester Mountain Road, NY
7. Smugglers Notch West, VT
8. Moore Hill Road, NY
9. Petersburgh Pass West, NY
10. Lake Tarleton East, NH

Additional Climbing Categories

Longest Climbs (min. 3.5% average grade)

1. Mount Greylock South, MA - 9.6 miles
2. Mount Greylock North, MA - 9.0 miles
3. Middlebury Gap West, VT - 8.3 miles
4. Whiteface Mountain, NY - 7.9 miles
5. Kancamagus Pass West, NH - 7.8 miles
6. Mount Washington, NH - 7.5 miles
7. Mohawk Trail East, MA - 7.4 miles
8. 105 West, VT - 7.1 miles
9. West Hawley Road, MA - 6.6 miles
10. Jay Peak South, VT - 6.0 miles

Most Scenic/Spectacular Climbs

1. Mount Washington, NH
2. Cadillac Mountain, ME
3. Whiteface Mountain, NY
4. Mount Equinox, VT
5. Prospect Mountain, NY
6. Mount Greylock North, MA
7. Peakamoose North, NY
8. Bish Bash West, MA
9. Jay Peak North, VT
10. Kancamagus Pass West, NH

Additional Climbing Resources

Books:

50 Climbs (By Bike) In Utah by John Summerson, Extreme Press, Winston-Salem, NC
Ascent, The Mountains of the Tour de France by Richard Yates, Cycle Publishing.
Cycling Colorado's Mountain Passes by Kurt Magsamen, Fulcrum Publishing, Golden, CO.
Kings of the Mountains by Matt Rendell, Arum Press. London, England.
The Complete Guide to Climbing By Bike (nationwide, California, Colorado, Southeast) by John Summerson, Extreme Press, Winston-Salem, NC.
Uphill Battle by Owen Mulholland, Velopress, Boulder, CO.

Magazines:

Bicycling
Cycle Sport America
Paved
Peloton
Pro Cycling
Road
Road Bike Action
Velo

Selected websites:

Azcycling.com

Bicyling.com
Bikeradar.com
Cyclingnews.com
Dailypeloton.com
Missingsaddle.com
Northeastcycling.com
Roadcycling.com
Spokepost.com
Steephill.tv
Truesport.com
Usacycling.org
Usacyclingclimbing.com
Utahcycling.com
Velonews.com
Westernwheelers.org

Training:

AthletiCamps.com
Bicyclecoach.com
Bikecamp.com
Carmichael Training Systems (trainright.com)
Cycle-Smart.com
Cyclist Training Bible by Joe Friel, Velopress, Boulder, CO.
Eddie B. Cycling World Fitness (Eddiebcyclingworld.com)
EliteFITcoach.com
Tecknowlogysource.com
Peakscoachinggroup.com
Trainingpeaks.com

Touring:

Adventure Cycling Association (aventurecycling.org)
Breaking Away Bicycle Tours (breakingaway.com)
Carpenter/Phinney Bike Camp (bikecamp.com)
Cycle America (cycleamerica.com)
Cycle Tours of Italy (cycleitalia.com)
Destination Cycling (destinationcycling.com)
Timberline Adventures (timbertours.com)
Trek Travel Cycling Vacations (trektravel.com)
Velo Classic Tours (veloclassictours.com)

Events:

Active.com
Azcycling.com
Bikereg.com
Bikeride.com
Cycleidaho.com
Hillclimbseries.com
Montanacycling.org
Northeastcycling.com
Nmcycling.com
Utahcycling.com

Additional Data Keys

Traffic:

1 - Almost nonexistent traffic
2 - Some intermittent traffic, mostly local
3 - Moderate traffic
4 - Moderately heavy traffic
5 - Seemingly non-stop traffic

Descent:

1 - Fast and smooth
2 - Fast with a few obstacles
3 - Speed somewhat blunted by obstacles (turns, traffic, etc)
4 - Difficult due to road and/or traffic conditions
5 - Danger of bodily harm at almost any speed

Connecticut

Lost Acres Road

Total elevation:	582 ft	Length:	3.0 miles
Top elevation:	954 ft	Average grade:	3.7%
Minimum grade:	0%	Maximum grade:	13%
Distance ≥ 5%:	1.1 miles	Distance ≥ 10%:	0.1 miles
Steepest mile:	4.8%	Steepest 3 miles:	3.7%
Traffic:	1	Descent:	3

Mountain Road

Total elevation:	893 ft	Length:	4.1 miles
Top elevation:	1,198 ft	Average grade:	4.1%
Minimum grade:	1%	Maximum grade:	13%
Distance ≥ 5%:	1.8 miles	Distance ≥ 10%:	0.4 miles
Steepest mile:	8.3%	Steepest 3 miles:	4.7%
Traffic:	3	Descent:	2

Hartland Road

Total elevation:	828 ft	Length:	4.8 miles
Top elevation:	1,198 ft	Average grade:	3.3%
Minimum grade:	1%	Maximum grade:	7%
Distance ≥ 5%:	1.3 miles	Distance ≥ 10%:	0.0 miles
Steepest mile:	4.7%	Steepest 3 miles:	3.6%
Traffic:	3	Descent:	2

North Hollow Road

Total elevation:	586 ft	Length:	2.3 miles
Top elevation:	1,178 ft	Average grade:	4.8%
Minimum grade:	3%	Maximum grade:	7%
Distance ≥ 5%:	1.1 miles	Distance ≥ 10%:	0.0 miles
Steepest mile:	5.3%	Steepest 3 miles:	NA
Traffic:	2	Descent:	2

Morrison Hill Road

Total elevation:	749 ft	Length:	2.9 miles
Top elevation:	1,316 ft	Average grade:	4.9%
Minimum grade:	1%	Maximum grade:	8%
Distance ≥ 5%:	1.4 miles	Distance ≥ 10%:	0.0 miles
Steepest mile:	5.1%	Steepest 3 miles:	NA
Traffic:	2	Descent:	2

Reservoir Climb

Total elevation:	724 ft	Length:	5.1 miles
Top elevation:	1,249 ft	Average grade:	2.7%
Minimum grade:	0%	Maximum grade:	11%
Distance ≥ 5%:	1.1 miles	Distance ≥ 10%:	0.0 miles
Steepest mile:	3.8%	Steepest 3 miles:	3.2%
Traffic:	2	Descent:	2

Riverton West

Total elevation:	749 ft	Length:	2.6 miles
Top elevation:	1,166 ft	Average grade:	4.7%
Minimum grade:	1%	Maximum grade:	10%
Distance ≥ 5%:	1.3 miles	Distance ≥ 10%:	0.0 miles
Steepest mile:	6.8%	Steepest 3 miles:	NA
Traffic:	2	Descent:	3

Music Mountain/Cream Hill Road

Total elevation:	8116 ft	Length:	2.7 miles
Top elevation:	1,414 ft	Average grade:	5.7%
Minimum grade:	0%	Maximum grade:	14%
Distance ≥ 5%:	1.5 miles	Distance ≥ 10%:	0.3 miles
Steepest mile:	6.1%	Steepest 3 miles:	NA
Traffic:	1	Descent:	3

Sharon Goshen Road (Route 128)

Total elevation:	630 ft	Length:	3.5 miles
Top elevation:	1,138 ft	Average grade:	3.4%
Minimum grade:	0%	Maximum grade:	8%
Distance ≥ 5%:	1.1 miles	Distance ≥ 10%:	0.0 miles
Steepest mile:	5.2%	Steepest 3 miles:	NA
Traffic:	2	Descent:	3

Sharon Mountain Road

Total elevation:	819 ft	Length:	3.0 miles
Top elevation:	1,293 ft	Average grade:	5.2%
Minimum grade:	1%	Maximum grade:	7%
Distance ≥ 5%:	1.8 miles	Distance ≥ 10%:	0.0 miles
Steepest mile:	5.5%	Steepest 3 miles:	5.2%
Traffic:	3	Descent:	2

4 East

Total elevation:	692 ft	Length:	2.1 miles
Top elevation:	1,349 ft	Average grade:	6.2%
Minimum grade:	0%	Maximum grade:	11%
Distance ≥ 5%:	1.2 miles	Distance ≥ 10%:	0.1 miles
Steepest mile:	6.3%	Steepest 3 miles:	NA
Traffic:	3	Descent:	3

Warren Hill Road West

Total elevation:	797 ft	Length:	2.1 miles
Top elevation:	1,356 ft	Average grade:	7.2%
Minimum grade:	1%	Maximum grade:	8%
Distance ≥ 5%:	1.7 miles	Distance ≥ 10%:	0.0 miles
Steepest mile:	7.3%	Steepest 3 miles:	NA
Traffic:	3	Descent:	2

Whitcomb Hill Road

Total elevation:	740 ft	Length:	1.8 miles
Top elevation:	1,270 ft	Average grade:	7.8%
Minimum grade:	1%	Maximum grade:	18%
Distance ≥ 5%:	1.2 miles	Distance ≥ 10%:	0.5 miles
Steepest mile:	8.3%	Steepest 3 miles:	NA
Traffic:	1	Descent:	4

Carter Road

Total elevation:	670 ft	Length:	1.7 miles
Top elevation:	1,203 ft	Average grade:	7.5%
Minimum grade:	0%	Maximum grade:	20%
Distance ≥ 5%:	1.4 miles	Distance ≥ 10%:	0.6 miles
Steepest mile:	7.7%	Steepest 3 miles:	NA
Traffic:	1	Descent:	2

Skiff Mountain Road

Total elevation:	748 ft	Length:	1.8 miles
Top elevation:	1,132 ft	Average grade:	7.9%
Minimum grade:	1%	Maximum grade:	13%
Distance ≥ 5%:	1.1 miles	Distance ≥ 10%:	0.3 miles
Steepest mile:	8.3%	Steepest 3 miles:	NA
Traffic:	1	Descent:	3

341 West

Total elevation:	766 ft	Length:	2.8 miles
Top elevation:	1,194 ft	Average grade:	5.2%
Minimum grade:	0%	Maximum grade:	8%
Distance ≥ 5%:	1.5 miles	Distance ≥ 10%:	0.0 miles
Steepest mile:	5.6%	Steepest 3 miles:	NA
Traffic:	3	Descent:	3

Castle Craig

Total elevation:	552 ft	Length:	1.3 miles
Top elevation:	972 ft	Average grade:	8.0%
Minimum grade:	1%	Maximum grade:	14%
Distance ≥ 5%:	1.1 miles	Distance ≥ 10%:	0.2 miles
Steepest mile:	8.3%	Steepest 3 miles:	NA
Traffic:	1	Descent:	3

Maine

Evans Notch North

Total elevation:	844 ft	Length:	5.1 miles
Top elevation:	1,423 ft	Average grade:	2.1%
Minimum grade:	0%	Maximum grade:	7%
Distance ≥ 5%:	1.3 miles	Distance ≥ 10%:	0.0 miles
Steepest mile:	4.2%	Steepest 3 miles:	2.8%
Traffic:	1	Descent:	3

Evans Notch South

Total elevation:	844 ft	Length:	2.1 mi
Top elevation:	1,423 ft	Average grade:	7.6%
Minimum grade:	3%	Maximum grade:	12%
Distance > 5%:	7.6 miles	Distance > 10%:	0.2 miles
Steepest mile:	9.7%	Steepest 3 miles:	NA
Traffic:	1	Descent:	4

Streaked Mountain East

Total elevation:	778 ft	Length:	3.6 miles
Top elevation:	1,163 ft	Average grade:	4.1%
Minimum grade:	1%	Maximum grade:	7%
Distance ≥ 5%:	1.6 miles	Distance ≥ 10%:	0.0 miles
Steepest mile:	4.8%	Steepest 3 miles:	4.3%
Traffic:	2	Descent:	3

Streaked Mountain West

Total elevation:	814 ft	Length:	4.8 miles
Top elevation:	1,163 ft	Average grade:	3.2%
Minimum grade:	4%	Maximum grade:	8%
Distance ≥ 5%:	1.8 miles	Distance ≥ 10%:	0.0 miles
Steepest mile:	4.8%	Steepest 3 miles:	3.3%
Traffic:	2	Descent:	3

Mount Battie

Total elevation:	595 ft	Length:	1.7 miles
Top elevation:	781 ft	Average grade:	6.6%
Minimum grade:	0%	Maximum grade:	14%
Distance ≥ 5%:	1.1 miles	Distance ≥ 10%:	0.2 miles
Steepest mile:	7.4%	Steepest 3 miles:	NA
Traffic:	1	Descent:	2

Cadillac Mountain

Total elevation:	1,404 ft	Length:	5.5 miles
Top elevation:	1,504 ft	Average grade:	4.8%
Minimum grade:	0%	Maximum grade:	8%
Distance > 5%:	2.5 miles	Distance > 10%:	0.0 miles
Steepest mile:	6.1%	Steepest 3 miles:	5.3%
Traffic:	4	Descent:	3

Massachusetts

Petersburgh Pass East

Total elevation:	1,226 ft	Length:	4.0 miles
Top elevation:	2,078 ft	Average grade:	5.8%
Minimum grade:	2%	Maximum grade:	7%
Distance ≥ 5%:	2.9 miles	Distance ≥ 10%:	0.0 miles
Steepest mile:	6.0%	Steepest 3 miles:	5.9%
Traffic:	2	Descent:	3

Mount Greylock South

Total elevation:	2,287 ft	Length:	9.6 miles
Top elevation:	3,475 ft	Average grade:	4.5%
Minimum grade:	0%	Maximum grade:	12%
Distance ≥ 5%:	3.9 miles	Distance ≥ 10%:	0.0 miles
Steepest mile:	6.9%	Steepest 3 miles:	5.3%
Traffic:	2	Descent:	3

Mount Greylock North

Total elevation:	2,780 ft	Length:	9.0 miles
Top elevation:	3,475 ft	Average grade:	5.9%
Minimum grade:	0%	Maximum grade:	17%
Distance ≥ 5%:	6.4 miles	Distance ≥ 10%:	0.5 miles
Steepest mile:	8.5%	Steepest 3 miles:	8.3%
Traffic:	3	Descent:	4

Mohawk Trail East

Total elevation:	1,589 ft	Length:	7.4 miles
Top elevation:	2,222 ft	Average grade:	4.1%
Minimum grade:	0%	Maximum grade:	8%
Distance ≥ 5%:	2.7 miles	Distance ≥ 10%:	0.0 miles
Steepest mile:	6.1%	Steepest 3 miles:	5.1%
Traffic:	4	Descent:	3

Mohawk Trail West

Total elevation:	1,259 ft	Length:	4.2 miles
Top elevation:	2,014 ft	Average grade:	5.7%
Minimum grade:	0%	Maximum grade:	8%
Distance ≥ 5%:	3.1 miles	Distance ≥ 10%:	0.0 miles
Steepest mile:	6.9%	Steepest 3 miles:	6.6%
Traffic:	4	Descent:	3

Whitcomb Hill Road

Total elevation:	1,299 ft	Length:	2.9 miles
Top elevation:	2,013 ft	Average grade:	8.5%
Minimum grade:	0%	Maximum grade:	11%
Distance > 5%:	2.5 miles	Distance > 10%:	0.2 miles
Steepest mile:	8.7%	Steepest 3 miles:	NA
Traffic:	1	Descent:	3

Kingsley Hill Road

Total elevation:	948 ft	Length:	1.4 miles
Top elevation:	2,045 ft	Average grade:	12.8%
Minimum grade:	1%	Maximum grade:	24%
Distance ≥ 5%:	1.1 miles	Distance ≥ 10%:	0.7 miles
Steepest mile:	14.1%	Steepest 3 miles:	NA
Traffic:	1	Descent:	4

Monroe Hill Road

Total elevation:	812 ft	Length:	1.3 miles
Top elevation:	1,885 ft	Average grade:	11.8%
Minimum grade:	3%	Maximum grade:	18%
Distance ≥ 5%:	1.1 miles	Distance ≥ 10%:	0.8 miles
Steepest mile:	12.1%	Steepest 3 miles:	NA
Traffic:	1	Descent:	3

116 West

Total elevation:	859 ft	Length:	2.9 miles
Top elevation:	2,004 ft	Average grade:	5.6%
Minimum grade:	0%	Maximum grade:	8%
Distance > 5%:	2.1 miles	Distance > 10%:	0.0 miles
Steepest mile:	5.8%	Steepest 3 miles:	NA
Traffic:	3	Descent:	2

West Hawley Road

Total elevation:	1,016 ft	Length:	6.6 miles
Top elevation:	1,723 ft	Average grade:	2.9%
Minimum grade:	2%	Maximum grade:	10%
Distance ≥ 5%:	2.2 miles	Distance ≥ 10%:	0.0 miles
Steepest mile:	6.9%	Steepest 3 miles:	4.8%
Traffic:	1	Descent:	3

East Hawley Road

Total elevation:	1,229 ft	Length:	3.7 miles
Top elevation:	1,822 ft	Average grade:	6.3%
Minimum grade:	0%	Maximum grade:	12%
Distance ≥ 5%:	2.3 miles	Distance ≥ 10%:	0.2 miles
Steepest mile:	7.3%	Steepest 3 miles:	6.6%
Traffic:	1	Descent:	3

Clesson Brook Road

Total elevation:	1,012 ft	Length:	5.2 miles
Top elevation:	1,747 ft	Average grade:	3.9%
Minimum grade:	1%	Maximum grade:	7%
Distance ≥ 5%:	7.5 miles	Distance ≥ 10%:	0.0 miles
Steepest mile:	4.8%	Steepest 3 miles:	4.3%
Traffic:	1	Descent:	3

112 North

Total elevation:	501 ft	Length:	1.6 miles
Top elevation:	1,292 ft	Average grade:	5.9%
Minimum grade:	3%	Maximum grade:	7%
Distance ≥ 5%:	1.0 miles	Distance ≥ 10%:	0.0 miles
Steepest mile:	6.4%	Steepest 3 miles:	NA
Traffic:	3	Descent:	2

South Shelburne Road

Total elevation:	565 ft	Length:	1.9 miles
Top elevation:	836 ft	Average grade:	5.6%
Minimum grade:	0%	Maximum grade:	7%
Distance ≥ 5%:	1.0 miles	Distance ≥ 10%:	0.0 miles
Steepest mile:	5.8%	Steepest 3 miles:	NA
Traffic:	1	Descent:	3

Wachusett Mountain

Total elevation:	1,072 ft	Length:	3.6 miles
Top elevation:	1,985 ft	Average grade:	5.6%
Minimum grade:	0%	Maximum grade:	12%
Distance ≥ 5%:	1.8 miles	Distance ≥ 10%:	0.1 miles
Steepest mile:	5.7%	Steepest 3 miles:	5.4%
Traffic:	2	Descent:	3

Mount Holyoke

Total elevation:	818 ft	Length:	2.1 miles
Top elevation:	929 ft	Average grade:	7.4%
Minimum grade:	0%	Maximum grade:	16%
Distance ≥ 5%:	1.3 miles	Distance ≥ 10%:	0.4 miles
Steepest mile:	7.5%	Steepest 3 miles:	NA
Traffic:	1	Descent:	4

66 East

Total elevation:	851 ft	Length:	4.2 miles
Top elevation:	1,243 ft	Average grade:	3.8%
Minimum grade:	1%	Maximum grade:	10%
Distance ≥ 5%:	1.8 miles	Distance ≥ 10%:	0.0 miles
Steepest mile:	4.6%	Steepest 3 miles:	3.9%
Traffic:	2	Descent:	3

66 West

Total elevation:	781 ft	Length:	2.7 miles
Top elevation:	1,243 ft	Average grade:	5.5%
Minimum grade:	0%	Maximum grade:	8%
Distance ≥ 5%:	1.5 miles	Distance ≥ 10%:	0.0 miles
Steepest mile:	5.8%	Steepest 3 miles:	NA
Traffic:	2	Descent:	3

Montgomery/Southampton Roads

Total elevation:	1,116 ft	Length:	2.2 miles
Top elevation:	1,448 ft	Average grade:	6.2%
Minimum grade:	0%	Maximum grade:	13%
Distance ≥ 5%:	2.8 miles	Distance ≥ 10%:	0.0 miles
Steepest mile:	6.5%	Steepest 3 miles:	NA
Traffic:	2	Descent:	3

Russell Stage Road

Total elevation:	1,116 ft	Length:	3.9 miles
Top elevation:	1,448 ft	Average grade:	5.4%
Minimum grade:	1%	Maximum grade:	11%
Distance ≥ 5%:	2.8 miles	Distance ≥ 10%:	0.0 miles
Steepest mile:	6.5%	Steepest 3 miles:	5.6%
Traffic:	2	Descent:	3

23 East

Total elevation:	1,109 ft	Length:	5.1 miles
Top elevation:	1,448 ft	Average grade:	4.1%
Minimum grade:	1%	Maximum grade:	9%
Distance ≥ 5%:	1.8 miles	Distance ≥ 10%:	0.0 miles
Steepest mile:	5.1%	Steepest 3 miles:	4.3%
Traffic:	3	Descent:	3

Bish Bash East

Total elevation:	788 ft	Length:	3.1 miles
Top elevation:	1,619 ft	Average grade:	4.8%
Minimum grade:	1%	Maximum grade:	9%
Distance ≥ 5%:	1.5 miles	Distance ≥ 10%:	0.0 miles
Steepest mile:	5.0%	Steepest 3 miles:	4.8%
Traffic:	1	Descent:	3

Bish Bash West

Total elevation:	1,017 ft	Length:	4.8 miles
Top elevation:	1,695 ft	Average grade:	4.0%
Minimum grade:	0%	Maximum grade:	13%
Distance ≥ 5%:	2.1 miles	Distance ≥ 10%:	0.1 miles
Steepest mile:	5.5%	Steepest 3 miles:	4.4%
Traffic:	1	Descent:	4

New Hampshire

Crawford Notch South

Total elevation:	541 ft	Length:	1.8 miles
Top elevation:	1,890 ft	Average grade:	5.7%
Minimum grade:	0%	Maximum grade:	11%
Distance ≥ 5%:	1.5 miles	Distance ≥ 10%:	0.1 miles
Steepest mile:	7.3%	Steepest 3 miles:	NA
Traffic:	3	Descent:	2

Pinkham Notch South

Total elevation:	843 ft	Length:	3.8 miles
Top elevation:	2,019 ft	Average grade:	4.2%
Minimum grade:	0%	Maximum grade:	8%
Distance ≥ 5%:	1.8 miles	Distance ≥ 10%:	0.0 miles
Steepest mile:	4.8%	Steepest 3 miles:	4.4%
Traffic:	3	Descent:	2

Mount Washington

Total elevation:	4,695 ft	Length:	7.5 miles
Top elevation:	6,258 ft	Average grade:	11.9%
Minimum grade:	2%	Maximum grade:	22%
Distance ≥ 5%:	7.3 miles	Distance ≥ 10%:	6.7 miles
Steepest mile:	13.3%	Steepest 3 miles:	12.4%
Traffic:	1	Descent:	5

Switchback Way

Total elevation:	1,050 ft	Length:	2.1 miles
Top elevation:	1,815 ft	Average grade:	9.5%
Minimum grade:	4%	Maximum grade:	15%
Distance ≥ 5%:	2.0 miles	Distance ≥ 10%:	0.8 miles
Steepest mile:	10.3%	Steepest 3 miles:	NA
Traffic:	1	Descent:	4

Bear Notch North

Total elevation:	1,103 ft	Length:	4.7 miles
Top elevation:	1,768 ft	Average grade:	4.5%
Minimum grade:	1%	Maximum grade:	8%
Distance ≥ 5%:	1.9 miles	Distance ≥ 10%:	0.0 miles
Steepest mile:	5.5%	Steepest 3 miles:	4.7%
Traffic:	1	Descent:	3

Hurricane Mountain Road West

Total elevation:	973 ft	Length:	1.7 miles
Top elevation:	1,718 ft	Average grade:	10.8%
Minimum grade:	0%	Maximum grade:	21%
Distance ≥ 5%:	1.6 miles	Distance ≥ 10%:	1.0 miles
Steepest mile:	12.4%	Steepest 3 miles:	NA
Traffic:	1	Descent:	5

Hurricane Mountain Road East

Total elevation:	1,193 ft	Length:	2.2 miles
Top elevation:	1,718 ft	Average grade:	10.3%
Minimum grade:	1%	Maximum grade:	22%
Distance ≥ 5%:	2.0 miles	Distance ≥ 10%:	1.4 miles
Steepest mile:	12.8%	Steepest 3 miles:	NA
Traffic:	1	Descent:	5

Kancamagus Highway East

Total elevation:	1,392 ft	Length:	4.9 miles
Top elevation:	2,855 ft	Average grade:	5.4%
Minimum grade:	2%	Maximum grade:	7%
Distance ≥ 5%:	3.8 miles	Distance ≥ 10%:	0.0 miles
Steepest mile:	5.7%	Steepest 3 miles:	5.5%
Traffic:	4	Descent:	2

Kancamagus Highway West

Total elevation:	1,116 ft	Length:	7.8 miles
Top elevation:	2,855 ft	Average grade:	4.1%
Minimum grade:	1%	Maximum grade:	8%
Distance ≥ 5%:	1.8 miles	Distance ≥ 10%:	0.0 miles
Steepest mile:	5.3%	Steepest 3 miles:	4.7%
Traffic:	4	Descent:	2

3 Mile Hill

Total elevation:	909 ft	Length:	2.1 miles
Top elevation:	2,005 ft	Average grade:	8.2%
Minimum grade:	0%	Maximum grade:	13%
Distance ≥ 5%:	1.8 miles	Distance ≥ 10%:	0.2 miles
Steepest mile:	8.5%	Steepest 3 miles:	NA
Traffic:	2	Descent:	3

Kinsman Notch East

Total elevation:	911 ft	Length:	3.4 miles
Top elevation:	1,869 ft	Average grade:	5.1%
Minimum grade:	1%	Maximum grade:	8%
Distance ≥ 5%:	1.8 miles	Distance ≥ 10%:	0.0 miles
Steepest mile:	6.2%	Steepest 3 miles:	5.2%
Traffic:	3	Descent:	2

Kinsman Notch West

Total elevation:	555 ft	Length:	1.9 miles
Top elevation:	1,851 ft	Average grade:	5.5%
Minimum grade:	0%	Maximum grade:	7%
Distance ≥ 5%:	1.8 miles	Distance ≥ 10%:	0.0 miles
Steepest mile:	5.7%	Steepest 3 miles:	NA
Traffic:	3	Descent:	3

118 East

Total elevation:	3,566 ft	Length:	5.5 miles
Top elevation:	2,534 ft	Average grade:	5.4%
Minimum grade:	1%	Maximum grade:	9%
Distance ≥ 5%:	3.3 miles	Distance ≥ 10%:	0.0 miles
Steepest mile:	6.0%	Steepest 3 miles:	5.6%
Traffic:	3	Descent:	3

118 West

Total elevation:	1,303 ft	Length:	3.8 miles
Top elevation:	2,534 ft	Average grade:	6.5%
Minimum grade:	2%	Maximum grade:	8%
Distance ≥ 5%:	2.8 miles	Distance ≥ 10%:	0.0 miles
Steepest mile:	6.8%	Steepest 3 miles:	6.6%
Traffic:	3	Descent:	3

Lake Tarleton East

Total elevation:	776 ft	Length:	2.3 miles
Top elevation:	1,585 ft	Average grade:	6.4%
Minimum grade:	2%	Maximum grade:	13%
Distance ≥ 5%:	1.8 miles	Distance ≥ 10%:	0.2 miles
Steepest mile:	7.2%	Steepest 3 miles:	NA
Traffic:	2	Descent:	2

Ellsworth Hill Road

Total elevation:	880 ft	Length:	2.6 miles
Top elevation:	1,403 ft	Average grade:	6.0%
Minimum grade:	0%	Maximum grade:	14%
Distance ≥ 5%:	1.6 miles	Distance ≥ 10%:	0.3 miles
Steepest mile:	7.6%	Steepest 3 miles:	NA
Traffic:	1	Descent:	2

Halls Brook Road North

Total elevation:	998 ft	Length:	4.6 miles
Top elevation:	1,516 ft	Average grade:	4.1%
Minimum grade:	0%	Maximum grade:	11%
Distance ≥ 5%:	2.1 miles	Distance ≥ 10%:	0.1 miles
Steepest mile:	6.5%	Steepest 3 miles:	4.4%
Traffic:	1	Descent:	3

North Groton Road (Groton Dump)

Total elevation:	897 ft	Length:	3.5 miles
Top elevation:	1,516 ft	Average grade:	4.9%
Minimum grade:	2%	Maximum grade:	13%
Distance ≥ 5%:	1.8 miles	Distance ≥ 10%:	0.6 miles
Steepest mile:	9.5%	Steepest 3 miles:	5.4%
Traffic:	2	Descent:	3

King Road

Total elevation:	641 ft	Length:	1.3 miles
Top elevation:	1,443 ft	Average grade:	9.3%
Minimum grade:	2%	Maximum grade:	15%
Distance ≥ 5%:	1.1 miles	Distance ≥ 10%:	0.4 miles
Steepest mile:	9.4%	Steepest 3 miles:	NA
Traffic:	1	Descent:	3

Eastman Hill Road North

Total elevation:	566 ft	Length:	1.1 miles
Top elevation:	1,405 ft	Average grade:	9.7%
Minimum grade:	1%	Maximum grade:	15%
Distance ≥ 5%:	0.9 miles	Distance ≥ 10%:	0.3 miles
Steepest mile:	9.8%	Steepest 3 miles:	NA
Traffic:	1	Descent:	3

Methodist Hill Road North

Total elevation:	676 ft	Length:	1.3 miles
Top elevation:	1,746 ft	Average grade:	9.8%
Minimum grade:	0%	Maximum grade:	14%
Distance ≥ 5%:	1.1 miles	Distance ≥ 10%:	0.4 miles
Steepest mile:	9.9%	Steepest 3 miles:	NA
Traffic:	1	Descent:	3

Methodist Hill Road South

Total elevation:	804 ft	Length:	1.9 miles
Top elevation:	1,746 ft	Average grade:	8.0%
Minimum grade:	1%	Maximum grade:	15%
Distance ≥ 5%:	1.7 miles	Distance ≥ 10%:	0.3 miles
Steepest mile:	9.3%	Steepest 3 miles:	NA
Traffic:	1	Descent:	3

Mount Kearsarge

Total elevation:	1,458 ft	Length:	3.4 miles
Top elevation:	2,610 ft	Average grade:	8.1%
Minimum grade:	0%	Maximum grade:	14%
Distance ≥ 5%:	2.6 miles	Distance ≥ 10%:	0.4 miles
Steepest mile:	9.8%	Steepest 3 miles:	8.2 miles
Traffic:	1	Descent:	4

Pack Monadnock

Total elevation:	774 ft	Length:	1.3 miles
Top elevation:	2,255 ft	Average grade:	11.3%
Minimum grade:	0%	Maximum grade:	23%
Distance ≥ 5%:	1.1 miles	Distance ≥ 10%:	0.9 miles
Steepest mile:	11.8%	Steepest 3 miles:	NA
Traffic:	1	Descent:	4

Leviathan

Total elevation:	**883 ft**	**Length:**	**3.9 miles**
Top elevation:	**1,129 ft**	**Average grade:**	**4.3%**
Minimum grade:	**2%**	**Maximum grade:**	**9%**
Distance ≥ 5%:	**1.7 miles**	**Distance ≥ 10%:**	**0.0 miles**
Steepest mile:	**6.1%**	**Steepest 3 miles:**	**4.5%**
Traffic:	**3**	**Descent:**	**3**

The end of New Hampshire's 3 Mile Hill

New York

Gillispie Drive

Total elevation:	636 ft	Length:	2.4 miles
Top elevation:	2,346 ft	Average grade:	5.0%
Minimum grade:	0%	Maximum grade:	9%
Distance ≥ 5%:	1.1 miles	Distance ≥ 10%:	0.0 miles
Steepest mile:	5.3%	Steepest 3 miles:	NA
Traffic:	1	Descent:	3

Styles Brook Road

Total elevation:	766 ft	Length:	1.8 miles
Top elevation:	1,511 ft	Average grade:	8.1%
Minimum grade:	4%	Maximum grade:	20%
Distance ≥ 5%:	1.2 miles	Distance ≥ 10%:	0.6 miles
Steepest mile:	8.6%	Steepest 3 miles:	NA
Traffic:	1	Descent:	4

Whiteface Mountain

Total elevation:	3,566 ft	Length:	7.9 miles
Top elevation:	4,606 ft	Average grade:	8.6%
Minimum grade:	1%	Maximum grade:	12%
Distance ≥ 5%:	7.5 miles	Distance ≥ 10%:	1.3 miles
Steepest mile:	9.8%	Steepest 3 miles:	9.4%
Traffic:	1	Descent:	2

73 East

Total elevation:	1,196 ft	Length:	4.3 miles
Top elevation:	2,043 ft	Average grade:	5.3%
Minimum grade:	0%	Maximum grade:	8%
Distance ≥ 5%:	2.5 miles	Distance ≥ 10%:	0.0 miles
Steepest mile:	5.8%	Steepest 3 miles:	5.4%
Traffic:	3	Descent:	2

Hurricane Road

Total elevation:	843 ft	Length:	1.8 miles
Top elevation:	1,715 ft	Average grade:	8.9%
Minimum grade:	3%	Maximum grade:	13%
Distance ≥ 5%:	1.7 miles	Distance ≥ 10%:	0.6 miles
Steepest mile:	11.2%	Steepest 3 miles:	NA
Traffic:	1	Descent:	4

9N West

Total elevation:	595 ft	Length:	1.9 miles
Top elevation:	1,578 ft	Average grade:	5.9%
Minimum grade:	2%	Maximum grade:	8%
Distance ≥ 5%:	1.5 miles	Distance ≥ 10%:	0.0 miles
Steepest mile:	6.4%	Steepest 3 miles:	NA
Traffic:	3	Descent:	1

Iron Mountain

Total elevation:	908 ft	Length:	2.5 miles
Top elevation:	1,211 ft	Average grade:	6.9%
Minimum grade:	3%	Maximum grade:	8%
Distance ≥ 5%:	2.2 miles	Distance ≥ 10%:	0.0 miles
Steepest mile:	7.3%	Steepest 3 miles:	NA
Traffic:	3	Descent:	1

Graphite Mountain Road

Total elevation:	1,351 ft	Length:	5.1 miles
Top elevation:	1,676 ft	Average grade:	5.0%
Minimum grade:	0%	Maximum grade:	8%
Distance ≥ 5%:	1.8 miles	Distance ≥ 10%:	0.0 miles
Steepest mile:	6.2%	Steepest 3 miles:	5.5%
Traffic:	2	Descent:	3

Prospect Mountain Highway

Total elevation:	1,604 ft	Length:	5.7 miles
Top elevation:	2,016 ft	Average grade:	5.3%
Minimum grade:	1%	Maximum grade:	9%
Distance ≥ 5%:	1.8 miles	Distance ≥ 10%:	0.0 miles
Steepest mile:	7.4%	Steepest 3 miles:	5.6%
Traffic:	2	Descent:	2

Glens Falls Mountain Road

Total elevation:	696 ft	Length:	1.3 miles
Top elevation:	1,172 ft	Average grade:	10.1%
Minimum grade:	1%	Maximum grade:	15%
Distance ≥ 5%:	1.1 miles	Distance ≥ 10%:	0.7 miles
Steepest mile:	10.5%	Steepest 3 miles:	NA
Traffic:	1	Descent:	4

Petersburgh Pass West

Total elevation:	1,297 ft	Length:	4.0 miles
Top elevation:	2,078 ft	Average grade:	6.1%
Minimum grade:	2%	Maximum grade:	7%
Distance ≥ 5%:	2.7 miles	Distance ≥ 10%:	0.0 miles
Steepest mile:	6.3%	Steepest 3 miles:	6.2%
Traffic:	2	Descent:	3

Crawford Road

Total elevation:	1,049 ft	Length:	2.4 miles
Top elevation:	1,826 ft	Average grade:	8.3%
Minimum grade:	1%	Maximum grade:	16%
Distance ≥ 5%:	1.8 miles	Distance ≥ 10%:	0.5 miles
Steepest mile:	8.6%	Steepest 3 miles:	NA
Traffic:	1	Descent:	3

85/157

Total elevation:	797 ft	Length:	3.4 miles
Top elevation:	1,210 ft	Average grade:	4.4%
Minimum grade:	1%	Maximum grade:	7%
Distance ≥ 5%:	1.6 miles	Distance ≥ 10%:	0.0 miles
Steepest mile:	5.1%	Steepest 3 miles:	4.4%
Traffic:	3	Descent:	3

Pinnacle Climb

Total elevation:	1,171 ft	Length:	3.7 miles
Top elevation:	1,584 ft	Average grade:	6.0%
Minimum grade:	1%	Maximum grade:	16%
Distance ≥ 5%:	2.3 miles	Distance ≥ 10%:	0.4 miles
Steepest mile:	7.7%	Steepest 3 miles:	7.4%
Traffic:	2	Descent:	3

85/Wolf Hill Road

Total elevation:	1,185 ft	Length:	4.9 miles
Top elevation:	1,598 ft	Average grade:	4.6%
Minimum grade:	0%	Maximum grade:	13%
Distance ≥ 5%:	2.2 miles	Distance ≥ 10%:	0.2 miles
Steepest mile:	6.8%	Steepest 3 miles:	5.0%
Traffic:	2	Descent:	4

10 North

Total elevation:	1,153 ft	Length:	4.0 miles
Top elevation:	2,165 ft	Average grade:	5.5%
Minimum grade:	0%	Maximum grade:	9%
Distance ≥ 5%:	2.2 miles	Distance ≥ 10%:	0.0 miles
Steepest mile:	6.3%	Steepest 3 miles:	5.6%
Traffic:	3	Descent:	2

4 North

Total elevation:	880 ft	Length:	2.0 miles
Top elevation:	1,918 ft	Average grade:	8.3%
Minimum grade:	0%	Maximum grade:	13%
Distance ≥ 5%:	1.6 miles	Distance ≥ 10%:	0.3 miles
Steepest mile:	8.5%	Steepest 3 miles:	NA
Traffic:	1	Descent:	4

Cotton Hill Road West

Total elevation:	1,143 ft	Length:	2.6 miles
Top elevation:	1,859 ft	Average grade:	8.3%
Minimum grade:	0%	Maximum grade:	15%
Distance ≥ 5%:	2.1 miles	Distance ≥ 10%:	0.6 miles
Steepest mile:	8.8%	Steepest 3 miles:	NA
Traffic:	1	Descent:	4

Potter Mountain Road

Total elevation:	1,082 ft	Length:	3.1 miles
Top elevation:	1,948 ft	Average grade:	6.6%
Minimum grade:	0%	Maximum grade:	10%
Distance ≥ 5%:	1.9 miles	Distance ≥ 10%:	0.0 miles
Steepest mile:	6.7%	Steepest 3 miles:	6.6%
Traffic:	2	Descent:	3

22/20

Total elevation:	1,370 ft	Length:	4.2 miles
Top elevation:	2,141 ft	Average grade:	6.2%
Minimum grade:	0%	Maximum grade:	15%
Distance ≥ 5%:	2.8 miles	Distance ≥ 10%:	0.4 miles
Steepest mile:	6.9%	Steepest 3 miles:	NA
Traffic:	1	Descent:	5

Cunningham Road

Total elevation:	1,158 ft	Length:	2.8 miles
Top elevation:	2,106 ft	Average grade:	7.8%
Minimum grade:	1%	Maximum grade:	14%
Distance ≥ 5%:	2.2 miles	Distance ≥ 10%:	0.5 miles
Steepest mile:	8.6%	Steepest 3 miles:	NA
Traffic:	1	Descent:	3

23 East

Total elevation:	1,082 ft	Length:	5.4 miles
Top elevation:	1,930 ft	Average grade:	3.8%
Minimum grade:	0%	Maximum grade:	8%
Distance ≥ 5%:	2.3 miles	Distance ≥ 10%:	0.0 miles
Steepest mile:	4.9%	Steepest 3 miles:	3.9%
Traffic:	3	Descent:	3

Kaaterskill Falls (23A)

Total elevation:	1,537 ft	Length:	4.6 miles
Top elevation:	1,921 ft	Average grade:	5.6%
Minimum grade:	0%	Maximum grade:	8%
Distance ≥ 5%:	2.2 miles	Distance ≥ 10%:	0.0 miles
Steepest mile:	6.5%	Steepest 3 miles:	5.6%
Traffic:	4	Descent:	3

Scribner Hollow Road North

Total elevation:	487 ft	Length:	1.1 miles
Top elevation:	2,293 ft	Average grade:	8.4%
Minimum grade:	1%	Maximum grade:	12%
Distance ≥ 5%:	0.8 miles	Distance ≥ 10%:	0.2 miles
Steepest mile:	8.5%	Steepest 3 miles:	NA
Traffic:	1	Descent:	3

Scribner Hollow Road South

Total elevation:	594 ft	Length:	2.0 miles
Top elevation:	2,293 ft	Average grade:	5.6%
Minimum grade:	0%	Maximum grade:	13%
Distance ≥ 5%:	0.9 miles	Distance ≥ 10%:	0.1 miles
Steepest mile:	5.9%	Steepest 3 miles:	NA
Traffic:	1	Descent:	3

Airport Road

Total elevation:	882 ft	Length:	2.1 miles
Top elevation:	2,125 ft	Average grade:	8.0%
Minimum grade:	0%	Maximum grade:	22%
Distance ≥ 5%:	1.0 miles	Distance ≥ 10%:	0.5 miles
Steepest mile:	10.7%	Steepest 3 miles:	NA
Traffic:	1	Descent:	2

206 North

Total elevation:	1,061 ft	Length:	2.7 miles
Top elevation:	2,290 ft	Average grade:	7.4%
Minimum grade:	1%	Maximum grade:	8%
Distance ≥ 5%:	2.3 miles	Distance ≥ 10%:	0.0 miles
Steepest mile:	7.6%	Steepest 3 miles:	NA
Traffic:	2	Descent:	2

206 South

Total elevation:	1,116 ft	Length:	5.2 miles
Top elevation:	2,261 ft	Average grade:	4.2%
Minimum grade:	2%	Maximum grade:	8%
Distance ≥ 5%:	1.8 miles	Distance ≥ 10%:	0.0 miles
Steepest mile:	6.1%	Steepest 3 miles:	5.1%
Traffic:	2	Descent:	4

206 South/Wilson HLW Road

Total elevation:	976 ft	Length:	5.1 miles
Top elevation:	2,205 ft	Average grade:	3.6%
Minimum grade:	2%	Maximum grade:	8%
Distance ≥ 5%:	1.8 miles	Distance ≥ 10%:	0.0 miles
Steepest mile:	5.2%	Steepest 3 miles:	4.2%
Traffic:	2	Descent:	3

Colchester Mountain Road

Total elevation:	942 ft	Length:	2.2 miles
Top elevation:	2,205 ft	Average grade:	8.1%
Minimum grade:	3%	Maximum grade:	15%
Distance ≥ 5%:	1.8 miles	Distance ≥ 10%:	0.4 miles
Steepest mile:	8.6%	Steepest 3 miles:	NA
Traffic:	1	Descent:	2

26 North

Total elevation:	943 ft	Length:	2.4 miles
Top elevation:	2,188 ft	Average grade:	7.4%
Minimum grade:	3%	Maximum grade:	12%
Distance ≥ 5%:	2.1 miles	Distance ≥ 10%:	0.2 miles
Steepest mile:	8.2%	Steepest 3 miles:	NA
Traffic:	2	Descent:	2

26 South

Total elevation:	509 ft	Length:	1.4 miles
Top elevation:	2,188 ft	Average grade:	6.9%
Minimum grade:	1%	Maximum grade:	12%
Distance ≥ 5%:	1.2 miles	Distance ≥ 10%:	0.3 miles
Steepest mile:	8.4%	Steepest 3 miles:	NA
Traffic:	2	Descent:	2

Berkaboom Road

Total elevation:	1,005 ft	Length:	3.9 miles
Top elevation:	2,298 ft	Average grade:	4.9%
Minimum grade:	0%	Maximum grade:	11%
Distance ≥ 5%:	1.8 miles	Distance ≥ 10%:	0.2 miles
Steepest mile:	5.6%	Steepest 3 miles:	5.0%
Traffic:	1	Descent:	3

Beech Hill Road North

Total elevation:	1,025 ft	Length:	3.5 miles
Top elevation:	2,337 ft	Average grade:	5.6%
Minimum grade:	0%	Maximum grade:	13%
Distance ≥ 5%:	1.9 miles	Distance ≥ 10%:	0.3 miles
Steepest mile:	7.5%	Steepest 3 miles:	5.7%
Traffic:	1	Descent:	3

Devils Kitchen

Total elevation:	1,149 ft	Length:	1.9 miles
Top elevation:	1,826 ft	Average grade:	11.5%
Minimum grade:	0%	Maximum grade:	22%
Distance ≥ 5%:	1.6 miles	Distance ≥ 10%:	1.2 miles
Steepest mile:	12.8%	Steepest 3 miles:	NA
Traffic:	2	Descent:	5

Devils Kitchen/Josh Road

Total elevation:	1,629 ft	Length:	3.2 miles
Top elevation:	2,306 ft	Average grade:	9.6%
Minimum grade:	0%	Maximum grade:	22%
Distance ≥ 5%:	2.3 miles	Distance ≥ 10%:	1.7 miles
Steepest mile:	12.8%	Steepest 3 miles:	9.6%
Traffic:	2	Descent:	5

Meads Mountain Road East

Total elevation:	1,116 ft	Length:	1.9 miles
Top elevation:	1,769 ft	Average grade:	11.1%
Minimum grade:	4%	Maximum grade:	13%
Distance ≥ 5%:	1.8 miles	Distance ≥ 10%:	1.6 miles
Steepest mile:	11.3%	Steepest 3 miles:	NA
Traffic:	1	Descent:	4

Meads Mountain Road West

Total elevation:	807 ft	Length:	2.4 miles
Top elevation:	1,769 ft	Average grade:	6.4%
Minimum grade:	0%	Maximum grade:	13%
Distance ≥ 5%:	1.6 miles	Distance ≥ 10%:	0.4 miles
Steepest mile:	6.9%	Steepest 3 miles:	NA
Traffic:	1	Descent:	4

Peakamoose Road North

Total elevation:	1,0011 ft	Length:	4.0 miles
Top elevation:	1,712 ft	Average grade:	4.8%
Minimum grade:	1%	Maximum grade:	12%
Distance ≥ 5%:	1.8 miles	Distance ≥ 10%:	0.1 miles
Steepest mile:	5.9%	Steepest 3 miles:	5.1%
Traffic:	1	Descent:	3

Sugar Loaf/Red Hill Road

Total elevation:	1,596 ft	Length:	4.2 miles
Top elevation:	2,524 ft	Average grade:	7.2%
Minimum grade:	0%	Maximum grade:	13%
Distance ≥ 5%:	7.6 miles	Distance ≥ 10%:	0.6 miles
Steepest mile:	8.6%	Steepest 3 miles:	7.4%
Traffic:	1	Descent:	4

Claryville Road/Cummings Road

Total elevation:	693 ft	Length:	2.2 miles
Top elevation:	1,861 ft	Average grade:	6.0%
Minimum grade:	0%	Maximum grade:	11%
Distance ≥ 5%:	1.6 miles	Distance ≥ 10%:	0.1 miles
Steepest mile:	8.4%	Steepest 3 miles:	NA
Traffic:	2	Descent:	2

Glade Hill Road

Total elevation:	1,251 ft	Length:	1.9 miles
Top elevation:	2,179 ft	Average grade:	12.5%
Minimum grade:	3%	Maximum grade:	23%
Distance ≥ 5%:	1.8 miles	Distance ≥ 10%:	1.7 miles
Steepest mile:	13.8%	Steepest 3 miles:	NA
Traffic:	1	Descent:	5

Moore Hill Road

Total elevation:	1,247 ft	Length:	3.0 miles
Top elevation:	2,179 ft	Average grade:	7.9%
Minimum grade:	1%	Maximum grade:	14%
Distance ≥ 5%:	2.2 miles	Distance ≥ 10%:	0.8 miles
Steepest mile:	9.4%	Steepest 3 miles:	7.9%
Traffic:	1	Descent:	3

Denman Mountain Road

Total elevation:	1,085 ft	Length:	2.5 miles
Top elevation:	2,099 ft	Average grade:	8.2%
Minimum grade:	1%	Maximum grade:	23%
Distance ≥ 5%:	1.9 miles	Distance ≥ 10%:	0.7 miles
Steepest mile:	8.7%	Steepest 3 miles:	NA
Traffic:	1	Descent:	4

Mohonk East

Total elevation:	854 ft	Length:	2.2 miles
Top elevation:	1,116 ft	Average grade:	7.4%
Minimum grade:	2%	Maximum grade:	9%
Distance ≥ 5%:	1.6 miles	Distance ≥ 10%:	0.0 miles
Steepest mile:	7.5%	Steepest 3 miles:	NA
Traffic:	3	Descent:	3

Mohonk West

Total elevation:	721 ft	Length:	2.1 miles
Top elevation:	1,116 ft	Average grade:	6.5%
Minimum grade:	2%	Maximum grade:	12%
Distance ≥ 5%:	1.7 miles	Distance ≥ 10%:	0.1 miles
Steepest mile:	7.2%	Steepest 3 miles:	NA
Traffic:	2	Descent:	3

52 East

Total elevation:	889 ft	Length:	2.8 miles
Top elevation:	1,492 ft	Average grade:	6.0%
Minimum grade:	3%	Maximum grade:	8%
Distance ≥ 5%:	1.9 miles	Distance ≥ 10%:	0.0 miles
Steepest mile:	6.3%	Steepest 3 miles:	NA
Traffic:	3	Descent:	2

52 West

Total elevation:	1,116 ft	Length:	4.2 miles
Top elevation:	1,769 ft	Average grade:	5.3%
Minimum grade:	2%	Maximum grade:	8%
Distance ≥ 5%:	2.5 miles	Distance ≥ 10%:	0.0 miles
Steepest mile:	5.3%	Steepest 3 miles:	NA
Traffic:	3	Descent:	2

South Gully Road

Total elevation:	1,539 ft	Length:	3.9 miles
Top elevation:	1,847 ft	Average grade:	7.5%
Minimum grade:	2%	Maximum grade:	14%
Distance ≥ 5%:	2.8 miles	Distance ≥ 10%:	0.5 miles
Steepest mile:	8.2%	Steepest 3 miles:	7.7%
Traffic:	2	Descent:	3

South Gully Road/Mount Meenagha

Total elevation:	1,483 ft	Length:	3.3 miles
Top elevation:	1,791 ft	Average grade:	8.5%
Minimum grade:	2%	Maximum grade:	19%
Distance ≥ 5%:	2.6 miles	Distance ≥ 10%:	0.8 miles
Steepest mile:	9.2%	Steepest 3 miles:	8.6%
Traffic:	2	Descent:	4

Wurtsboro Mountain Road

Total elevation:	9476 ft	Length:	5.0 miles
Top elevation:	1,539 ft	Average grade:	3.6%
Minimum grade:	0%	Maximum grade:	7%
Distance ≥ 5%:	1.7 miles	Distance ≥ 10%:	0.0 miles
Steepest mile:	4.4%	Steepest 3 miles:	3.8%
Traffic:	5	Descent:	1

Guymard Turnpike West

Total elevation:	716 ft	Length:	2.4 miles
Top elevation:	1,178 ft	Average grade:	5.7%
Minimum grade:	0%	Maximum grade:	8%
Distance ≥ 5%:	1.5 miles	Distance ≥ 10%:	0.0 miles
Steepest mile:	5.8%	Steepest 3 miles:	NA
Traffic:	2	Descent:	3

Grand Army of the Republic Highway

Total elevation:	779 ft	Length:	3.4 miles
Top elevation:	1,232 ft	Average grade:	4.3%
Minimum grade:	2%	Maximum grade:	7%
Distance ≥ 5%:	0.8 miles	Distance ≥ 10%:	0.0 miles
Steepest mile:	4.6%	Steepest 3 miles:	4.4%
Traffic:	3	Descent:	2

Greenville Turnpike

Total elevation:	836 ft	Length:	2.5 miles
Top elevation:	1,323 ft	Average grade:	6.3%
Minimum grade:	1%	Maximum grade:	9%
Distance ≥ 5%:	1.4 miles	Distance ≥ 10%:	0.0 miles
Steepest mile:	6.5%	Steepest 3 miles:	NA
Traffic:	1	Descent:	3

17A East

Total elevation:	534 ft	Length:	1.7 miles
Top elevation:	1,172 ft	Average grade:	5.9%
Minimum grade:	2%	Maximum grade:	9%
Distance ≥ 5%:	1.5 miles	Distance ≥ 10%:	0.0 miles
Steepest mile:	6.3%	Steepest 3 miles:	NA%
Traffic:	3	Descent:	3

17A West

Total elevation:	542 ft	Length:	1.4 miles
Top elevation:	1,172 ft	Average grade:	7.3%
Minimum grade:	3%	Maximum grade:	9%
Distance ≥ 5%:	0.8 miles	Distance ≥ 10%:	0.0 miles
Steepest mile:	7.8%	Steepest 3 miles:	NA
Traffic:	3	Descent:	3

Harriman State Park West

Total elevation:	542 ft	Length:	3.1 miles
Top elevation:	1,028 ft	Average grade:	3.3%
Minimum grade:	0%	Maximum grade:	7%
Distance ≥ 5%:	1.1 miles	Distance ≥ 10%:	0.0 miles
Steepest mile:	3.8%	Steepest 3 miles:	3.3%
Traffic:	2	Descent:	3

Gate Hill Road

Total elevation:	463 ft	Length:	1.5 miles
Top elevation:	809 ft	Average grade:	5.8%
Minimum grade:	2%	Maximum grade:	7%
Distance ≥ 5%:	1.0 miles	Distance ≥ 10%:	0.0 miles
Steepest mile:	6.0%	Steepest 3 miles:	NA
Traffic:	3	Descent:	3

Bear Mountain

Total elevation:	1,267 ft	Length:	4.5 miles
Top elevation:	1,280 ft	Average grade:	5.3%
Minimum grade:	0%	Maximum grade:	8%
Distance ≥ 5%:	2.3 miles	Distance ≥ 10%:	0.0 miles
Steepest mile:	5.8%	Steepest 3 miles:	5.5%
Traffic:	2	Descent:	3

Vermont

105 East

Total elevation:	1,022 ft	Length:	3.0 miles
Top elevation:	2,089 ft	Average grade:	6.5%
Minimum grade:	2%	Maximum grade:	8%
Distance ≥ 5%:	1.8 miles	Distance ≥ 10%:	0.0 miles
Steepest mile:	6.8%	Steepest 3 miles:	6.5%
Traffic:	1	Descent:	2

105 West

Total elevation:	1,283 ft	Length:	7.1 miles
Top elevation:	2,089 ft	Average grade:	4.3%
Minimum grade:	0%	Maximum grade:	8%
Distance ≥ 5%:	3.1 miles	Distance ≥ 10%:	0.0 miles
Steepest mile:	5.6%	Steepest 3 miles:	4.7%
Traffic:	1	Descent:	3

Blue House Hill North

Total elevation:	700 ft	Length:	3.1 miles
Top elevation:	1,176 ft	Average grade:	4.3%
Minimum grade:	0%	Maximum grade:	9%
Distance ≥ 5%:	1.2 miles	Distance ≥ 10%:	0.0 miles
Steepest mile:	5.3%	Steepest 3 miles:	4.4%
Traffic:	1	Descent:	3

Blue House Hill South

Total elevation:	678 ft	Length:	3.7 miles
Top elevation:	1,176 ft	Average grade:	3.5%
Minimum grade:	0%	Maximum grade:	14%
Distance ≥ 5%:	1.4 miles	Distance ≥ 10%:	0.3 miles
Steepest mile:	7.3%	Steepest 3 miles:	3.9%
Traffic:	1	Descent:	3

Jay Peak North

Total elevation:	1,328 ft	Length:	5.0 miles
Top elevation:	2,256 ft	Average grade:	5.0%
Minimum grade:	0%	Maximum grade:	11%
Distance ≥ 5%:	2.3 miles	Distance ≥ 10%:	0.4 miles
Steepest mile:	7.3%	Steepest 3 miles:	5.5%
Traffic:	2	Descent:	3

Jay Peak South

Total elevation:	1,714 ft	Length:	6.3 miles
Top elevation:	2,256 ft	Average grade:	5.2%
Minimum grade:	1%	Maximum grade:	12%
Distance ≥ 5%:	2.6 miles	Distance ≥ 10%:	0.3 miles
Steepest mile:	8.3%	Steepest 3 miles:	5.7%
Traffic:	2	Descent:	2

122 North

Total elevation:	660 ft	Length:	2.6 miles
Top elevation:	1,819 ft	Average grade:	4.8%
Minimum grade:	1%	Maximum grade:	9%
Distance ≥ 5%:	1.3 miles	Distance ≥ 10%:	0.0 miles
Steepest mile:	5.8%	Steepest 3 miles:	NA
Traffic:	2	Descent:	3

Burke Mountain

Total elevation:	2.381 ft	Length:	4.7 miles
Top elevation:	3,211 ft	Average grade:	9.6%
Minimum grade:	0%	Maximum grade:	24%
Distance ≥ 5%:	4.0 miles	Distance ≥ 10%:	2.7 miles
Steepest mile:	15.6%	Steepest 3 miles:	13.0%
Traffic:	1	Descent:	5

Smugglers Notch East

Total elevation:	1,221 ft	Length:	4.5 miles
Top elevation:	2,162 ft	Average grade:	5.1%
Minimum grade:	0%	Maximum grade:	20%
Distance ≥ 5%:	1.9 miles	Distance ≥ 10%:	0.5 miles
Steepest mile:	10.1%	Steepest 3 miles:	6.2%
Traffic:	3	Descent:	3

Smugglers Notch West

Total elevation:	1,120 ft	Length:	3.1 miles
Top elevation:	2,162 ft	Average grade:	6.8%
Minimum grade:	1%	Maximum grade:	11%
Distance ≥ 5%:	2.3 miles	Distance ≥ 10%:	0.1 miles
Steepest mile:	7.1%	Steepest 3 miles:	6.8%
Traffic:	3	Descent:	3

Bolton Mountain

Total elevation:	1,787 ft	Length:	4.2 miles
Top elevation:	2,136 ft	Average grade:	8.1%
Minimum grade:	4%	Maximum grade:	16%
Distance ≥ 5%:	3.6 miles	Distance ≥ 10%:	1.4 miles
Steepest mile:	9.8%	Steepest 3 miles:	9.3%
Traffic:	2	Descent:	2

Appalachian Gap East

Total elevation:	1,332 ft	Length:	2.7 miles
Top elevation:	2,422 ft	Average grade:	9.3%
Minimum grade:	4%	Maximum grade:	13%
Distance ≥ 5%:	2.4 miles	Distance ≥ 10%:	1.0 miles
Steepest mile:	9.8%	Steepest 3 miles:	NA
Traffic:	2	Descent:	3

Appalachian Gap West

Total elevation:	1,224 ft	Length:	2.7 miles
Top elevation:	2,422 ft	Average grade:	8.6%
Minimum grade:	4%	Maximum grade:	17%
Distance ≥ 5%:	2.5 miles	Distance ≥ 10%:	0.6 miles
Steepest mile:	10.6%	Steepest 3 miles:	NA
Traffic:	2	Descent:	3

Sugarbush

Total elevation:	620 ft	Length:	1.9 miles
Top elevation:	1,558 ft	Average grade:	6.2%
Minimum grade:	1%	Maximum grade:	13%
Distance ≥ 5%:	1.3 miles	Distance ≥ 10%:	0.3 miles
Steepest mile:	6.5%	Steepest 3 miles:	NA
Traffic:	2	Descent:	3

Lincoln Gap West

Total elevation:	1,385 ft	Length:	3.5 miles
Top elevation:	2,424 ft	Average grade:	7.5%
Minimum grade:	0%	Maximum grade:	21%
Distance ≥ 5%:	2.3 miles	Distance ≥ 10%:	0.8 miles
Steepest mile:	12.5%	Steepest 3 miles:	8.2%
Traffic:	1	Descent:	4

Lincoln Gap East

Total elevation:	1,098 ft	Length:	1.5 miles
Top elevation:	2,424 ft	Average grade:	13.9%
Minimum grade:	3%	Maximum grade:	21%
Distance ≥ 5%:	1.4 miles	Distance ≥ 10%:	1.3 miles
Steepest mile:	15.9%	Steepest 3 miles:	NA
Traffic:	1	Descent:	4

Roxbury Gap East

Total elevation:	1,409 ft	Length:	3.5 miles
Top elevation:	2,397 ft	Average grade:	7.6%
Minimum grade:	1%	Maximum grade:	14%
Distance ≥ 5%:	2.4 miles	Distance ≥ 10%:	1.1 miles
Steepest mile:	10.9%	Steepest 3 miles:	8.5%
Traffic:	1	Descent:	3

Roxbury Gap West

Total elevation:	1,466 ft	Length:	4.5 miles
Top elevation:	2,397 ft	Average grade:	6.2%
Minimum grade:	3%	Maximum grade:	13%
Distance ≥ 5%:	3.6 miles	Distance ≥ 10%:	0.9 miles
Steepest mile:	10.4%	Steepest 3 miles:	8.2%
Traffic:	1	Descent:	3

Middlebury Gap East

Total elevation:	1,250 ft	Length:	6.0 miles
Top elevation:	2,146 ft	Average grade:	3.9%
Minimum grade:	0%	Maximum grade:	13%
Distance ≥ 5%:	3.4 miles	Distance ≥ 10%:	1.1 miles
Steepest mile:	9.6%	Steepest 3 miles:	6.1%
Traffic:	2	Descent:	3

Middlebury Gap West

Total elevation:	1,612 ft	Length:	8.3 miles
Top elevation:	2,146 ft	Average grade:	3.7%
Minimum grade:	0%	Maximum grade:	12%
Distance ≥ 5%:	3.7 miles	Distance ≥ 10%:	0.1 miles
Steepest mile:	6.9%	Steepest 3 miles:	5.2%
Traffic:	2	Descent:	3

Brandon Gap East

Total elevation:	1,188 ft	Length:	5.4 miles
Top elevation:	2,184 ft	Average grade:	4.2%
Minimum grade:	0%	Maximum grade:	11%
Distance ≥ 5%:	2.8 miles	Distance ≥ 10%:	0.0 miles
Steepest mile:	5.8%	Steepest 3 miles:	4.8%
Traffic:	2	Descent:	3

Brandon Gap West

Total elevation:	1,591 ft	Length:	4.9 miles
Top elevation:	2,184 ft	Average grade:	6.2%
Minimum grade:	0%	Maximum grade:	13%
Distance ≥ 5%:	2.7 miles	Distance ≥ 10%:	0.7 miles
Steepest mile:	10.1%	Steepest 3 miles:	7.0%
Traffic:	2	Descent:	5

Rochester Gap East

Total elevation:	1,557 ft	Length:	5.6 miles
Top elevation:	2,148 ft	Average grade:	5.3%
Minimum grade:	0%	Maximum grade:	13%
Distance ≥ 5%:	2.5 miles	Distance ≥ 10%:	0.4 miles
Steepest mile:	9.8%	Steepest 3 miles:	5.7%
Traffic:	2	Descent:	3

Rochester Gap West

Total elevation:	1,273 ft	Length:	3.8 miles
Top elevation:	2,146 ft	Average grade:	6.3%
Minimum grade:	0%	Maximum grade:	11%
Distance ≥ 5%:	2.3 miles	Distance ≥ 10%:	0.1 miles
Steepest mile:	7.6%	Steepest 3 miles:	6.6%
Traffic:	2	Descent:	3

North Road

Total elevation:	971 ft	Length:	4.4 miles
Top elevation:	1,512 ft	Average grade:	4.2%
Minimum grade:	0%	Maximum grade:	12%
Distance ≥ 5%:	1.7 miles	Distance ≥ 10%:	0.1 miles
Steepest mile:	6.2%	Steepest 3 miles:	4.4%
Traffic:	3	Descent:	2

Sharon to Strafford

Total elevation:	1,052 ft	Length:	4.0 miles
Top elevation:	1,545 ft	Average grade:	5.0%
Minimum grade:	0%	Maximum grade:	12%
Distance ≥ 5%:	1.8 miles	Distance ≥ 10%:	0.2 miles
Steepest mile:	7.2%	Steepest 3 miles:	5.2%
Traffic:	2	Descent:	3

Howe Hill Road

Total elevation:	900 ft	Length:	3.2 miles
Top elevation:	1,339 ft	Average grade:	5.3%
Minimum grade:	0%	Maximum grade:	14%
Distance ≥ 5%:	2.4 miles	Distance ≥ 10%:	0.3 miles
Steepest mile:	6.8%	Steepest 3 miles:	5.5%
Traffic:	2	Descent:	3

Jericho Street

Total elevation:	706 ft	Length:	1.7 miles
Top elevation:	1,082 ft	Average grade:	7.9%
Minimum grade:	1%	Maximum grade:	12%
Distance ≥ 5%:	1.4 miles	Distance ≥ 10%:	0.1 miles
Steepest mile:	8.3%	Steepest 3 miles:	NA
Traffic:	1	Descent:	4

Jericho Road

Total elevation:	766 ft	Length:	2.4 miles
Top elevation:	1,126 ft	Average grade:	6.0%
Minimum grade:	1%	Maximum grade:	14%
Distance ≥ 5%:	1.5 miles	Distance ≥ 10%:	0.2 miles
Steepest mile:	7.9%	Steepest 3 miles:	NA
Traffic:	1	Descent:	3

4 East

Total elevation:	942 ft	Length:	3.6 miles
Top elevation:	2,159 ft	Average grade:	5.0%
Minimum grade:	2%	Maximum grade:	8%
Distance ≥ 5%:	1.7 miles	Distance ≥ 10%:	0.0 miles
Steepest mile:	6.7%	Steepest 3 miles:	5.2%
Traffic:	4	Descent:	2

4 West

Total elevation:	**1,055 ft**	**Length:**	**5.0 miles**
Top elevation:	**2,159 ft**	**Average grade:**	**4.0%**
Minimum grade:	**0%**	**Maximum grade:**	**8%**
Distance ≥ 5%:	**2.2 miles**	**Distance ≥ 10%:**	**0.0 miles**
Steepest mile:	**5.6%**	**Steepest 3 miles:**	**4.3%**
Traffic:	**4**	**Descent:**	**2**

Killington Ski Area

Total elevation:	**1,289 ft**	**Length:**	**5.1 miles**
Top elevation:	**2,506 ft**	**Average grade:**	**4.8%**
Minimum grade:	**0%**	**Maximum grade:**	**17%**
Distance ≥ 5%:	**2.7 miles**	**Distance ≥ 10%:**	**0.3 miles**
Steepest mile:	**8.3%**	**Steepest 3 miles:**	**5.5%**
Traffic:	**3**	**Descent:**	**3**

East Mountain Road

Total elevation:	**993 ft**	**Length:**	**2.2 miles**
Top elevation:	**2,257 ft**	**Average grade:**	**8.6%**
Minimum grade:	**0%**	**Maximum grade:**	**13%**
Distance ≥ 5%:	**1.8 miles**	**Distance ≥ 10%:**	**0.9 miles**
Steepest mile:	**10.3%**	**Steepest 3 miles:**	**NA**
Traffic:	**2**	**Descent:**	**3**

Tyson Road East

Total elevation:	1,204 ft	Length:	5.8 miles
Top elevation:	1,971 ft	Average grade:	3.9%
Minimum grade:	0%	Maximum grade:	8%
Distance ≥ 5%:	1.8 miles	Distance ≥ 10%:	0.0 miles
Steepest mile:	4.7%	Steepest 3 miles:	4.3%
Traffic:	2	Descent:	3

Tyson Road West

Total elevation:	896 ft	Length:	3.8 miles
Top elevation:	1,971 ft	Average grade:	4.5%
Minimum grade:	1%	Maximum grade:	9%
Distance ≥ 5%:	1.7 miles	Distance ≥ 10%:	0.0 miles
Steepest mile:	5.1%	Steepest 3 miles:	4.6%
Traffic:	2	Descent:	3

Mount Auscutney

Total elevation:	2,250 ft	Length:	3.7 miles
Top elevation:	2,771 ft	Average grade:	11.5%
Minimum grade:	0%	Maximum grade:	18%
Distance ≥ 5%:	3.2 miles	Distance ≥ 10%:	2.7 miles
Steepest mile:	12.5%	Steepest 3 miles:	11.6%
Traffic:	1	Descent :	5

Okemo Mountain

Total elevation:	2,099 ft	Length:	3.8 miles
Top elevation:	3,144 ft	Average grade:	10.5%
Minimum grade:	2%	Maximum grade:	17%
Distance ≥ 5%:	3.2 miles	Distance ≥ 10%:	2.7 miles
Steepest mile:	12.3%	Steepest 3 miles:	11.6%
Traffic:	1	Descent:	4

Rupert Mountain East

Total elevation:	861 ft	Length:	2.0 miles
Top elevation:	1,698 ft	Average grade:	8.2%
Minimum grade:	3%	Maximum grade:	12%
Distance ≥ 5%:	1.8 miles	Distance ≥ 10%:	0.1 miles
Steepest mile:	8.4%	Steepest 3 miles:	NA
Traffic:	2	Descent:	2

Rupert Mountain West

Total elevation:	630 ft	Length:	1.7 miles
Top elevation:	1,698 ft	Average grade:	7.0%
Minimum grade:	4%	Maximum grade:	14%
Distance ≥ 5%:	1.2 miles	Distance ≥ 10%:	0.4 miles
Steepest mile:	8.2%	Steepest 3 miles:	NA
Traffic:	2	Descent:	2

30/11 West

Total elevation:	1,337 ft	Length:	5.9 miles
Top elevation:	2,091 ft	Average grade:	4.3%
Minimum grade:	0%	Maximum grade:	8%
Distance ≥ 5%:	2.6 miles	Distance ≥ 10%:	0.0 miles
Steepest mile:	4.8%	Steepest 3 miles:	4.5%
Traffic:	4	Descent:	3

Stratton Mountain

Total elevation:	824 ft	Length:	3.8 miles
Top elevation:	2,116 ft	Average grade:	4.1%
Minimum grade:	0%	Maximum grade:	9%
Distance ≥ 5%:	2.7 miles	Distance ≥ 10%:	0.0 miles
Steepest mile:	6.5%	Steepest 3 miles:	4.4%
Traffic:	2	Descent:	3

Mount Equinox

Total elevation:	3,157 ft	Length:	5.2 miles
Top elevation:	3,811 ft	Average grade:	11.5%
Minimum grade:	0%	Maximum grade:	17%
Distance ≥ 5%:	4.9 miles	Distance ≥ 10%:	4.6 miles
Steepest mile:	13.3%	Steepest 3 miles:	12.2%
Traffic:	1	Descent:	5

Hill Climb Profiles (Top 50)
(in alphabetical order)

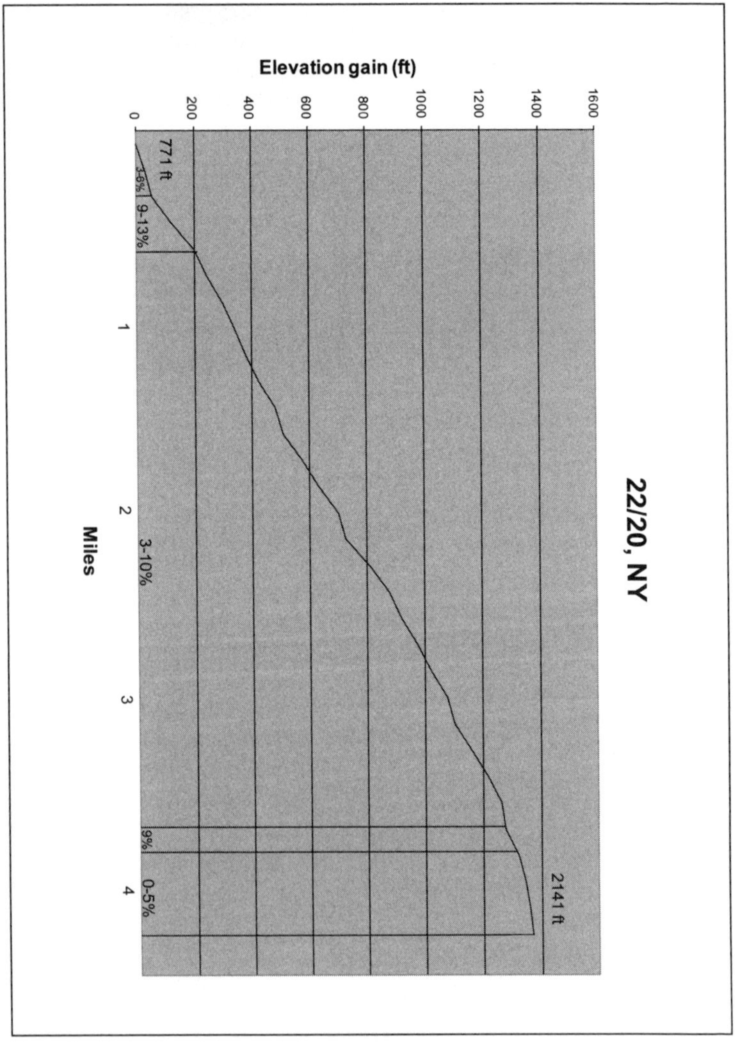

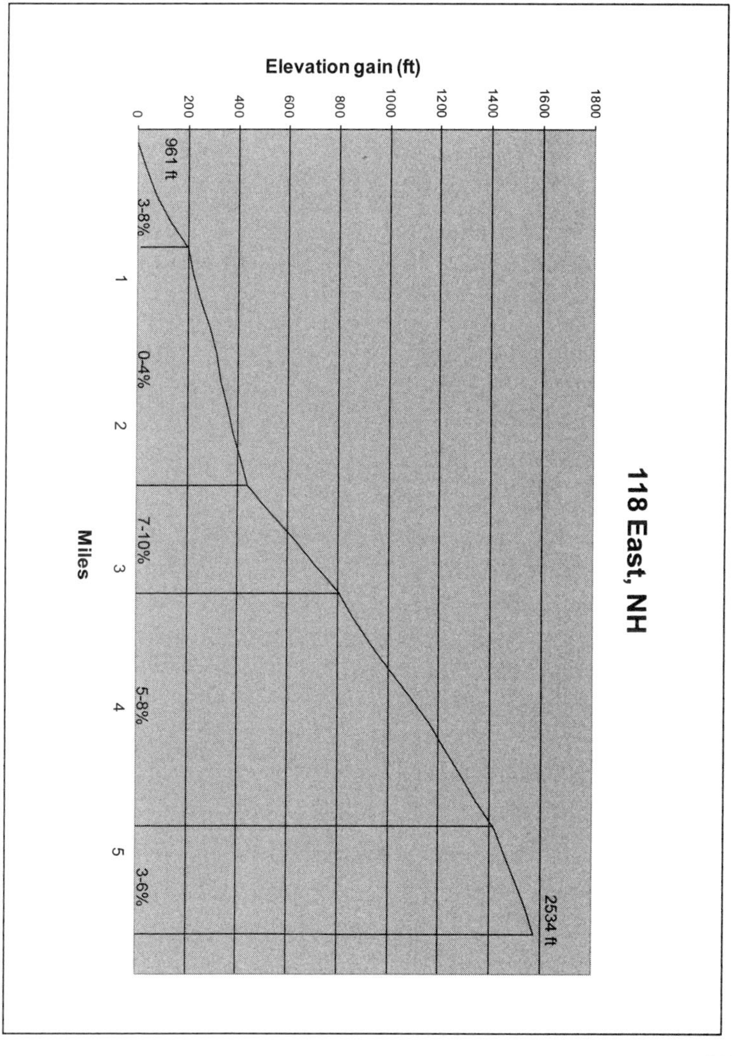
118 East, NH
Elevation gain (ft)
0
200
400
600
800
1000
1200
1400
1600
1800
961 ft
2534 ft
3-8%
0-4%
7-10%
5-8%
3-6%
1
2
3
4
5
Miles

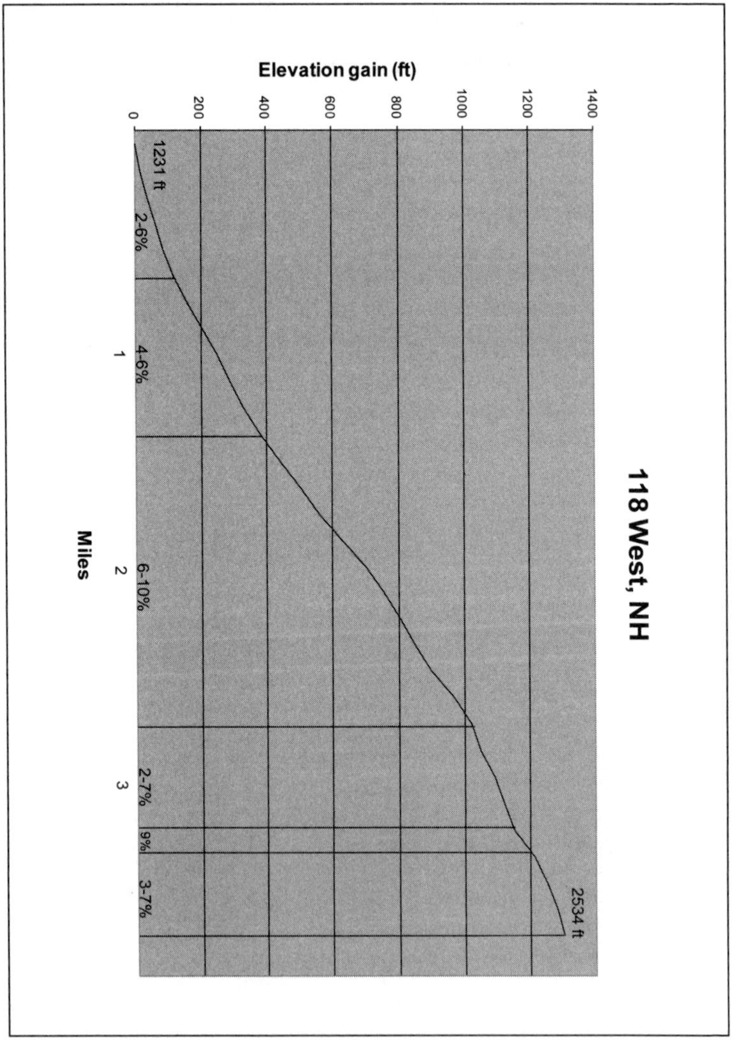
118 West, NH
Elevation gain (ft)
0
200
400
600
800
1000
1200
1400
1231 ft
2-6%
4-6%
6-10%
2-7%
9%
3-7%
2534 ft
1
2
3
Miles

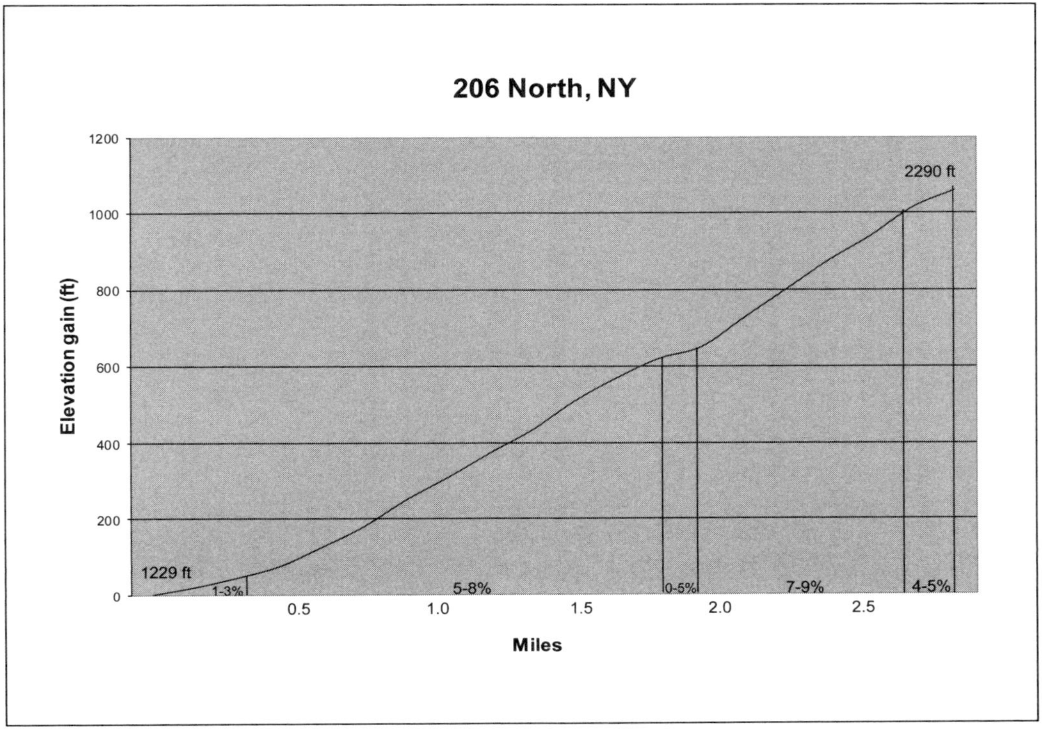
206 North, NY
Elevation gain (ft)
0
200
400
600
800
1000
1200
0.5
1.0
1.5
2.0
2.5
Miles
1229 ft
1-3%
5-8%
0-5%
7-9%
4-5%
2290 ft

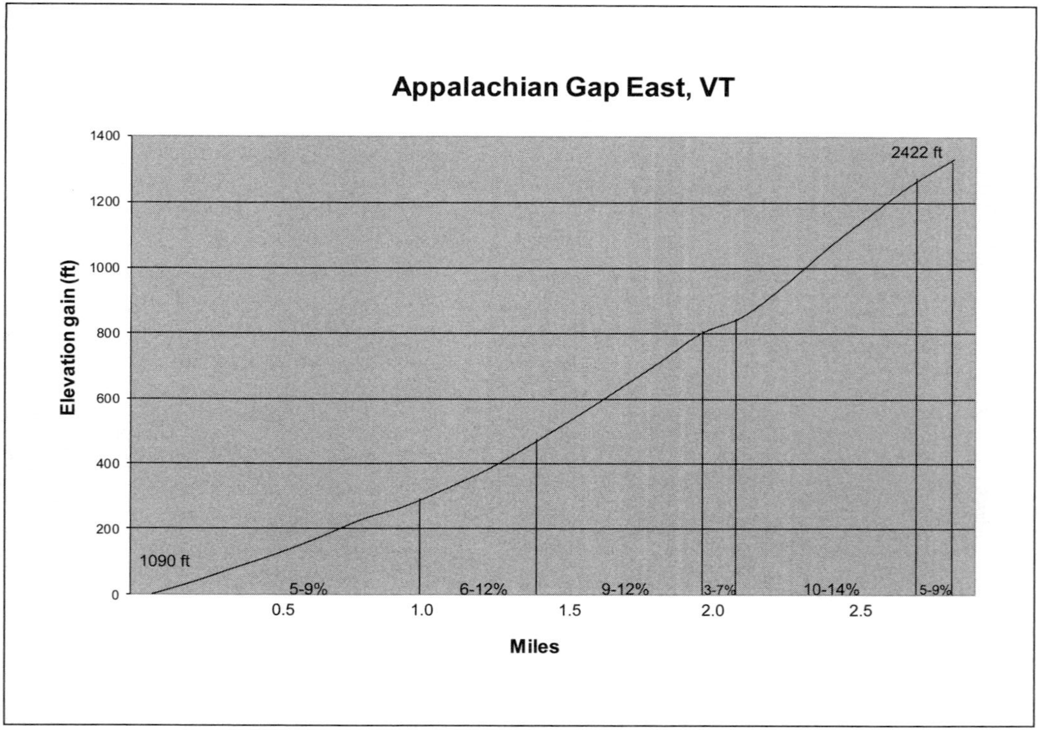
Appalachian Gap East, VT
Elevation gain (ft)
1400
1200
1000
800
600
400
200
0
2422 ft
1090 ft
5-9%
6-12%
9-12%
3-7%
10-14%
5-9%
0.5
1.0
1.5
2.0
2.5
Miles

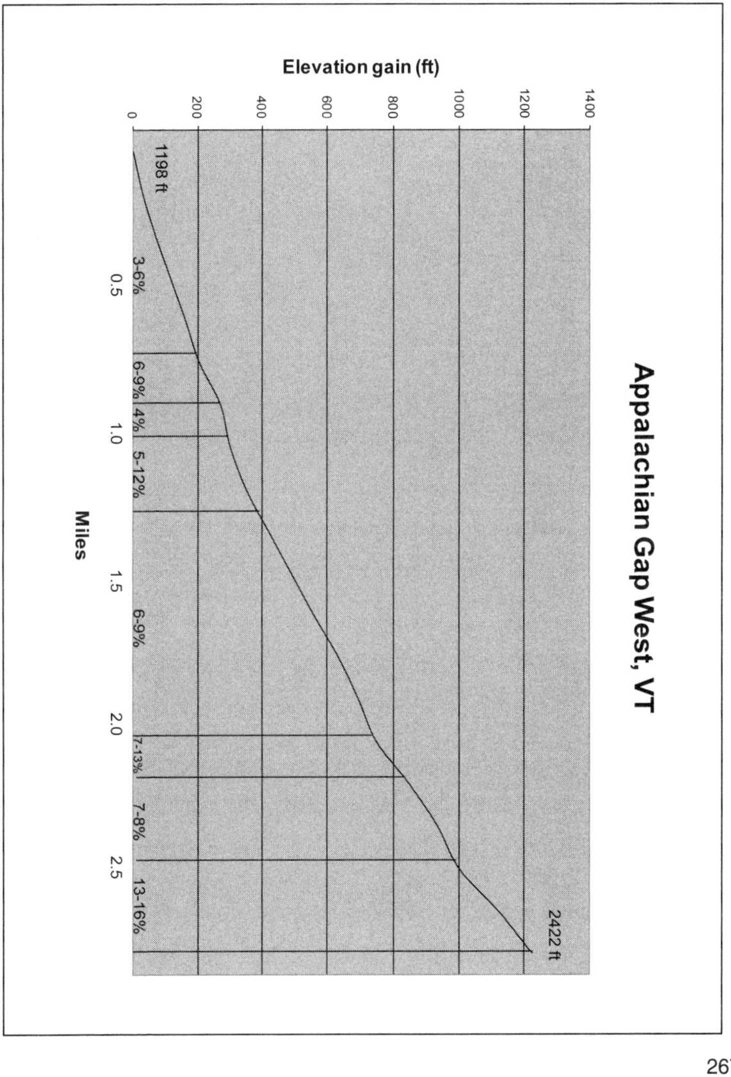
Appalachian Gap West, VT
Elevation gain (ft)
0
200
400
600
800
1000
1200
1400
Miles
0.5
1.0
1.5
2.0
2.5
1198 ft
3-6%
6-9%
4%
5-12%
6-9%
7-13%
7-8%
13-16%
2422 ft

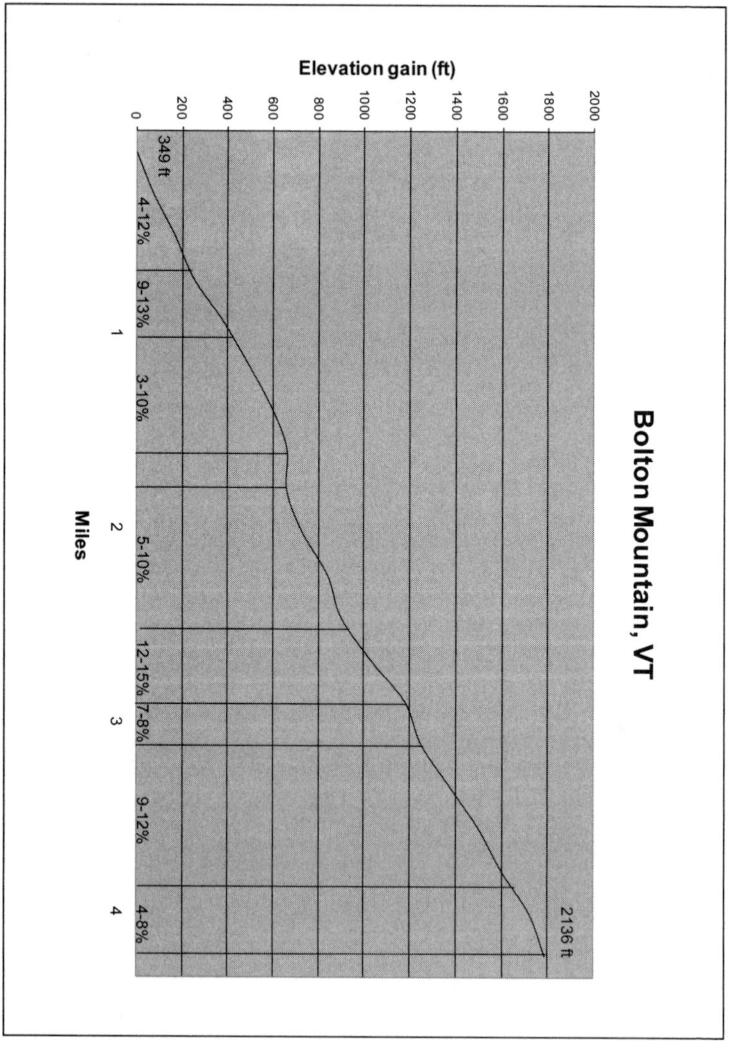
Bolton Mountain, VT
Elevation gain (ft)
0
200
400
600
800
1000
1200
1400
1600
1800
2000
349 ft
4-12%
9-13%
3-10%
5-10%
12-15%
7-8%
9-12%
4-8%
2136 ft
1
2
3
4
Miles

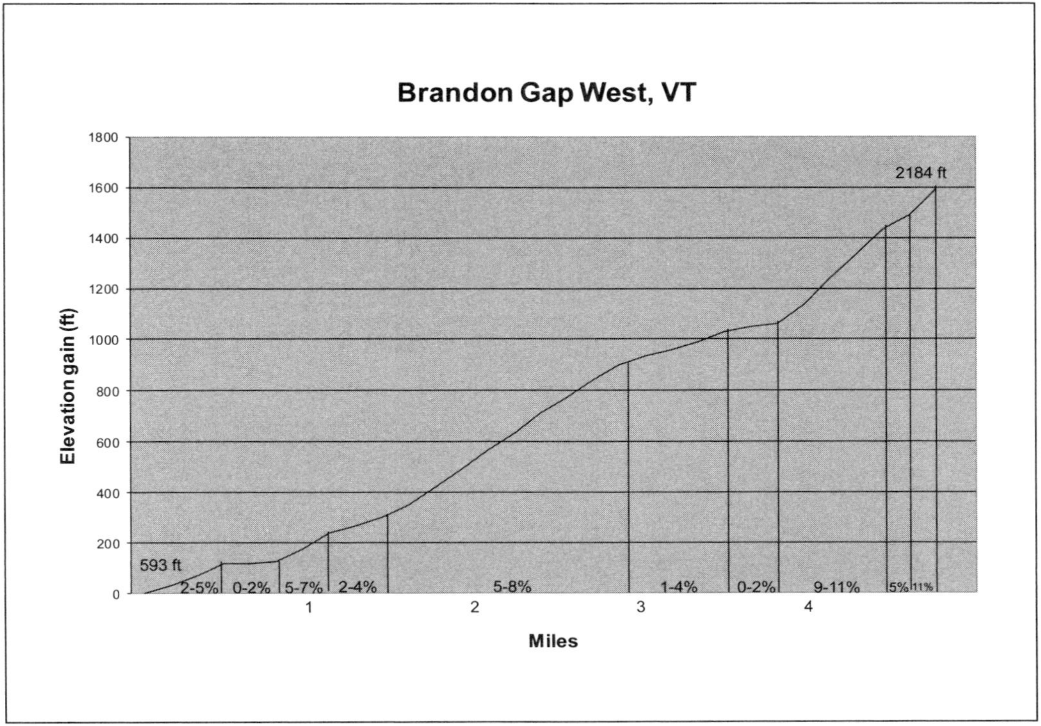
Brandon Gap West, VT
Elevation gain (ft)
0
200
400
600
800
1000
1200
1400
1600
1800
593 ft
2-5%
0-2%
5-7%
2-4%
5-8%
1-4%
0-2%
9-11%
5%
11%
2184 ft
1
2
3
4
Miles

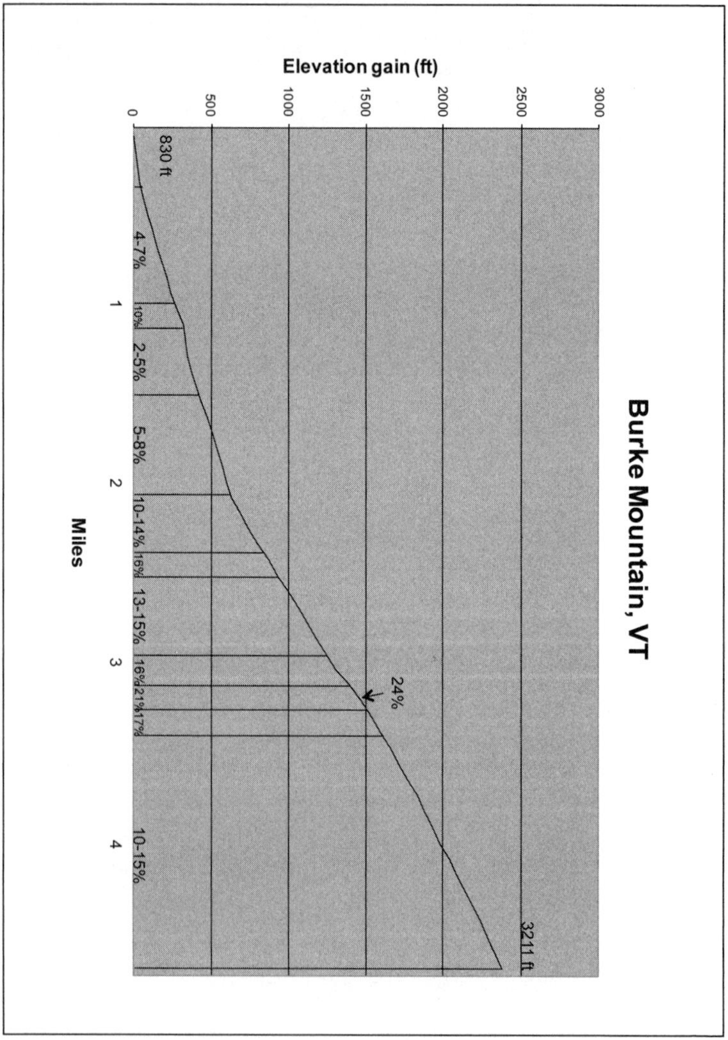
Burke Mountain, VT
Elevation gain (ft)
0
500
1000
1500
2000
2500
3000
Miles
1
2
3
4
830 ft
4-7%
10%
2-5%
5-8%
10-14%
16%
13-15%
16%
21%
17%
24%
10-15%
3211 ft

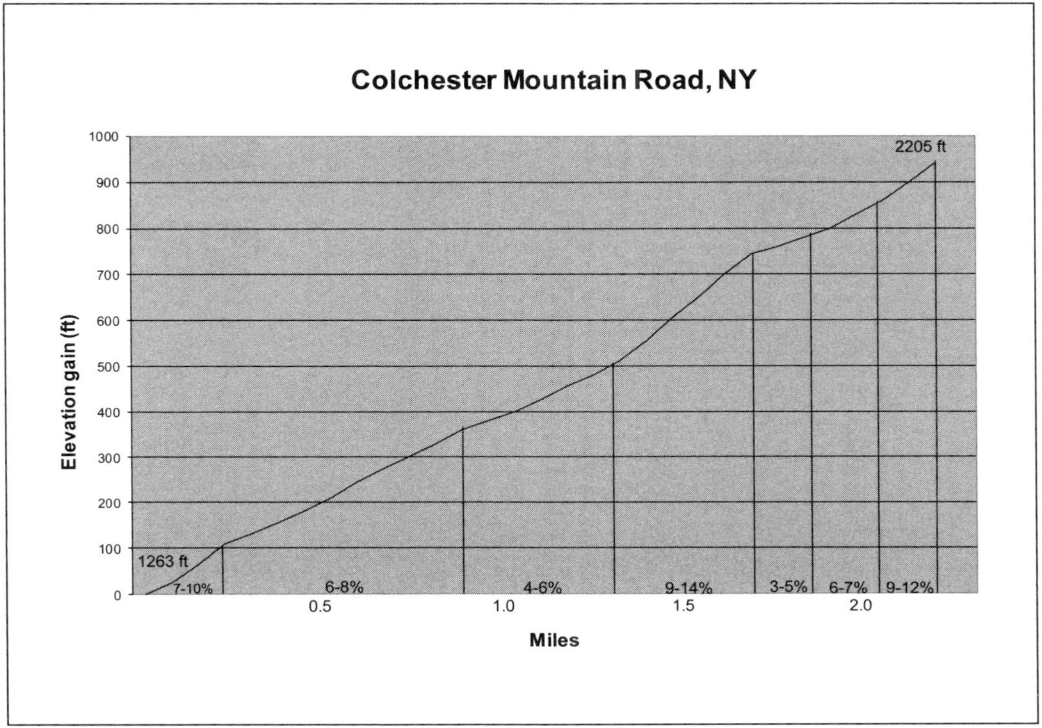
Colchester Mountain Road, NY
Elevation gain (ft)
0
100
200
300
400
500
600
700
800
900
1000
1263 ft
2205 ft
7-10%
6-8%
4-6%
9-14%
3-5%
6-7%
9-12%
0.5
1.0
1.5
2.0
Miles

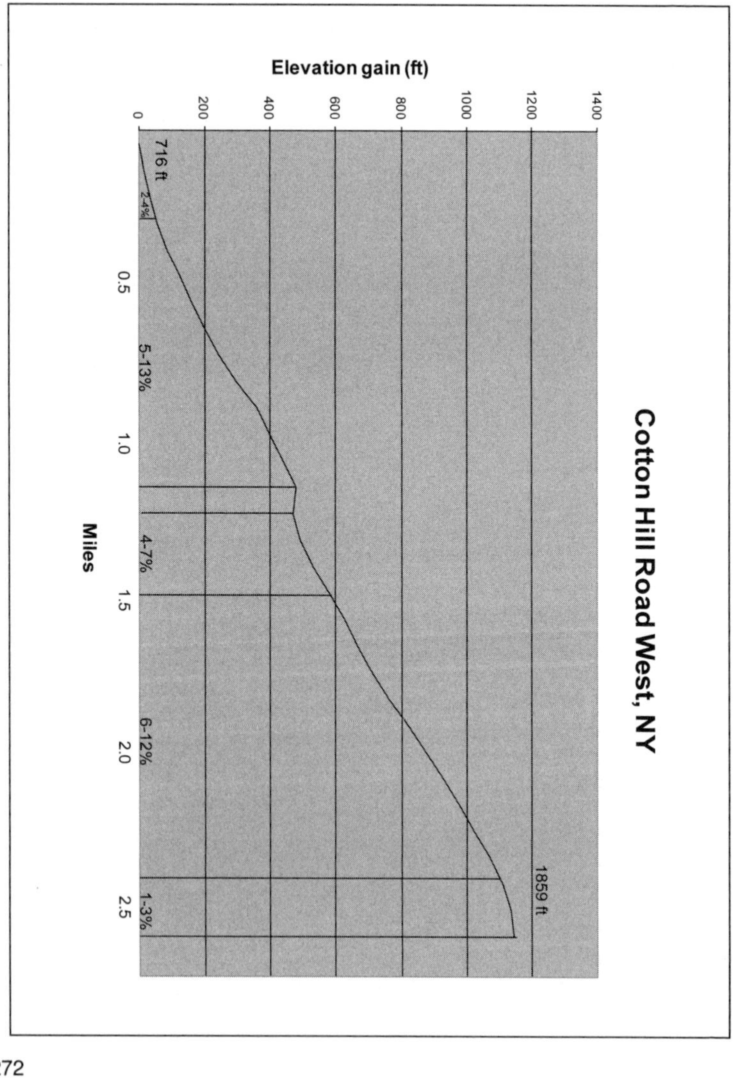
Cotton Hill Road West, NY
Elevation gain (ft)
1400
1200
1000
800
600
400
200
0
716 ft
2.4%
5-13%
4-7%
6-12%
1859 ft
1-3%
0.5
1.0
1.5
2.0
2.5
Miles

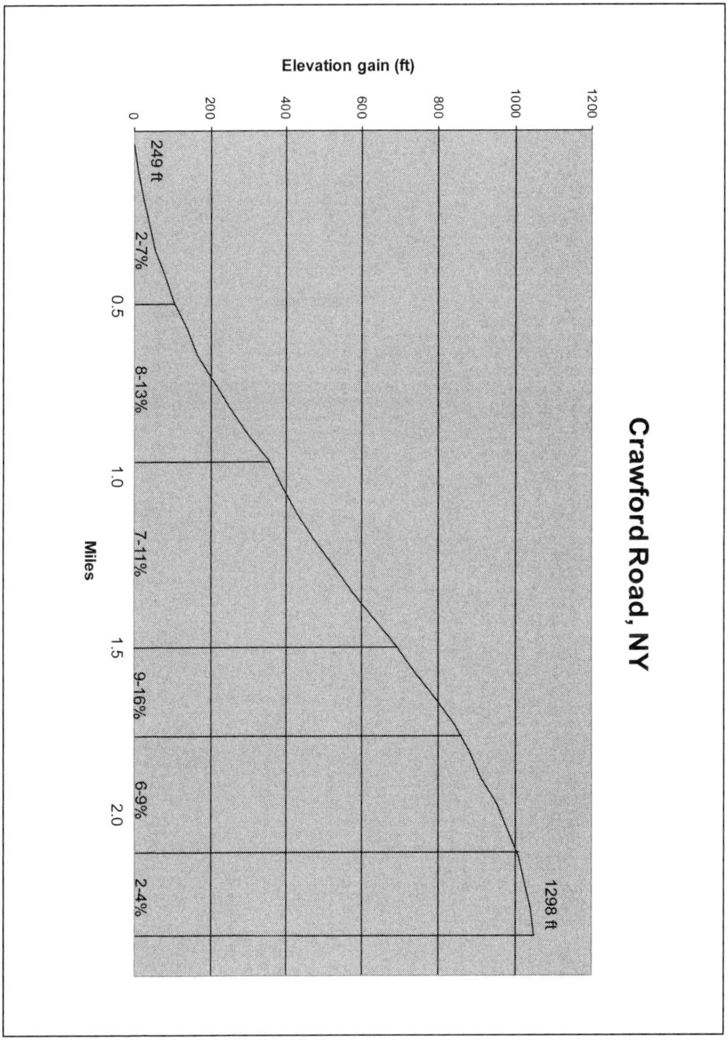

Crawford Road, NY
Elevation gain (ft)
0
200
400
600
800
1000
1200
249 ft
2-7%
8-13%
7-11%
9-16%
6-9%
2-4%
1298 ft
0.5
1.0
1.5
2.0
Miles

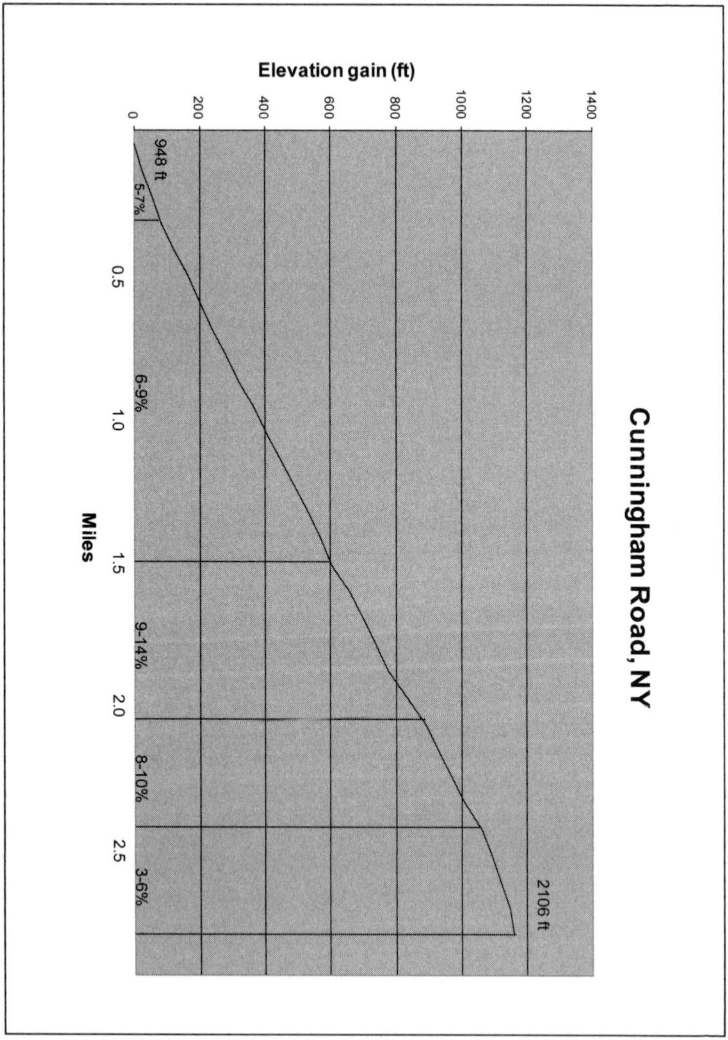
Cunningham Road, NY
Elevation gain (ft)
0
200
400
600
800
1000
1200
1400
948 ft
5-7%
6-9%
9-14%
8-10%
3-6%
2106 ft
0.5
1.0
1.5
2.0
2.5
Miles

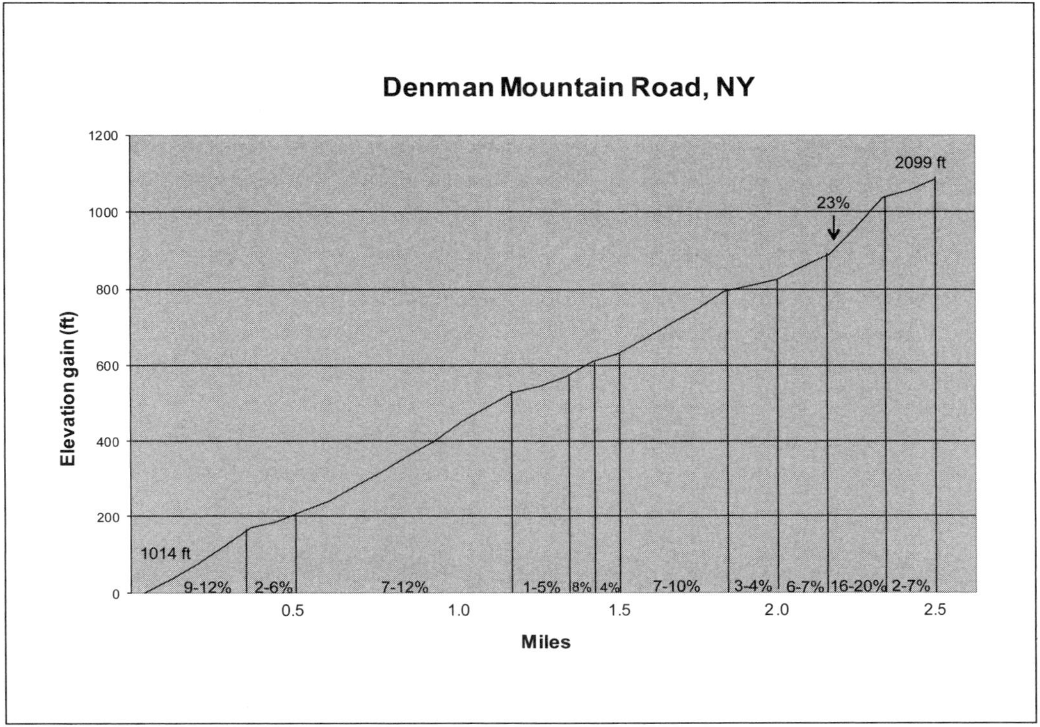
Denman Mountain Road, NY
Elevation gain (ft)
0
200
400
600
800
1000
1200
1014 ft
2099 ft
23%
9-12%
2-6%
7-12%
1-5%
8%
4%
7-10%
3-4%
6-7%
16-20%
2-7%
0.5
1.0
1.5
2.0
2.5
Miles

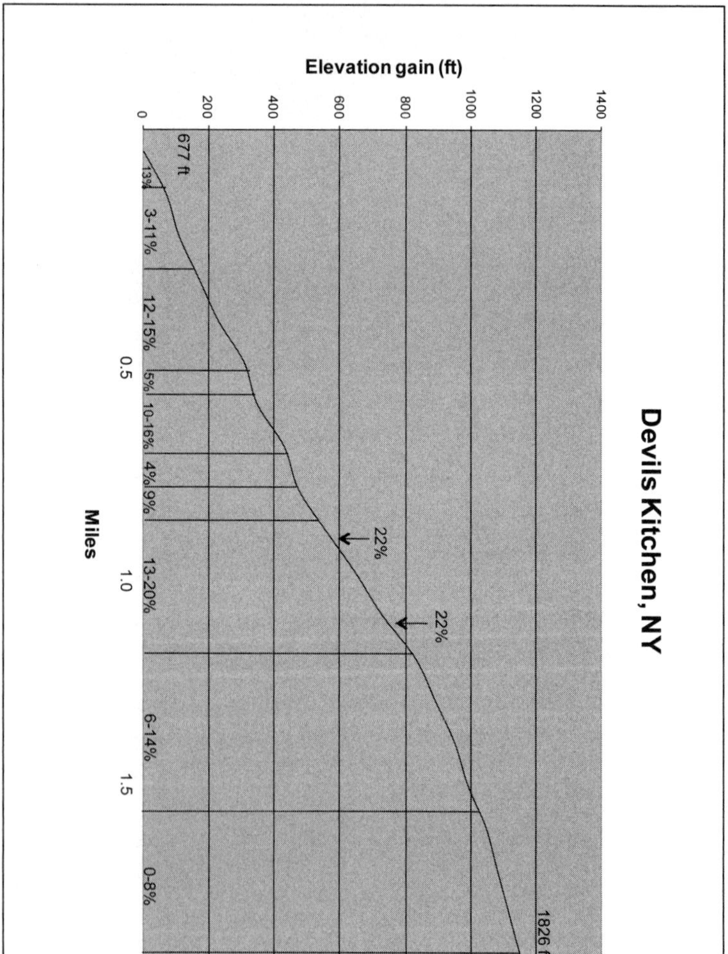
Devils Kitchen, NY
Elevation gain (ft)
0
200
400
600
800
1000
1200
1400
Miles
0.5
1.0
1.5
677 ft
1826 ft
13%
3-11%
12-15%
5%
10-16%
4%
9%
13-20%
6-14%
0-8%
22%
22%

Devils Kitchen/Josh Road, NY

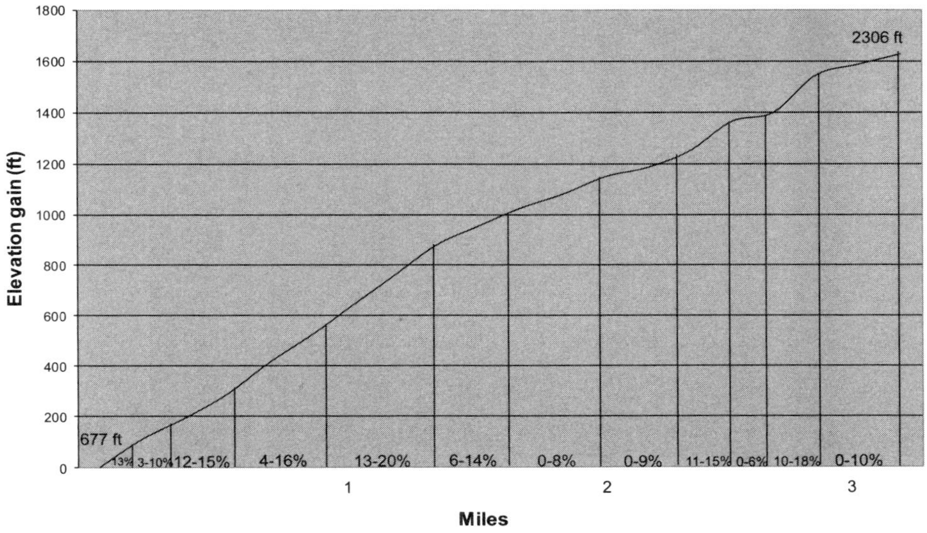

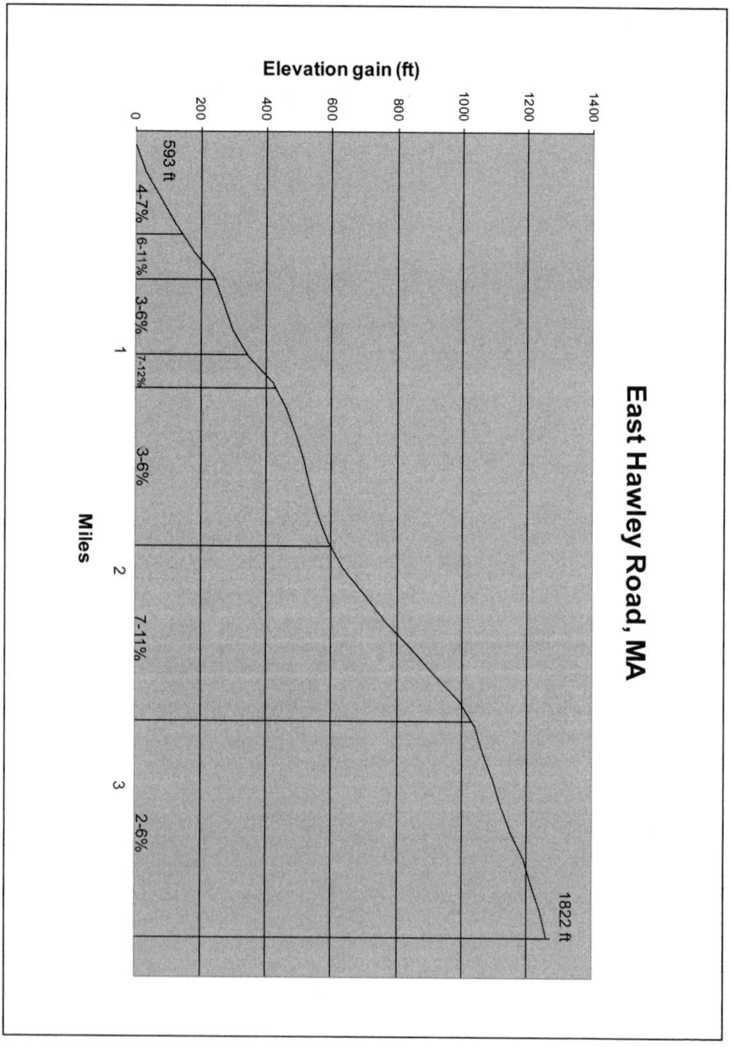
East Hawley Road, MA
Elevation gain (ft)
0
200
400
600
800
1000
1200
1400
593 ft
4-7%
6-11%
3-6%
7-12%
3-6%
7-11%
2-6%
1822 ft
1
2
3
Miles

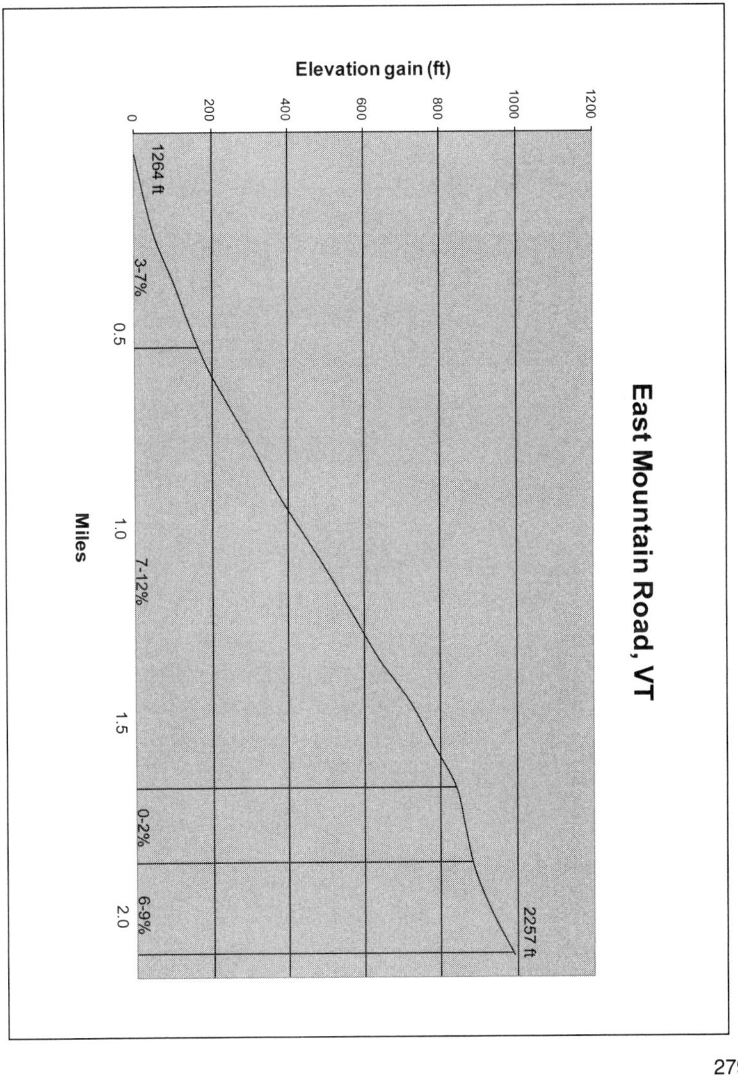
East Mountain Road, VT
Elevation gain (ft)
0
200
400
600
800
1000
1200
Miles
0.5
1.0
1.5
2.0
1264 ft
3-7%
7-12%
0-2%
6-9%
2257 ft

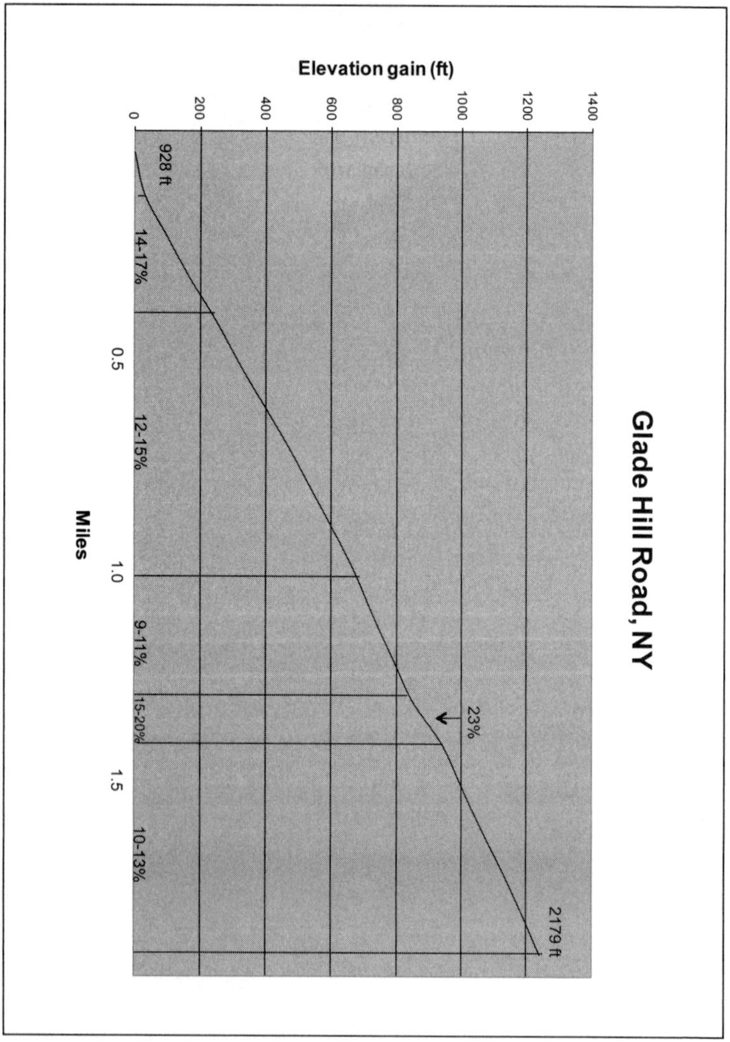
Glade Hill Road, NY
Elevation gain (ft)
0
200
400
600
800
1000
1200
1400
928 ft
14-17%
12-15%
9-11%
15-20%
23%
10-13%
2179 ft
0.5
1.0
1.5
Miles

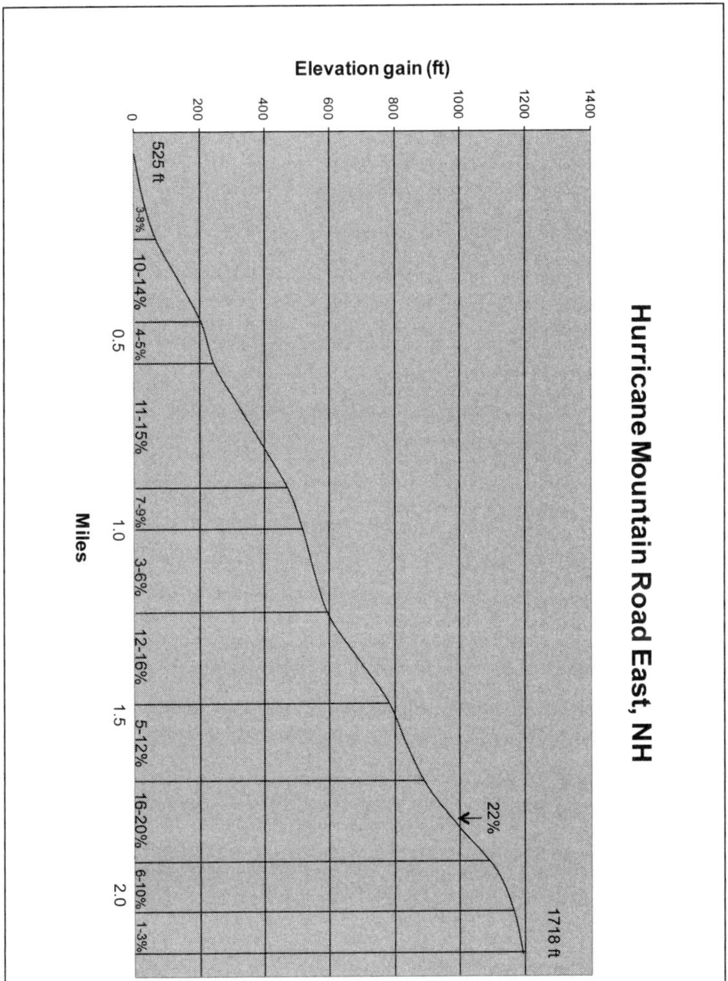
Hurricane Mountain Road East, NH
Elevation gain (ft)
0
200
400
600
800
1000
1200
1400
Miles
0.5
1.0
1.5
2.0
525 ft
3-8%
10-14%
4-5%
11-15%
7-9%
3-6%
12-16%
5-12%
16-20%
22%
6-10%
1-3%
1718 ft

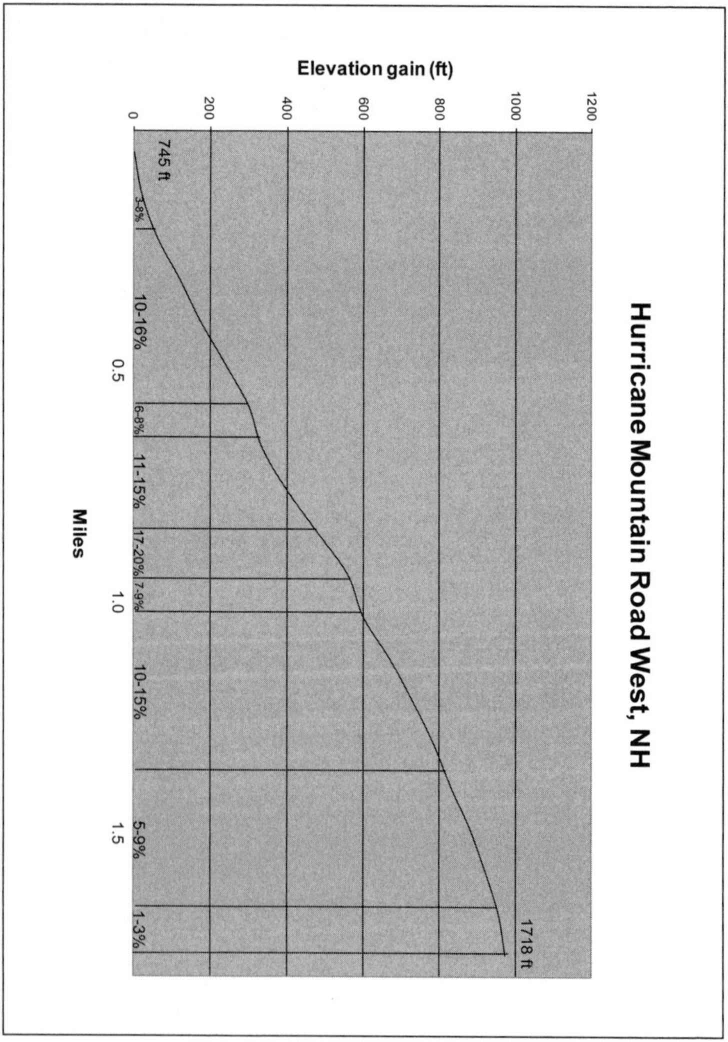
Hurricane Mountain Road West, NH
Elevation gain (ft)
0
200
400
600
800
1000
1200
745 ft
3-8%
10-16%
6-8%
11-15%
17-20%
7-9%
10-15%
5-9%
1-3%
1718 ft
0.5
1.0
1.5
Miles

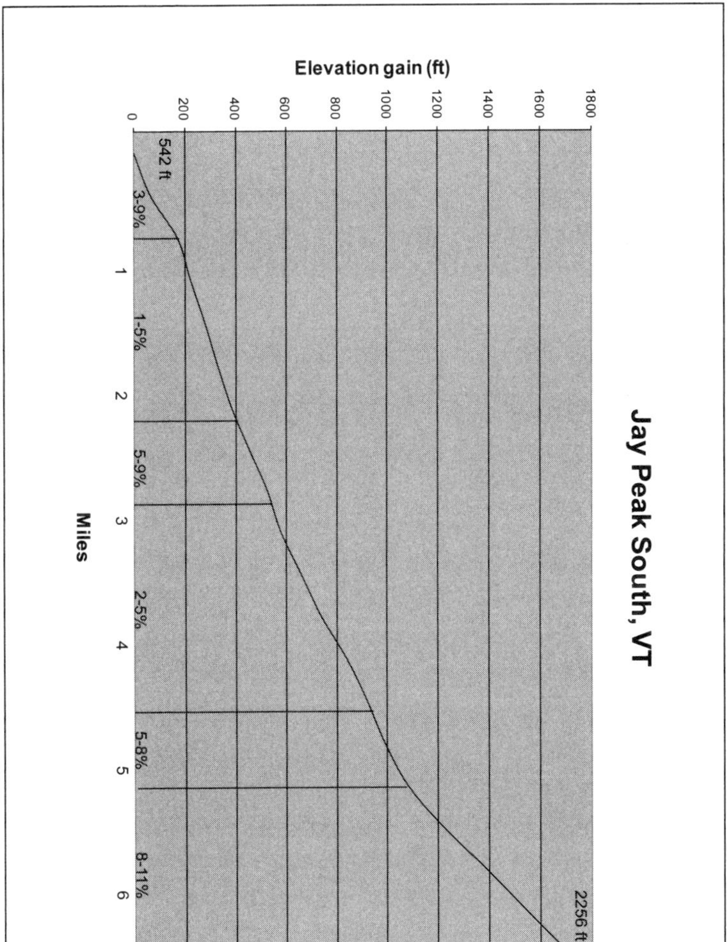
Jay Peak South, VT
Elevation gain (ft)
0
200
400
600
800
1000
1200
1400
1600
1800
542 ft
3-9%
1-5%
5-9%
2-5%
5-8%
8-11%
2256 ft
1
2
3
4
5
6
Miles

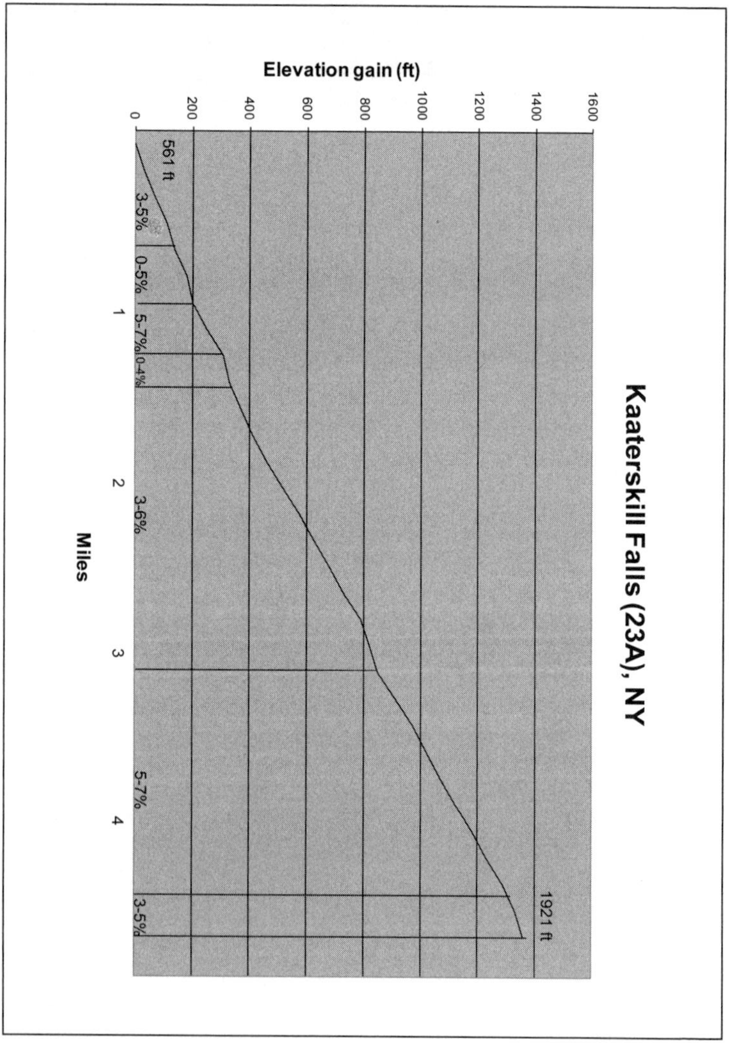
Kaaterskill Falls (23A), NY
Elevation gain (ft)
0
200
400
600
800
1000
1200
1400
1600
561 ft
3-5%
0-5%
5-7%
0-4%
3-6%
5-7%
3-5%
1921 ft
1
2
3
4
Miles

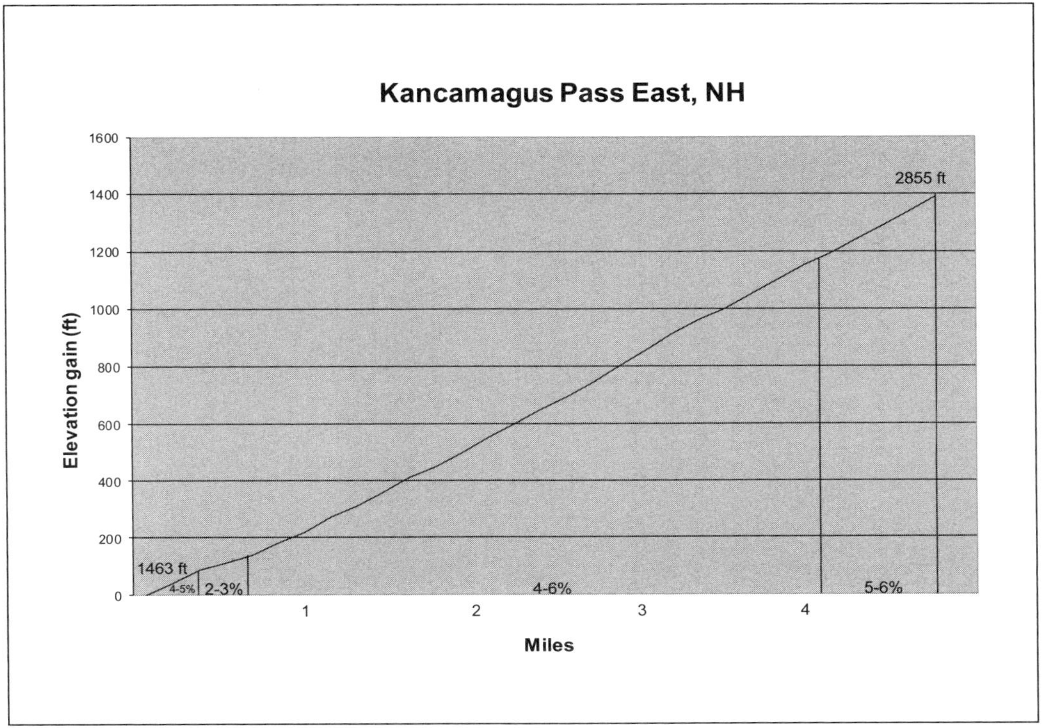
Kancamagus Pass East, NH
Elevation gain (ft)
1600
1400
1200
1000
800
600
400
200
0
1463 ft
4-5%
2-3%
4-6%
5-6%
2855 ft
1
2
3
4
Miles

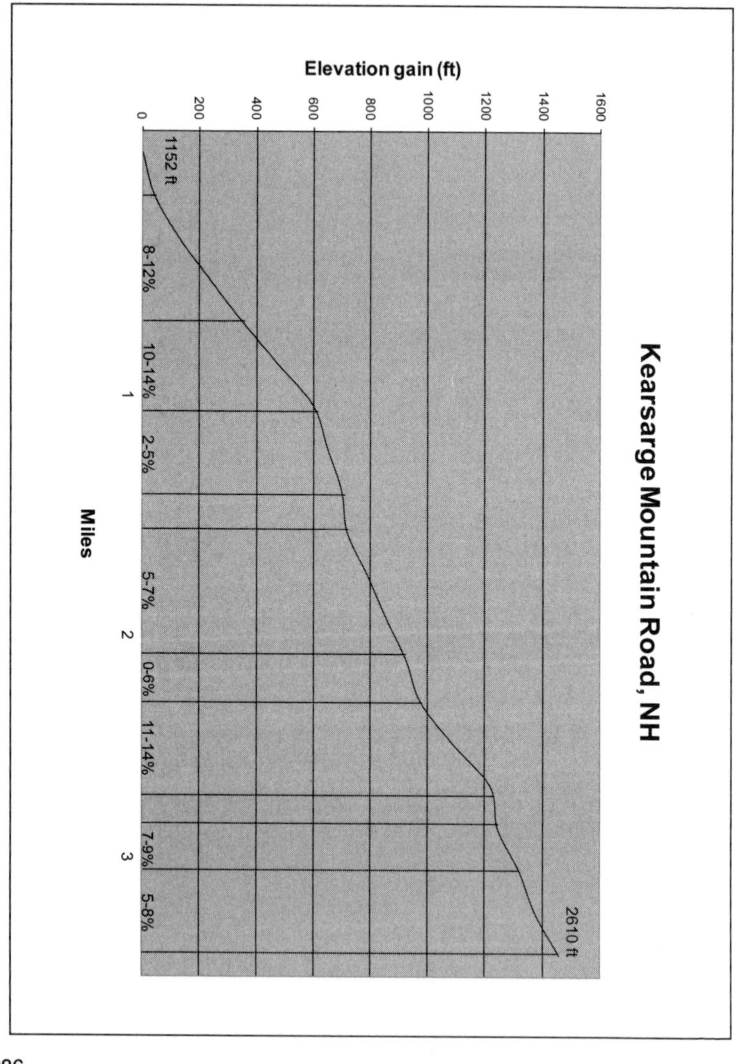
Kearsarge Mountain Road, NH
Elevation gain (ft)
0
200
400
600
800
1000
1200
1400
1600
1152 ft
8-12%
10-14%
2-5%
5-7%
0-6%
11-14%
7-9%
5-8%
2610 ft
1
2
3
Miles

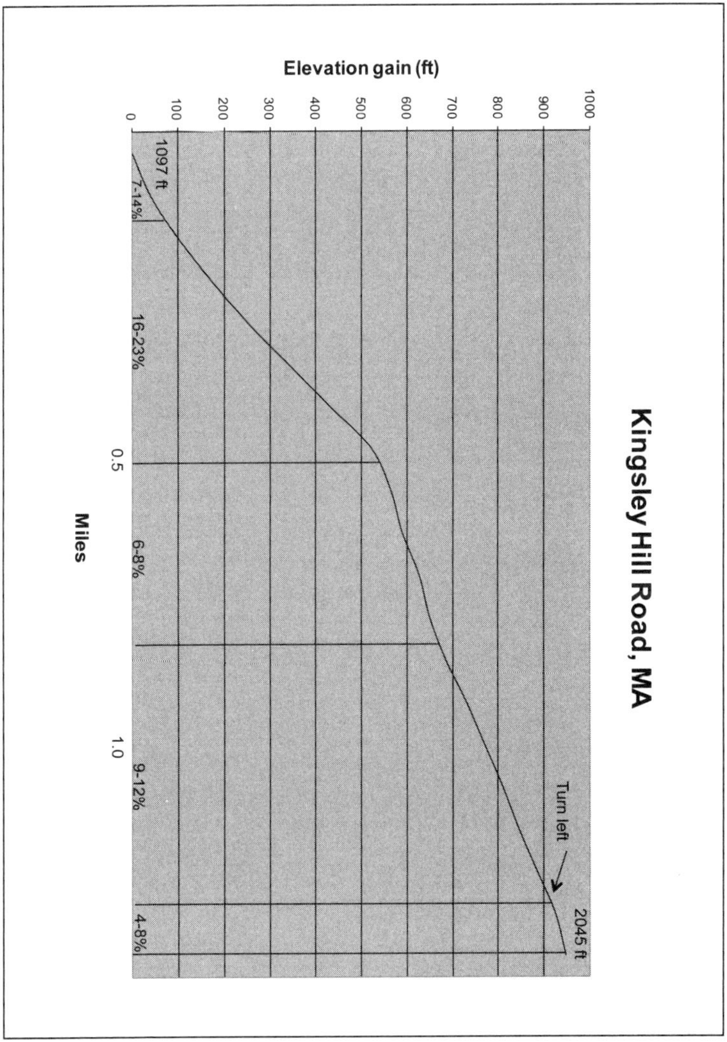

Kingsley Hill Road, MA
Elevation gain (ft)
0
100
200
300
400
500
600
700
800
900
1000
1097 ft
7-14%
16-23%
6-8%
9-12%
Turn left
2045 ft
4-8%
0.5
1.0
Miles

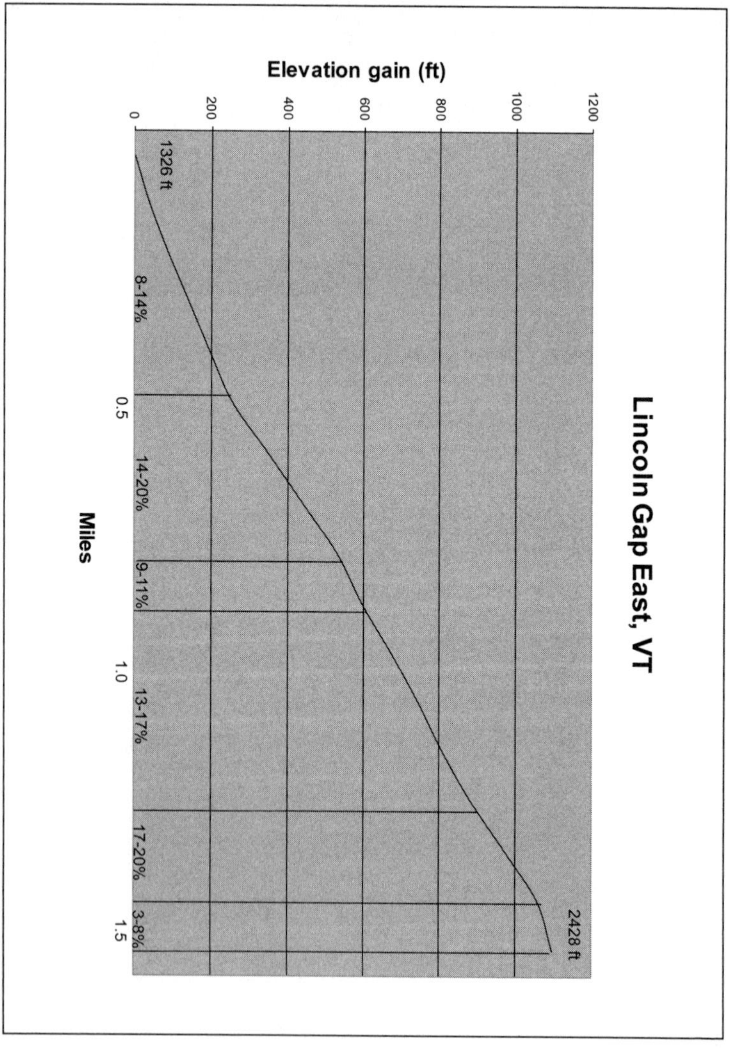
Lincoln Gap East, VT
Elevation gain (ft)
0
200
400
600
800
1000
1200
1326 ft
2428 ft
8-14%
14-20%
9-11%
13-17%
17-20%
3-8%
0.5
1.0
1.5
Miles

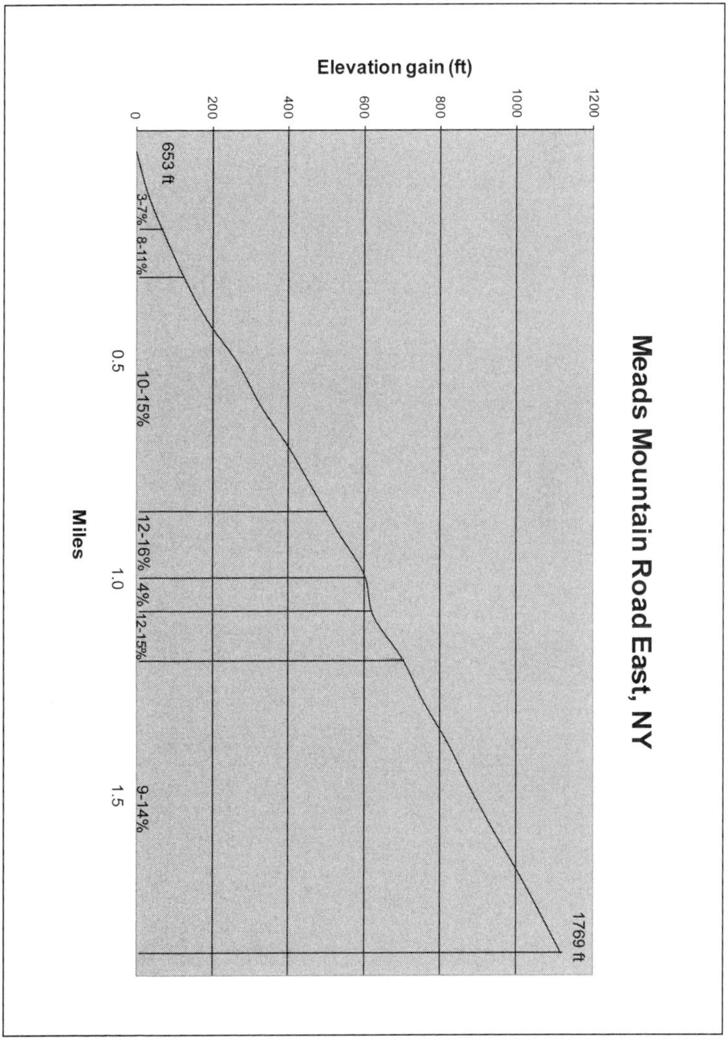

Meads Mountain Road East, NY
Elevation gain (ft)
0
200
400
600
800
1000
1200
Miles
0.5
1.0
1.5
653 ft
3-7%
8-11%
10-15%
12-16%
4%
12-15%
9-14%
1769 ft

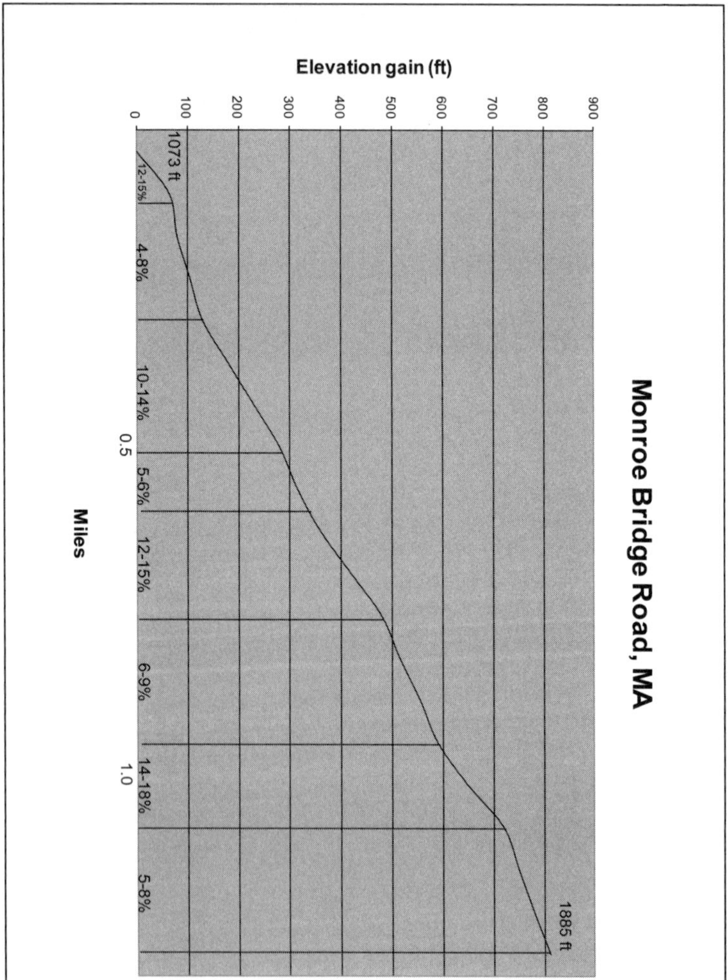
Monroe Bridge Road, MA
Elevation gain (ft)
0
100
200
300
400
500
600
700
800
900
Miles
0.5
1.0
1073 ft
1885 ft
12-15%
4-8%
10-14%
5-6%
12-15%
6-9%
14-18%
5-8%

Moore Hill Road, NY

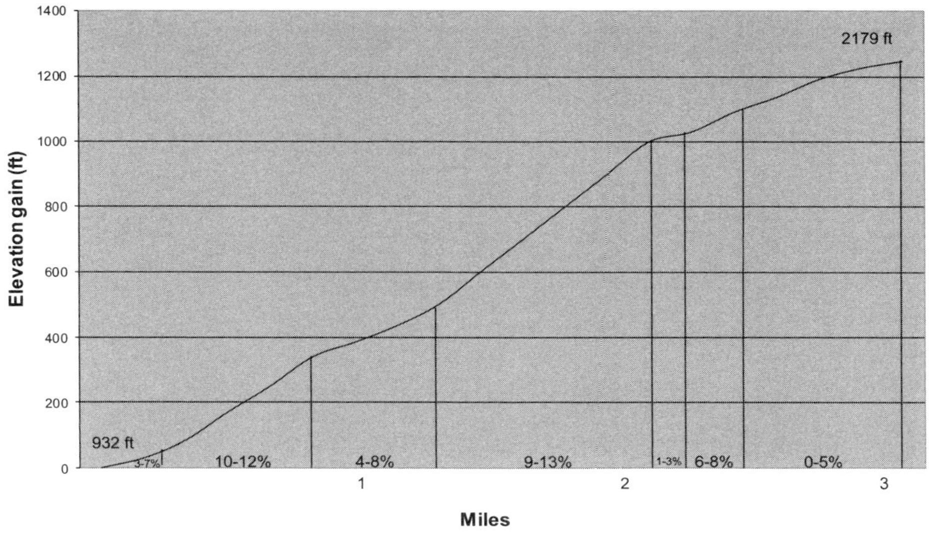

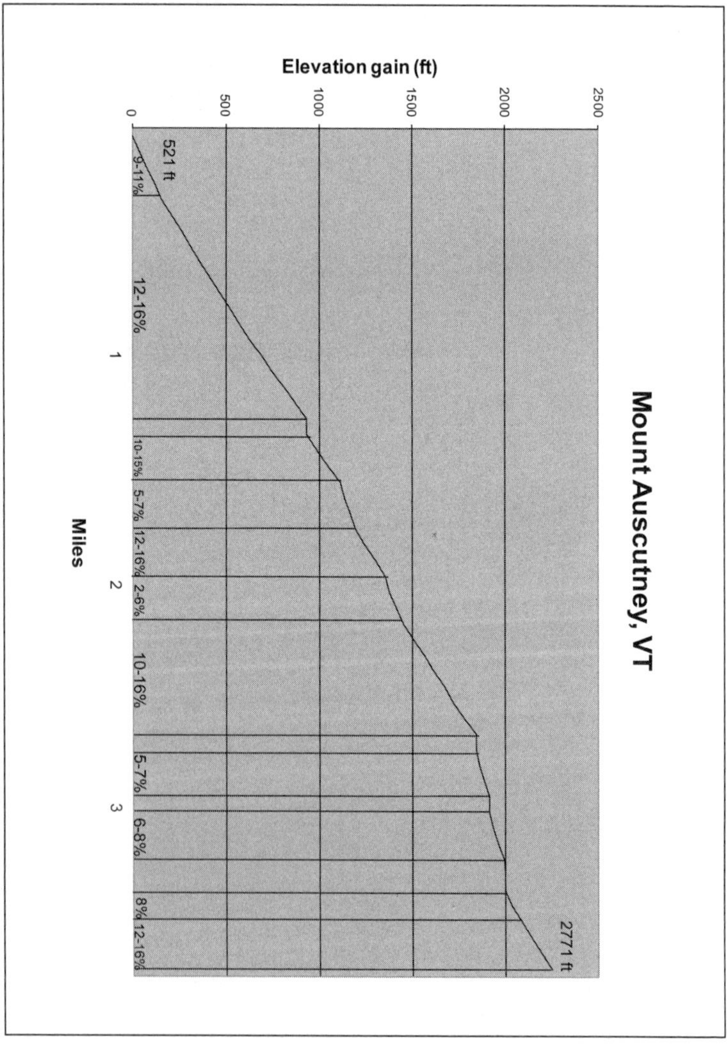

Mount Ascutney, VT
Elevation gain (ft)
0
500
1000
1500
2000
2500
Miles
1
2
3
521 ft
9-11%
12-16%
10-15%
5-7%
12-16%
2-6%
10-16%
5-7%
6-8%
8%
12-16%
2771 ft

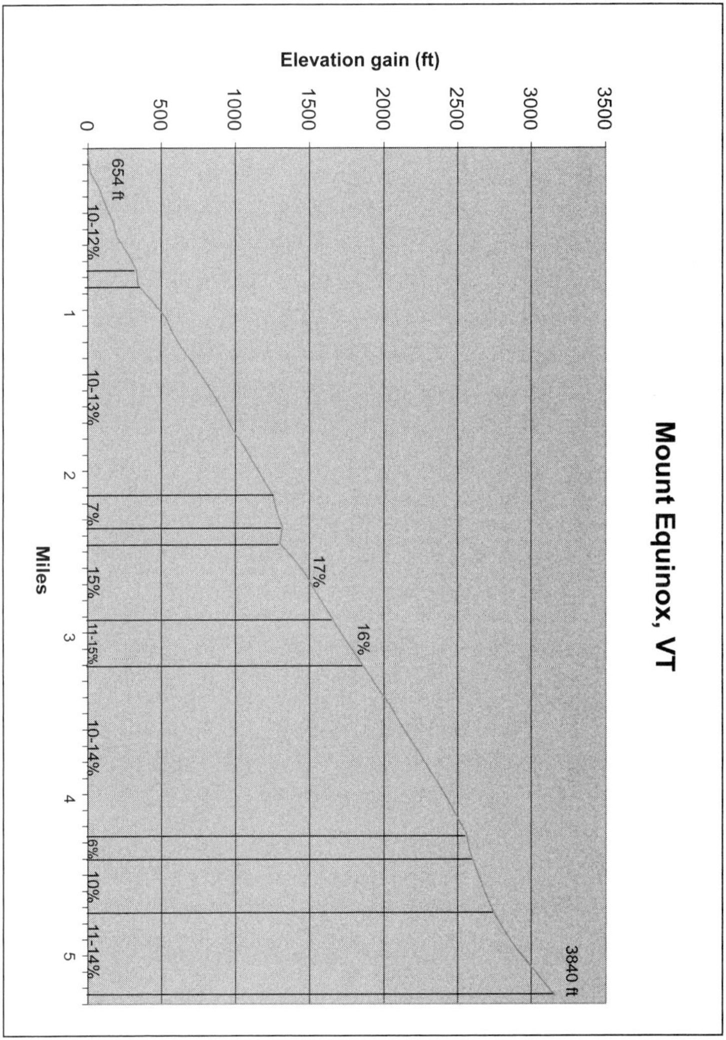

Mount Equinox, VT
Elevation gain (ft)
3500
3000
2500
2000
1500
1000
500
0
654 ft
10-12%
10-13%
7%
17%
15%
16%
11-15%
10-14%
6%
10%
11-14%
3840 ft
1
2
3
4
5
Miles

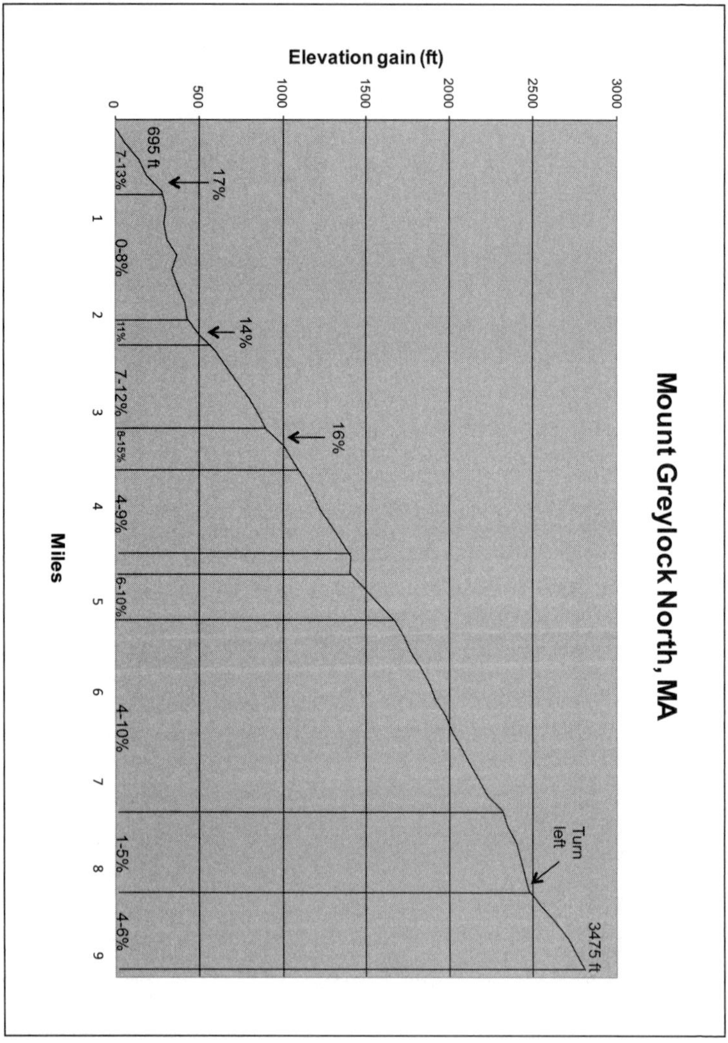

Mount Greylock North, MA
Elevation gain (ft)
0
500
1000
1500
2000
2500
3000
Miles
1
2
3
4
5
6
7
8
9
695 ft
7-13%
17%
0-8%
11%
14%
7-12%
8-15%
16%
4-9%
6-10%
4-10%
1-5%
Turn left
4-6%
3475 ft

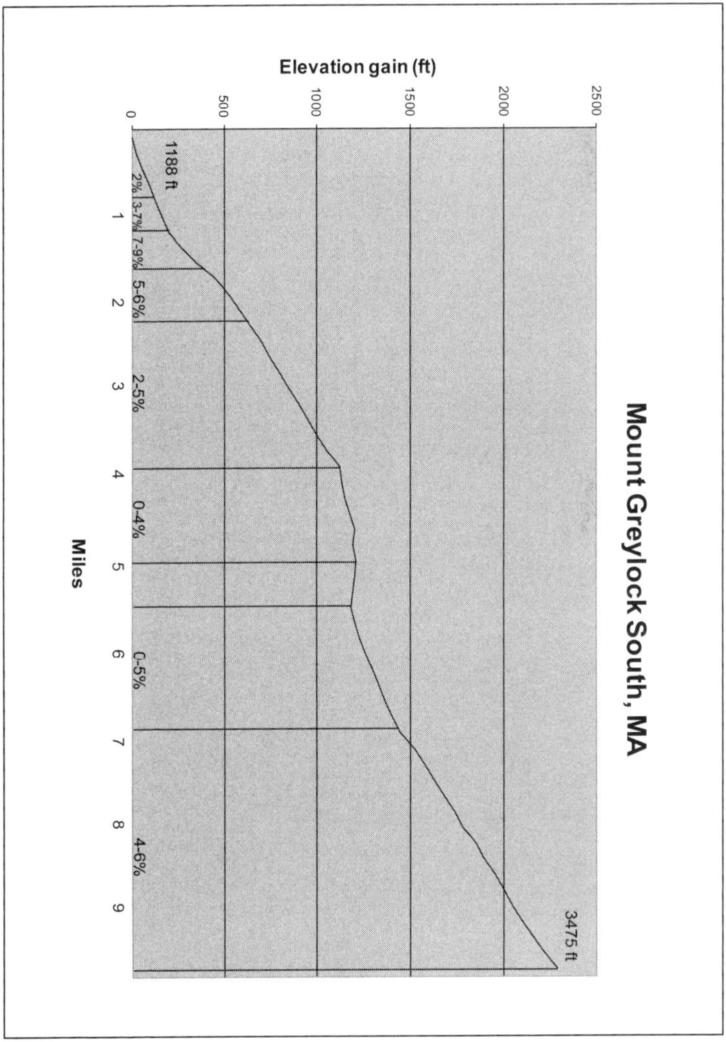

Mount Greylock South, MA
Elevation gain (ft)
0
500
1000
1500
2000
2500
1188 ft
3475 ft
2%
3-7%
7-9%
5-6%
2-5%
0-4%
0-5%
4-6%
1
2
3
4
5
6
7
8
9
Miles

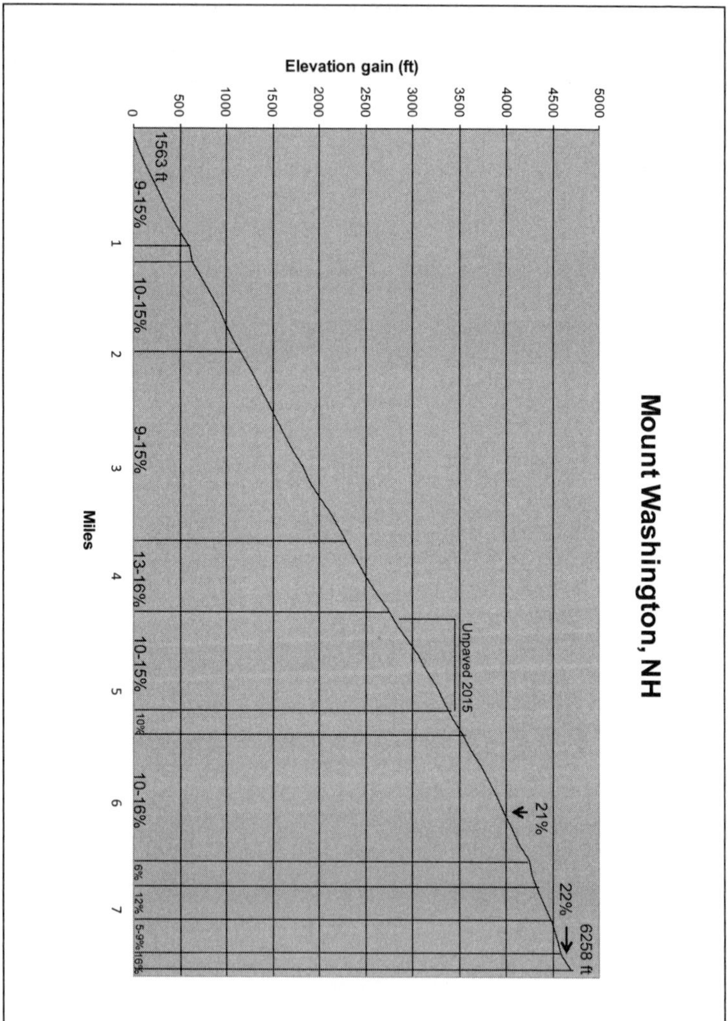
Mount Washington, NH
Elevation gain (ft)
0
500
1000
1500
2000
2500
3000
3500
4000
4500
5000
Miles
1
2
3
4
5
6
7
1563 ft
9-15%
10-15%
9-15%
13-16%
10-15%
10%
10-16%
6%
12%
5-9%
16%
21%
22%
6258 ft
Unpaved 2015

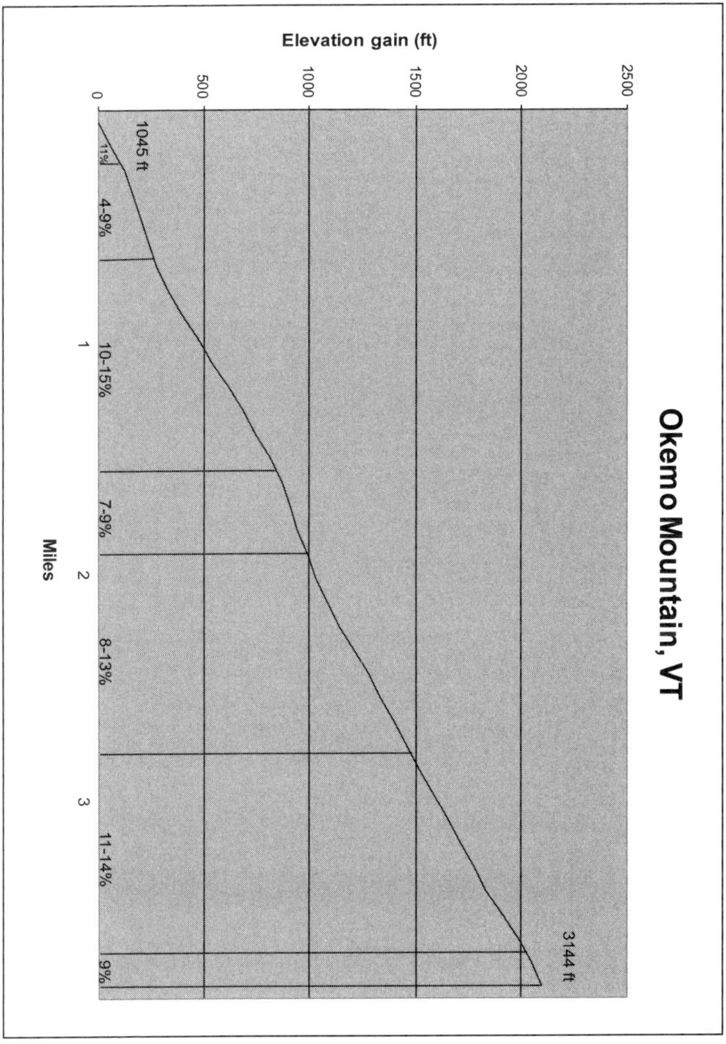

Okemo Mountain, VT
Elevation gain (ft)
0
500
1000
1500
2000
2500
Miles
0
1
2
3
1045 ft
3144 ft
11%
4-9%
10-15%
7-9%
8-13%
11-14%
9%

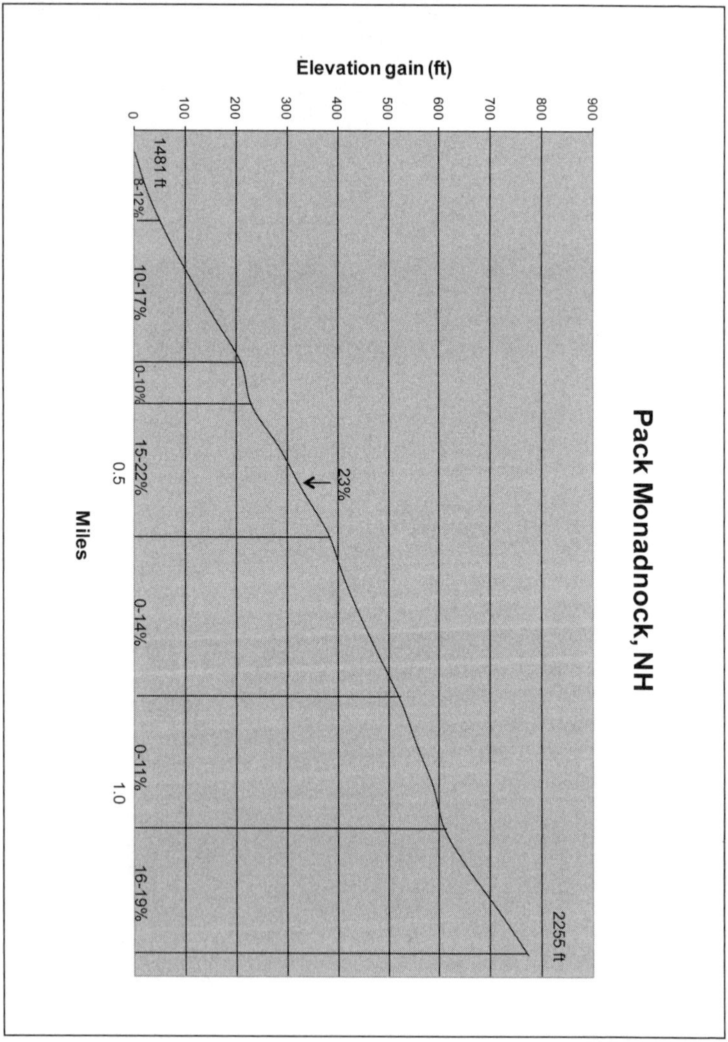

Pack Monadnock, NH
Elevation gain (ft)
0
100
200
300
400
500
600
700
800
900
1481 ft
8-12%
10-17%
0-10%
15-22%
23%
0-14%
0-11%
16-19%
2255 ft
0.5
1.0
Miles

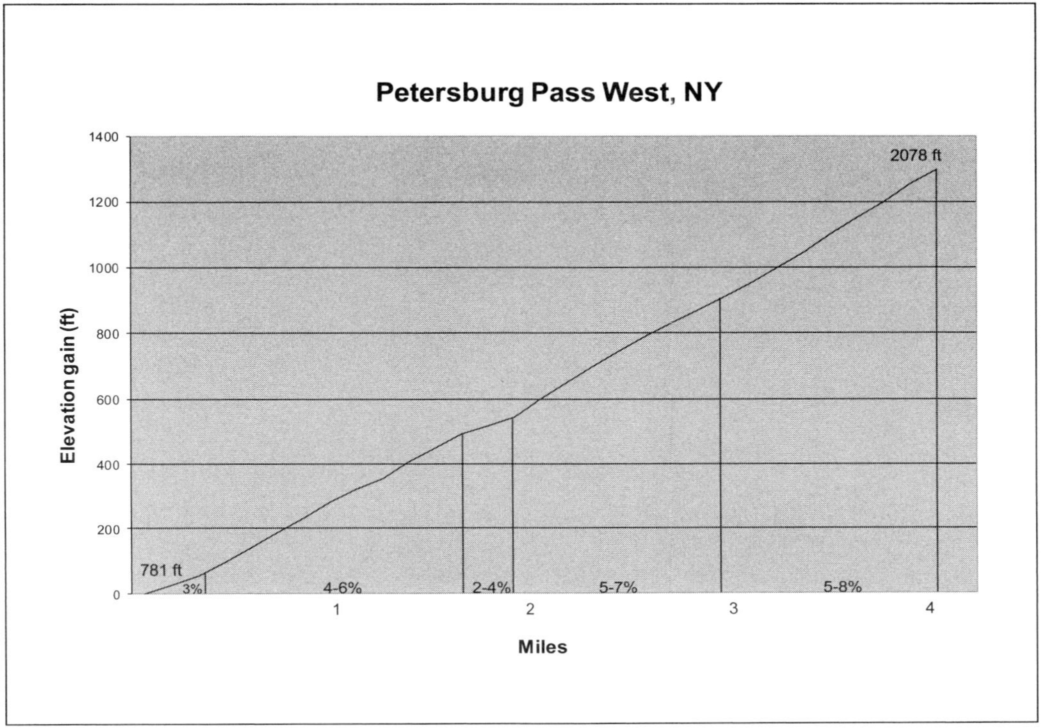

Petersburg Pass West, NY
Elevation gain (ft)
1400
1200
1000
800
600
400
200
0
781 ft
2078 ft
3%
4-6%
2-4%
5-7%
5-8%
1
2
3
4
Miles

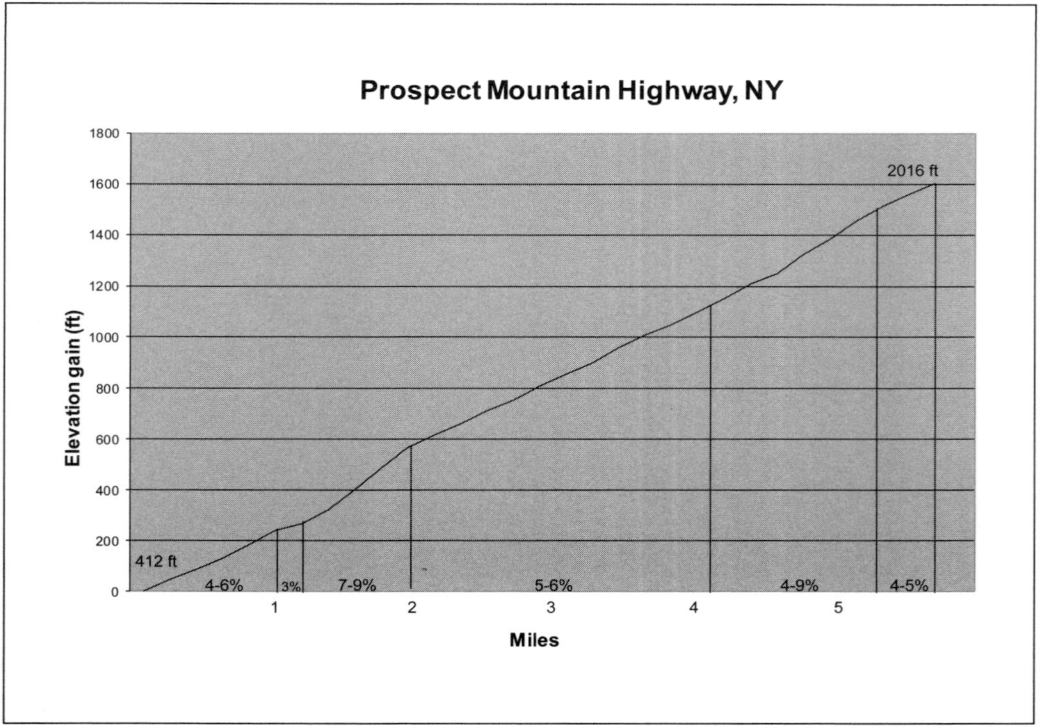

Prospect Mountain Highway, NY
Elevation gain (ft)
1800
1600
1400
1200
1000
800
600
400
200
0
2016 ft
412 ft
4-6%
3%
7-9%
5-6%
4-9%
4-5%
1
2
3
4
5
Miles

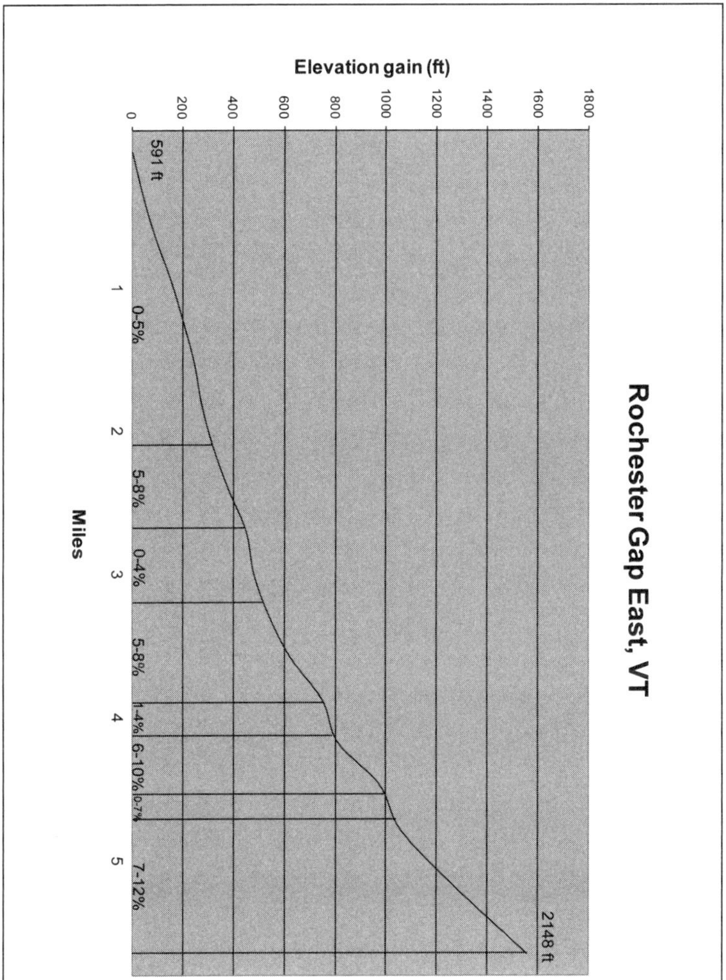
Rochester Gap East, VT
Elevation gain (ft)
0
200
400
600
800
1000
1200
1400
1600
1800
591 ft
2148 ft
0-5%
5-8%
0-4%
5-8%
1-4%
6-10%
0-7%
7-12%
1
2
3
4
5
Miles

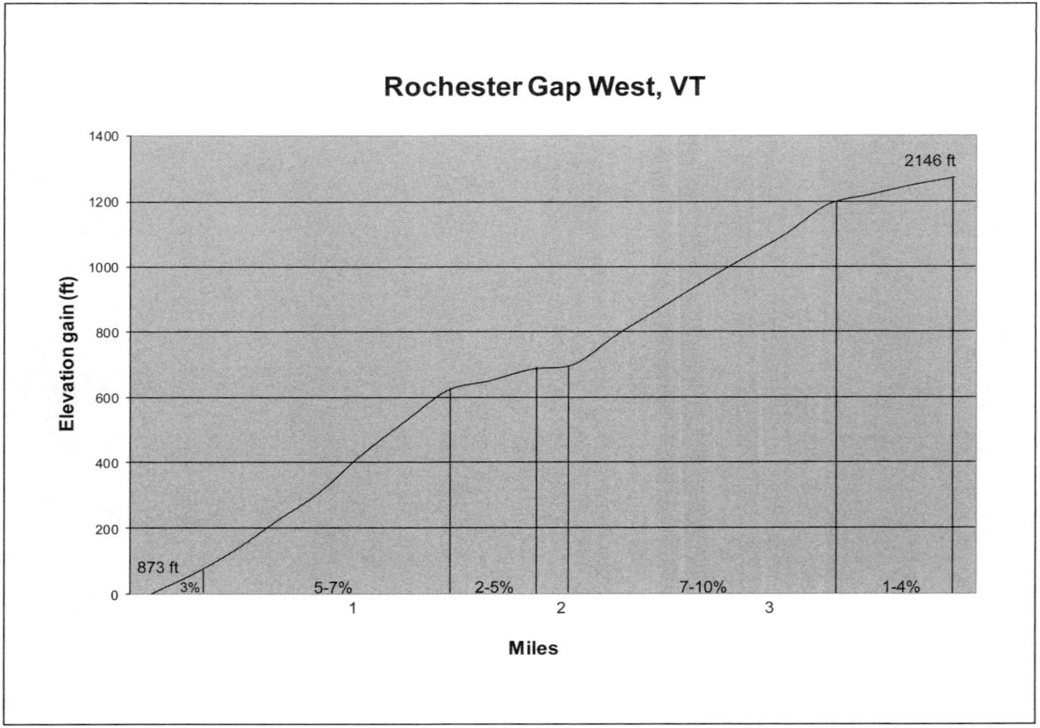
Rochester Gap West, VT
Elevation gain (ft)
1400
1200
1000
800
600
400
200
0
873 ft
3%
5-7%
2-5%
7-10%
1-4%
2146 ft
1
2
3
Miles

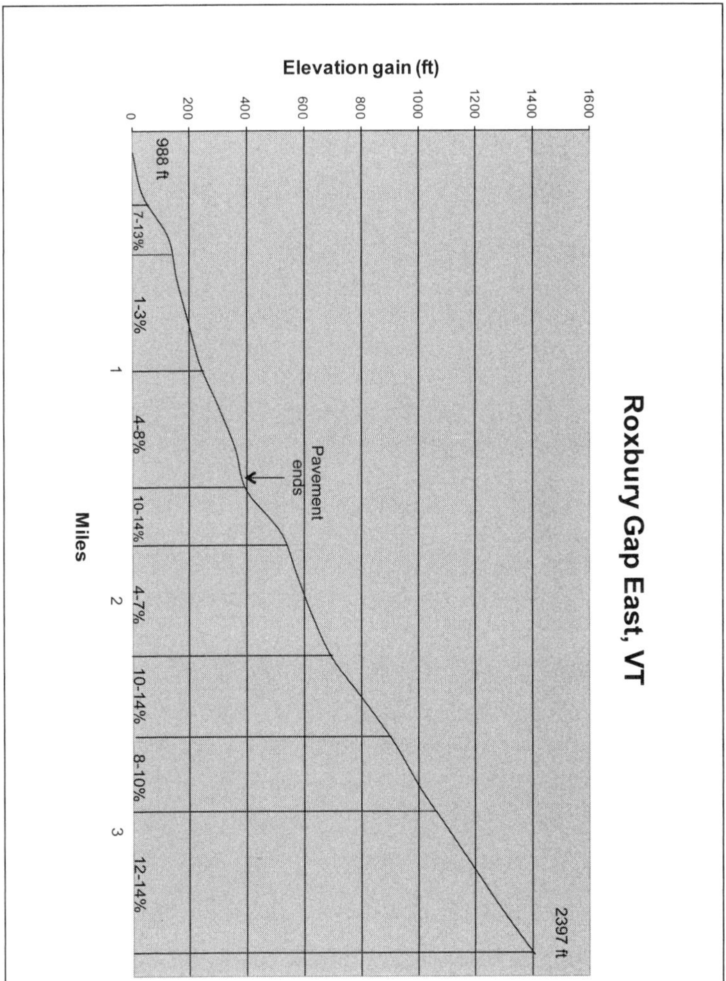
Roxbury Gap East, VT
Elevation gain (ft)
0
200
400
600
800
1000
1200
1400
1600
988 ft
7-13%
1-3%
4-8%
Pavement ends
10-14%
4-7%
10-14%
8-10%
12-14%
2397 ft
1
2
3
Miles

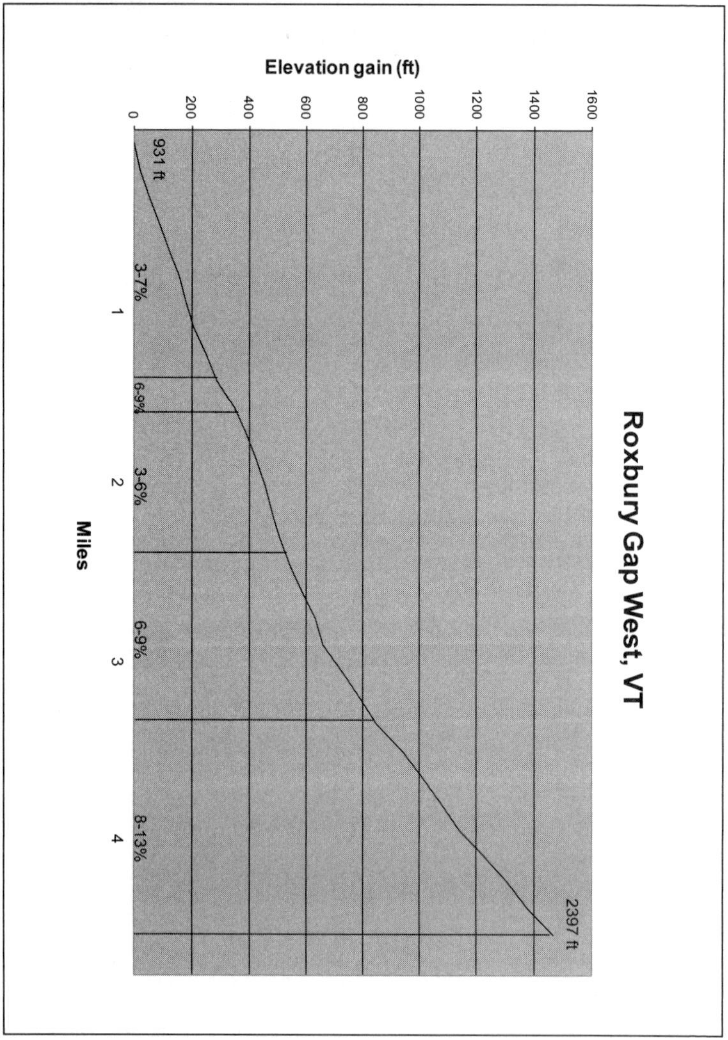

Roxbury Gap West, VT
Elevation gain (ft)
0
200
400
600
800
1000
1200
1400
1600
931 ft
3-7%
6-9%
3-6%
6-9%
8-13%
2397 ft
1
2
3
4
Miles

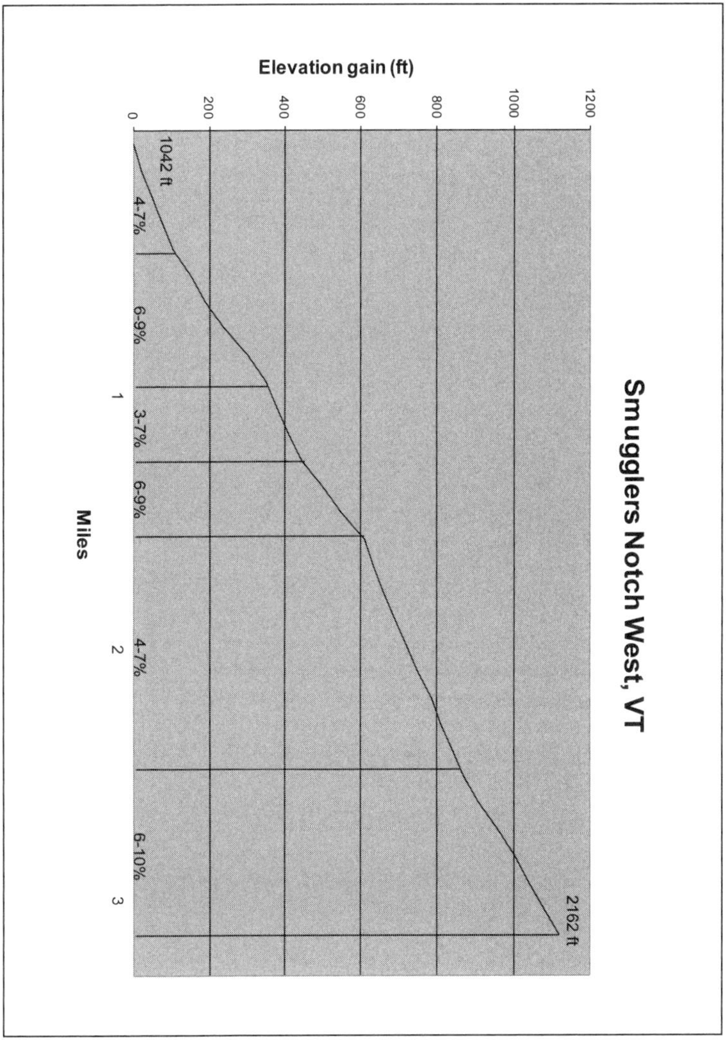
Smugglers Notch West, VT
Elevation gain (ft)
0
200
400
600
800
1000
1200
1042 ft
4-7%
6-9%
3-7%
6-9%
4-7%
6-10%
2162 ft
1
2
3
Miles

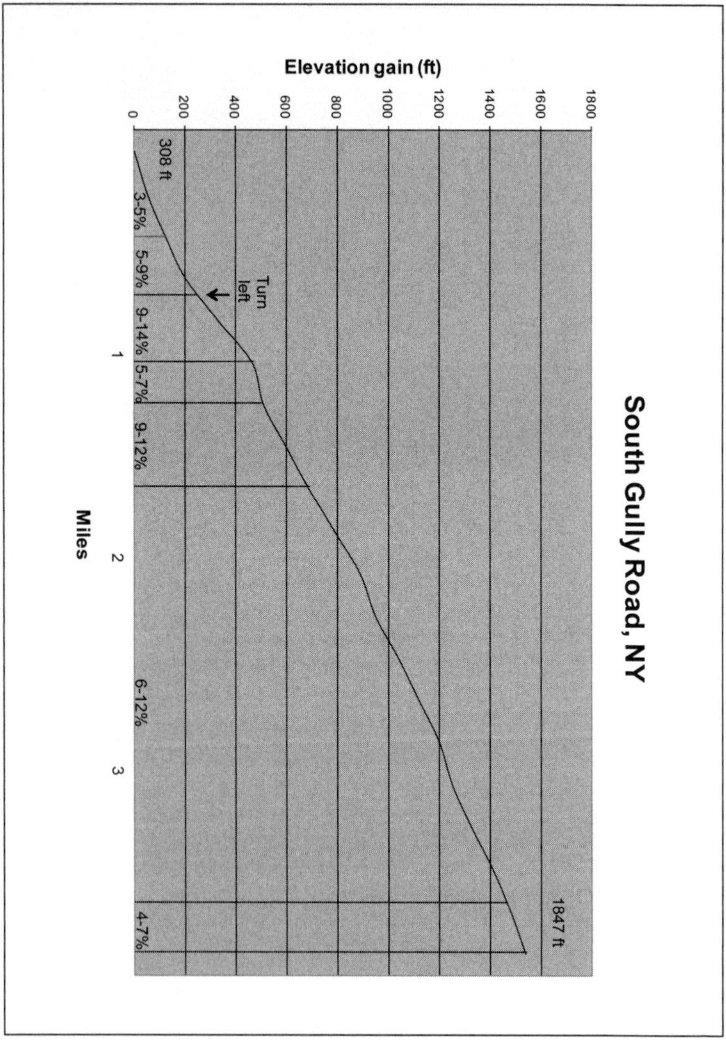
South Gully Road, NY
Elevation gain (ft)
0
200
400
600
800
1000
1200
1400
1600
1800
Miles
1
2
3
308 ft
1847 ft
Turn left
3-5%
5-9%
9-14%
5-7%
9-12%
6-12%
4-7%

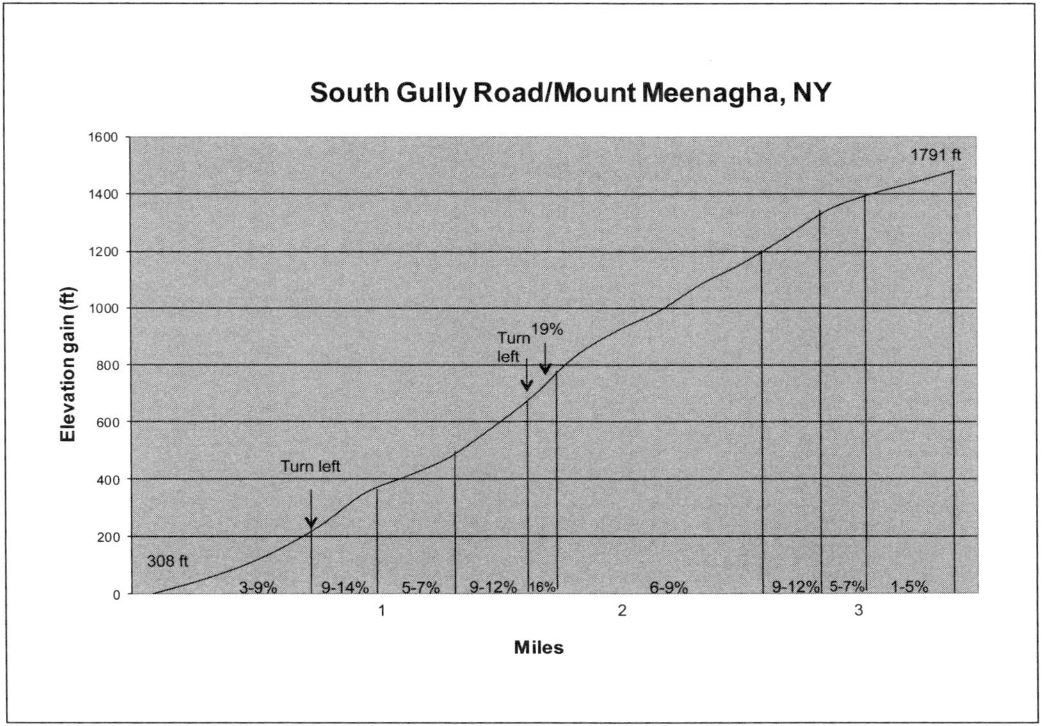
South Gully Road/Mount Meenagha, NY
Elevation gain (ft)
1600
1400
1200
1000
800
600
400
200
0
1791 ft
Turn
left
19%
Turn left
308 ft
3-9%
9-14%
5-7%
9-12%
16%
6-9%
9-12%
5-7%
1-5%
1
2
3
Miles

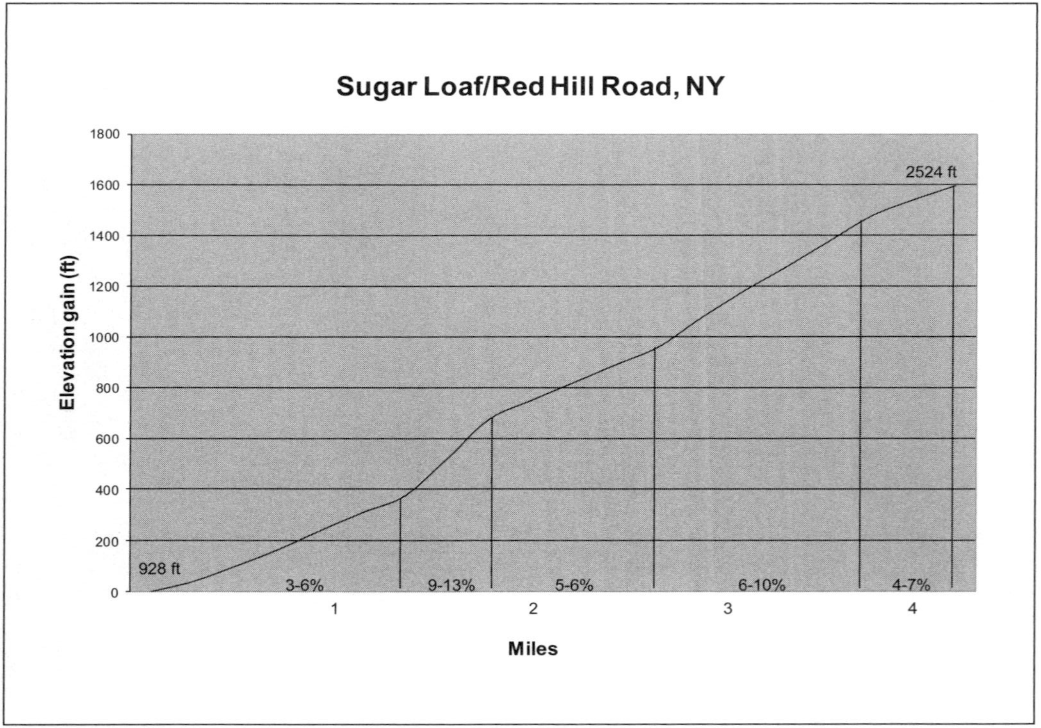
Sugar Loaf/Red Hill Road, NY
Elevation gain (ft)
1800
1600
1400
1200
1000
800
600
400
200
0
928 ft
2524 ft
3-6%
9-13%
5-6%
6-10%
4-7%
1
2
3
4
Miles

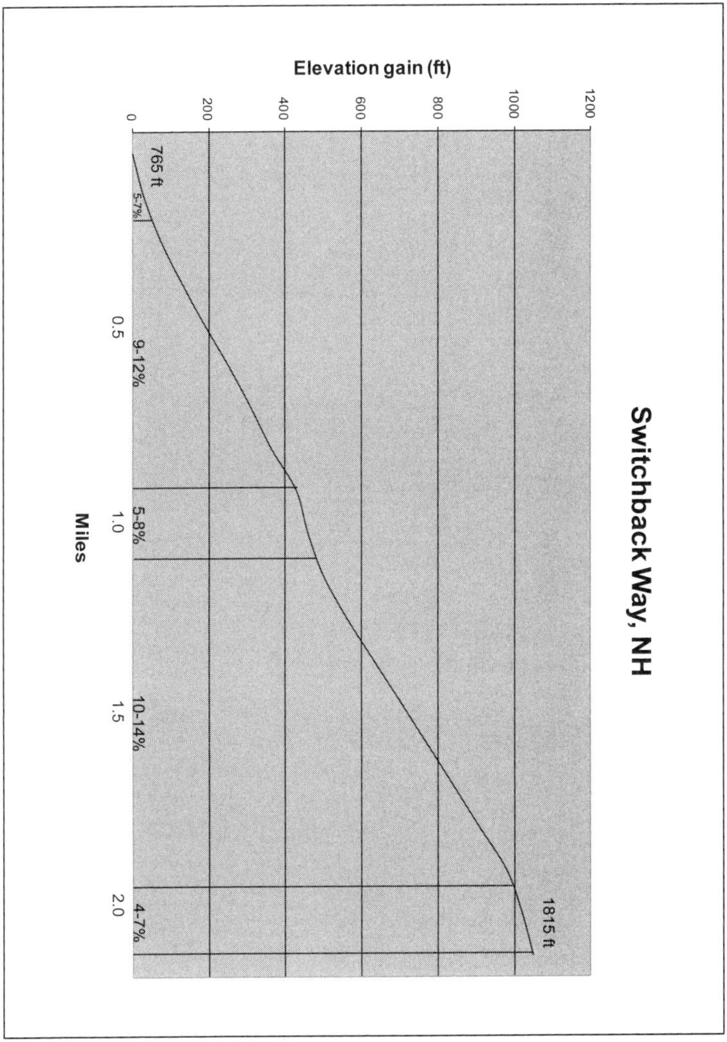
Switchback Way, NH
Elevation gain (ft)
1200
1000
800
600
400
200
0
765 ft
5-7%
9-12%
5-8%
10-14%
4-7%
1815 ft
0.5
1.0
1.5
2.0
Miles

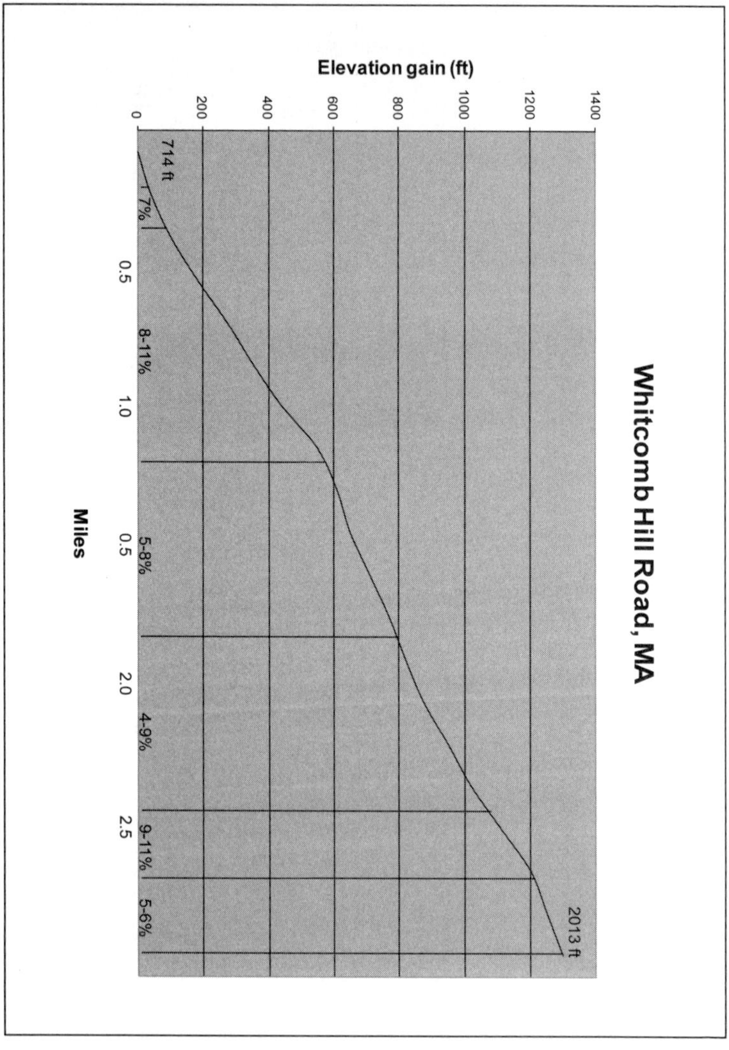
Whitcomb Hill Road, MA
Elevation gain (ft)
0
200
400
600
800
1000
1200
1400
714 ft
7%
8-11%
5-8%
4-9%
9-11%
5-6%
2013 ft
0.5
1.0
0.5
2.0
2.5
Miles